NEW YORK IS VERY MUCH ALIVE

NEW YORK
IS VERY MUCH
ALIVE

A Manpower View

ELI GINZBERG
and the Conservation of Human
Resources Staff, Columbia University

McGRAW-HILL BOOK COMPANY

New York St. Louis San Francisco Düsseldorf London
Sydney Toronto Mexico Panama Kuala Lumpur
Montreal New Delhi Rio de Janeiro Singapore

To my friends, Michael I. Sovern, William E. Petersen, Andrew W. Cordier, who, in 1968, brought Columbia University through its crisis, and thereby helped to ensure that New York would remain very much alive.

This book was set in Caledonia by University Graphics, Inc. It was printed on antique paper and bound by Book Press. The designer was Christine Aulicino. The editors were Tom Quinn and Rose Arny. Alice Cohen and Joseph Campanella supervised the production.

Cover design by Bob Aulicino.

07-023286-5

Contributors: Conservation of Human Resources Staff

Ivar E. Berg, George E. Warren, Professor of Business and Sociology, Graduate School of Business, Columbia University; Senior Research Associate.

Charles M. Brecher, Research Associate.

Alfred S. Eichner, Associate Professor of Economics, State University of New York—Purchase; Senior Research Associate.

Stanley L. Friedlander, Associate Professor of Economics, City College of the City University of New York; Senior Research Associate.

Marcia K. Freedman, Senior Research Associate.

Eli Ginzberg, A. Barton Hepburn Professor of Economics, Graduate School of Business, Columbia University; Director.

Dale L. Hiestand, Professor (Business Economics), Graduate School of Business, Columbia University; Senior Research Associate.

Richard V. Knight, Assistant Professor of Economics, Case Western Reserve University; Research Associate.

Dean W. Morse, Chairman, Department of Social Sciences, Liberal Arts College, Fordham University; Senior Research Associate.

Miriam Ostow, Research Associate.

Beatrice G. Reubens, Senior Research Associate.

Thomas M. Stanback, Jr., Professor of Economics, New York University; Senior Research Associate.

Boris Yavitz, Professor (Management), Graduate School of Business, Columbia University; Senior Research Associate.

Alice M. Yohalem, Research Associate.

CONTENTS

LIST OF TABLES
AND ILLUSTRATIONS

FOREWORD

THE PRESENT BOOK is a collaborative effort of the staff of the Conservation of Human Resources Project of Columbia University, who have become increasingly involved in recent years in the study of metropolitan labor markets—their structures and dynamics, and the outcomes for different groups in the population in search of employment and careers. While the Conservation staff initially directed almost all its efforts to manpower problems at the national, occasionally the international, level, and while it continues to be concerned with large macrostudies, it has recently allocated increasing resources to subnational issues, particularly those involving regions and metropolitan areas.

The explanation for this shift in focus is needed to place the present undertaking in perspective. The 1960s can be characterized as the manpower decade. It was only during the last decade that the federal government underwrote at a substantial level the financing of manpower training and related manpower services. The rapid increase and the scale of its investment is suggested by the fact that the budget for fiscal 1973 provides for $5.1 billion, compared with less than $400 million in the early sixties. For those who, like myself, have been close to this effort, it has become increasingly clear that while the federal government can finance ever larger manpower programs, it is up to state and particularly local efforts to determine whether the funds appropriated are translated into useful services for those who are eligible under the law to benefit from them.

However, since knowledge is a necessary precondition for sound policy and programming, the new federal effort faced an uphill battle because we know little about the workings of local labor markets, particularly those that have come to dominate our contemporary economy—the large metropolitan labor markets. In an effort to narrow the gap between what we know and what we need to know, the Conservation Project, as part of its broader interest in the dynamics of metropolitan economics, began in the mid-1960s to explore different dimensions of metropolitan labor markets in the hope and expectation of deepening its understanding of the factors governing their operations.

The principal publications emerging from this research focus follow:

> *Electronic Data Processing in New York City: Lessons for Metropolitan Economics*, Boris Yavitz and Thomas Stanback, Columbia, 1967
>
> *Manpower Strategy for the Metropolis*, Eli Ginzberg and the Conservation of Human Resources Staff, Columbia, 1968
>
> *The Metropolitan Economy: The Process of Employment Expansion*, Thomas Stanback and Richard Knight, Columbia, 1970
>
> *State Development Agencies and Employment Expansion*, Alfred S. Eichner, Institute of Labor Industrial Relations, University of Michigan–Wayne State, 1970
>
> *Urban Health Services: The Case of New York*, Eli Ginzberg and the Conservation of Human Resources Staff, Columbia, 1971

At the beginning of 1972 the Conservation staff had the following related books in press:

> *Metropolitan Trade and Employment Expansion*, Richard Knight
>
> *Upgrading Blue Collar and Service Workers*, Charles Brecher, Johns Hopkins Press
>
> *The Labor Market: An Information System*, Boris Yavitz and Dean Morse, Praeger
>
> *Unemployment in the Urban Core: An Analysis of Thirty Cities with Policy Recommendations*, Stanley Friedlander assisted by Robert Shick, Praeger

In addition, the staff is currently engaged in the following research projects which, when completed, will add to our knowledge of metropolitan labor markets:

"The Suburban Labor Market"—Thomas Stanback
"Human Resources Budgeting for New York"—Alfred Eichner and Charles Brecher
"An Urban Labor Market Information System"—Raymond Horton, David Lewin, Dean Morse, and Robert Shick
"Work and Welfare"—Miriam Ostow and Anna Dutka
"Urban Labor Markets: A Comparative Study"—Dale L. Hiestand

The present effort, while related in one or another respect to the research efforts cited above, is closest in concept to our *Manpower Strategy for the Metropolis*. In fact, this book can be considered an extension of that earlier work. Once again we have focused on the metropolitan labor market in seeking to illuminate dimensions of its operations by drawing upon our steadily enlarging armamentarium of labor market theory and techniques. In following this route we have taken New York City as our example. We live and work in New York City; we are concerned about the viability of New York's economy; moreover, we believe that what we learn about New York will be relevant in the main to other metropolitan centers.

We must add an important caveat which sets a severe constraint on our analysis of the New York labor market. It will be many months, perhaps even years, before the detailed results of the 1970 census become available. All that we have at the end of 1971 are a few totals. Even when the detailed data become available, they will enable the researcher to go only part of the way. There is much that he wants and needs to know about the labor market for which relevant data have not been collected. The shortfall in local labor market information, particularly on a current basis, is the bane of all who work in this arena. The challenge that every investigator faces is to make effective use of the limited information available and to extend his efforts with the help of theory, case studies, comparative analysis.

A few paragraphs about the structure of this book. The contributions are divided into four sections: Perspective, Problems,

Planning, Policy. The first group of chapters deals sequentially with New York City as a unique metropolis; the similarities and differences between New York and other metropolises; the interaction between the labor market of the city and that of the suburb; an assessment of the manpower record of New York for the 1960s; and the range of occupational and income opportunities which New York provides for different groups.

In Part II, Problems, the chapters consider the opportunities and constraints encountered by minorities as they seek to advance up the occupational and income ladders; the potentialities for upgrading blue-collar and service workers; the place of guidance in improving career decision making; the interface of work and welfare; aging in the ghetto.

Part III, Planning, presents explorations aimed at strengthening the decision-making process and considers seriatim issues in the field of educational planning in relation to changing manpower requirements, the need for strengthening informational services, improved linkages among the principal manpower institutions, and the interface between the manpower system with its malfunctioning institutions and the operation of the labor market.

Part IV, Policy, points up the more important recommendations that flow from the earlier analyses which, if implemented, can lead to the more effective development and utilization of the city's manpower resources.

The entire work must be viewed not as a finished product, but as an incremental addition to the slowly but steadily expanding knowledge base of urban labor markets. The Conservation Project has been privileged to contribute to the construction of this knowledge base in the past and it looks forward to making further contributions in the future.

A special note for the reader. The individual chapters and the book as a whole have an optimistic lilt. Moreover, at no point in the analysis is there a chamber of horrors in which the negatives in New York City are cataloged, much less extrapolated. Such negatives include the replacement of middle-income families with those at or below the poverty level; the aging infrastructure most visible in the equipment of the rapid transit system but also present to a marked degree in invisible items such as the electric wiring, telephone cables, sewers; crime on the streets; malperformance of the schools; the vulnerability of the municipal government to the excessive demands of its organized employees; the slippage of the port; smog and pollution; traffic congestion; dirty streets; lack of new construction for middle-income families; high municipal taxes; widespread drug addiction—and a host of other urban pathogens.

So much attention and concern have been directed to these negatives which in the opinion of many spell doom for New York City and for most other large cities that we opted in favor of a less eschatological approach. It may be that what is bad will get worse. But there is a good chance that it will get better. The reader should understand that while we are fully aware of the major challenges that New York faces, we saw little point in taking to sackcloth and ashes. Rather this book focuses on the feedback mechanisms that have begun to operate—and that we believe will accelerate—that augur well for the city's future.

ACKNOWLEDGMENTS

THE FUND FOR THE CITY OF NEW YORK provided funding for the present study, for which act acknowledgment is gratefully made to its trustees and to its executive director, Mr. Gregory Farrell.

This work draws heavily on the long-term research of the Conservation of Human Resources staff, most of which is supported by the U.S. Department of Labor. Hence the Office of Research and Development, Manpower Administration, U.S. Department of Labor was a silent but critically important contributor to this effort.

The Conservation of Human Resources staff benefited from the cooperation of representatives of several federal, state, municipal, and private organizations. The agencies and individuals who were particularly helpful are: U.S. Department of Labor, Bureau of Labor Statistics—Herbert Bienstock; U.S. Department of Health, Education and Welfare, New York Regional Office—Herbert Rosenbloom; New York State Department of Labor—Estelle Schrifte; New York City Planning Department—John Baer, Ann Fribourg; New York City Human Resources Administration—Jule Sugarman, Administrator and Abraham Burstein; New York City Department of Social Services—Arthur Schiff, Eileen North, Edward Korn; New York City Bureau of the Budget—Jane Kosloff; the Rand Corporation—William Johnson.

As the table of contents makes clear, Charles Brecher is the author or coauthor of three chapters. In addition he undertook and carried out with much skill the final editing of the manuscript. His good sense saved the manuscript from several errors and helped to sharpen the recommendations.

Ruth Szold Ginzberg devoted the larger part of a Florida vacation to editing the several chapters. Only those who have benefited from her light pencil can appreciate her skill in reducing slippage between authors and readers.

March 1972   Eli Ginzberg, Director
                              Conservation of Human Resources
                                          Columbia University

Part 1

PERSPECTIVE

1

THE GROWTH POLE

Richard Knight

NEW YORK IS THE NATION'S primary growth pole. It has been the birthplace of many new products and technologies and has evolved as the center of corporate management, planning, and innovation. The city is not dominated by one industry; it is characterized by a dynamic and diverse, but interdependent, set of activities relating to the management and growth of the private sector. An inordinately high concentration of economic resources— capital, manpower, and information—are attracted to and emanate from the city. It is from the convergence of these forces that New York develops its innovative spirit and maintains its competitive advantage.

The purpose of this chapter is to explore New York's role as a national growth pole. This will require a discussion of the historical forces leading to the evolution of the city's present functions, an analysis of the contemporary New York economy, and a prognosis of the vitality of the city's private sector.

HISTORICAL BACKGROUND

New York was founded in 1626 when Dutch traders first settled New Amsterdam. The city served as an agricultural center until the British captured it in 1664. Growth remained slow during the ensuing Dutch-British conflict, which lasted until 1691, but during this period communities were settled in the outlying areas which later became the boroughs of Greater New York.

Initially, New York's greatest locational advantages were related to transportation and commerce. The city had an excellent harbor, an asset which was later enhanced by the canals which were built upstate. It was established as a point of embarkation for steamships in the early 1800s and later emerged as a railroad convergence point. New York's early competitors were Boston, America's dominant commercial city through the first half of the eighteenth century, and Philadelphia, the largest city in the colonies from the 1750s to the early 1800s. New York outgrew Boston soon after Philadelphia did and then surpassed Philadelphia in the early 1800s. It has remained the largest city in the United States ever since, primarily because of its initial advantages in commerce and transportation.

New York's rapid ascendancy to prominence in the world hierarchy of cities must be stressed. In 1800 New York was an infant compared to European metropolises. Its size was only about one-tenth that of Paris and an even smaller fraction of London's. But in its role as a growth pole, New York set the pace for economic expansion in the United States. The city grew into a region whose population rose from 60,000 in 1800 to 629,000 in 1855 and to 16,000,000 in 1970. At present, New York's population is considerably larger than that of Paris, London, or Moscow and is approximately equal to that of the world's largest metropolitan area, Tokyo-Yokohama.

New York became a major port and transportation center at a crucial time in history, for trade was increasing rapidly and interest was shifting away from the physical process of production toward the problems of financing and marketing. The city's expanding mercantile functions provided a base for activities related to the extension to credit, reduction of risk, and other services available from banking and insurance organizations. Agglomeration economies accrued and augmented the locational advantages of the New York port. The headquarters of railways, public utilities, manufacturers and foreign investment trusts were established in New York because the city housed key financial institutions such as commercial and investment banks, a stock exchange, property and life insurance firms, and real estate investment companies.

Around this core of financial institutions and corporate head-quarters sprang up specialized producer services: law, accounting, advertising, public relations, engineering, trade associations, government, and a variety of information and research organizations. The rapid growth of these activities was accompanied by a rash of office-related innovations—shorthand and telegraphy (1837), cheap universal postage (1840), elevators (1857), typewriters (1867), telephones (1876), adding machines (1872), electric lights (1880), mimeographing and dictating machines (1887) and carbon paper (1890). These technological advances as well as the proliferation of producer services provided considerable stimulus to the communications industry and New York became a base for printing and publishing and telecommunications.

Spurred by the rapidly growing export industries (commerce, finance, communications), rising incomes, and an unlimited supply of immigrant labor, the local sector (retailing, transportation, food processing, etc.) also expanded. The construction of elevated transit lines began in 1868, and with each extension there was a wave of residential construction. The island of Manhattan was soon fully developed and the city expanded into surrounding boroughs. The South Bronx was annexed in 1874 and in 1898 the remainder of the five boroughs were incorporated into New York.

The momentum has continued to the present day. Subways, bridges, commuter railroads, and highways have enabled office activities to intensify in the central city while drawing on a labor force that resides farther and farther out. Manhattan reached its peak residential population (over 2.2 million) in 1910. Today the number is less than 1.6 million and only about 20 percent of New York City residents and 10 percent of the region's population live in Manhattan.

The decline in residential population was to be expected. As the financial sector grew and the advantages of a firm's locating in Manhattan increased, space was bid away from residential use and allocated to commercial, industrial, or public establishments. Moreover, the typical American desire to own one's home on a piece of land led many of the city's wealthier residents to succumb to the lure of the suburbs.

Historically New York, the growth pole, served the important national function of assimilating immigrants and developing their capacities and skills. In 1900 over 75 percent of the city's population had foreign-born parents. After the Immigration Act of 1921, the flow of immigrants was reduced to a trickle and the city began a new and difficult phase of its development.

Although the city's economy remained vital and competitive, obsolescence of its residential and social infrastructure began to occur at an increasing rate in the middle of the twentieth century. Greatly expanded use of the automobile, federal mortgage assistance and tax incentives to homeowners, and national subsidies for highway construction led to a rapid rate of suburbanization after World War II. Growth spilled over the city's political boundaries. Since no regional mechanism for planning or coordination existed, suburban communities multiplied. Today the metropolitan area encompasses parts of three states, a number of special-purpose regional authorities, about 550 local governments, and approximately 900 special districts. The residential shifts and political fragmentation in the metropolitan area are being reinforced by the movement of retailing functions, some industrial plants, and other tax ratables to the suburbs. Disinvestment (not maintaining capital) in the boroughs and new investment in the suburban counties have resulted in a selected dismantling of the city.

At the same time the central city's residential and social infrastructure, which served for over a century to help assimilate immigrants into the expanding economy, has not been adequately maintained. Sixty percent of the city's housing units are over 40 years old. Age does not necessarily imply obsolescence. But if, as in New York, a large portion of the older housing stock was substandard when first constructed, age can make them only more obsolete. The housing situation is further aggravated by the age-homogeneity of neighborhoods. It is not individual housing units, but entire neighborhoods that become obsolete at the same time, and the social and economic dynamics of neighborhood decay are difficult to reverse.

Housing is not the only problem. The city's social infrastructure suffers from analogous problems of underinvestment and obsolescence. For example, with respect to mass transit, not only have no new subway lines been built since 1935, but maintenance funds have been limited. Consequently, reliability of service (not to mention comfort) has decreased. Despite substantial financial support, the city's school system has not innovated sufficiently to adapt to the needs of its changed population. Today over half the students in city schools are black or Puerto Rican, and from their vantage the system often is obsolete. Of every 100 students entering ghetto schools only 13 emerge with academic diplomas. The problems of the city's new in-migrants are further compounded by geographic and educational changes in the labor market which frequently place skill requirements and credential barriers in the way of their obtaining central city jobs and force those pursuing less-skilled job openings in the suburbs to undertake difficult daily travel.

One must note that despite these formidable problems the city's public and private sectors have performed remarkably well. New York has been the nation's major innovator in the use of government to humanize an industrial society; its government offers a wide range of services and its personnel are expert. The city's private sector, while undergoing continual transition, has remained vital and responsive to the needs of the national and international economy. That the city can accommodate the mounting social pressure is a tribute to the vitality of its economy. In fact, it may well be on the needs, wisdom, and commitment of the private sector that the city's future depends.

THE REGIONAL SETTING

An analysis of the contemporary New York economy must begin by placing it in a regional perspective. Definitions of the region abound, and each is relevant to at least one of the city's many interdependent functions. The geographic bounds of labor markets vary by occupation and industry and range from the local neighborhood to the entire nation. Moreover, definitions change as transportation and other technologies are upgraded. Commuting distances now extend as far as 100 miles from Times Square. A four- or three-day workweek is likely to lengthen the commuting distance and push the boundaries farther. Even now, it can take as long to commute from the outskirts of the region as from Chicago.

The most frequently used definitions are presented in Table 1-1. The Tri-State Transportation Authority's definition is probably the most appropriate.[1] It encompasses 7,886 square miles which include New York City, 7 suburban counties in New York State, 10 counties in northeastern New Jersey, and 6 planning regions in southwestern Connecticut. This region embraces 11 standard metropolitan statistical areas (SMSA's). Although intraregional linkages are weak at the periphery, approximately 90 percent of the population and employment are concentrated in the 3,660 square miles surrounding Manhattan. The region offers a wide variety of residential and work places; only one-third of the land area is urbanized and residential densities vary from 70,000 people per square mile in Manhattan to 200 in some peripheral areas.

The region's 6.7 million jobs and 3 billion square feet of work space are highly concentrated in New York City, particularly in the Central Business District (CBD) of Manhattan, which lies south of 61st Street. New York City accounts for one-half of the region's floor space. Manhattan, with one-quarter of 1 percent of the region's land area, provides 16 percent of the floor space. The 1-square-mile area encompassing Grand Central Station provides 173.2 million square feet of floor space and 800,000 jobs.

Table 1-1
Size of Selected Areas Used to Define the New York Region

	Estimated population, 1970	Land area, sq mi
Manhattan	1,524,541	23
New York City	7,867,760	300
New York Standard Metropolitan Statistical Area	11,528,649	2,136
New York–Northeast New Jersey Standard Consolidated Area	16,179,401	3,930
Tri-State Transportation Authority Regional Area	19,028,970	7,886
Regional Plan Association Metropolitan Area	20,275,800	12,748

SOURCE: Bureau of the Census, *1970 Census of Population and Housing*, Final Report PHC (2)-24, "New York: General Demographic Trends for Metropolitan Areas, 1960 to 1970"; New York City Council on Economic Education, *Fact Book: 1972*; Tri-State Transportation Commission, *Regional Development Guide*; Regional Plan Association, *The Region's Growth*.

The movement of people and goods in the region is truly remarkable. An estimated 30 million person-trips are made daily, and 11 tons of goods are brought in and 5 tons sent out annually for each person in the region. To facilitate this movement, there are 44,000 miles of public streets, 2,500 miles of rails, and 480 miles of improved waterways. Transportation equipment includes 5.3 million registered vehicles, 3,000 suburban passenger rail cars and 6,600 rapid transit cars.

These facilities make possible the daily mobilization of manpower required to staff the various organizations that comprise the nation's business capital. It has been estimated that less than 47 percent of the city's jobs are filled by people who live and work in the same county. At least 1.4 million people cross into Manhattan to work: over 800,000 cross the East River, nearly 400,000 cross the Harlem River, and almost 200,000 cross the Hudson.

The unique component of the city's transportation system is its highly developed public transport facilities. Mass transit accounts for 67 percent of the region's work trips, including 75 percent of the trips terminating in the city and 24 percent of those which terminate in the outer ring. Within New York City three-quarters of the nonresidents and nine-tenths of the residents use mass transit to get to their jobs.

The significance of this transportation system is frequently overlooked in evaluations of the region's comparative advantages. A low-cost commutation represents substantial savings to employee and employer and is reflected in both wage levels and cost-of-living indices. By holding its costs down, the transportation system has helped to make low-wage industries characteristic of New York's manufacturing sector. It is possible that the recent residential shifts to the outer areas beyond the reach of the mass transit system has contributed to inflation of wages and prices in the region.

THE NEW YORK CITY ECONOMY

The New York City economy can be usefully analyzed in terms of a trade model of metropolitan economies. Within any area employment may be divided into the local sector and the export sector.

The local sector includes those activities which generate goods or services which are consumed within the metropolitan area. Exports are goods or services sent out of the region to other areas or consumed by nonresidents. The type of exports indicates the activities in which the region specializes because of its comparative advantages.

A recent study of trade patterns among the 368 metropolitan areas of the United States found that New York plays a major role in most of the industries in which exports are significant.[2] In 8 of the 13 industries in which trade is most important, New York accounts for a larger share of exports than any other city. It supplies over half (52 percent) the exports in apparel manufacture and accounts for the largest single share of employment in the five business service categories—airlines and other transport (42 percent), finance, insurance, and real estate (FIRE) (35 percent), business and repair services (31 percent), wholesaling (36 percent), and communications (24 percent). New York also accounts for more "exports" than any other city in printing and publishing (26 percent) and eating and drinking places (18 percent). It is second only to Los Angeles in recreation and entertainment and to Miami in hotels and personal services.

New York's export sector is exceptionally dynamic. As might be expected of a growth pole, some of the numerous businesses "incubated" in the city eventually move to different locations. This process of developing and eventually "spinning off" a function is evident in the electrical products manufacturing industry. New York was the birthplace of much electronic technology including telephone, radio, television, and hi-fi products. However, products and production technology eventually became standardized, skill requirements were reduced, and mass production techniques mandated increased floor space. Production was decentralized and a large portion of the industry moved from New York to other parts of the country.

The industries in which New York's share of exports has been growing are generally those which are in the forefront of national economic growth. During the twenty-year period ending in 1960, New York's share of total metropolitan exports increased in transportation, business services, and communications. Its share of export activity declined primarily in fields such as apparel manufacture, where national export activity has become less significant.

The dynamics of New York's export sector help to explain its role as a national growth pole. Industrial transitions in the export sector have been a key facet of local and national growth. New York firms must compete with companies in other cities as well as with other industries within the city for the same factors of production. The United Nations now stands on a site previously occupied by "nuisance industries," and the World Trade Center and Battery Park City are being constructed on an area once occupied by piers. The city has remained competitive by continually innovating and upgrading its human resources and its physical plant to meet the requirements of a changing national economy.

GROWTH PROSPECTS

New York's future growth will depend primarily on its ability to maintain the locational advantages it now offers those industries at the core of its export sector—corporate headquarters, financial institutions, and related business services. The region's major strengths are derived not from any individual function but from the agglomeration of these interdependent functions. The whole is greater than the sum of its parts, and consequently the gain or loss of one function may have an impact greater than its size might indicate. Little is known about the linkages between the corporate headquarters industry and related activities except that they require extensive face-to-face communications and must, therefore, be in close proximity to each other. It is possible that new technologies in communications, information processing, and transportation might weaken the centripetal pull that has caused headquarters activities to be concentrated in New York. But even if a few firms opt to relocate in other regions, New York's present preeminence in this activity and its sophisticated supporting infrastructure of transportation, communications, business services, and amenities bring advantages to the city's future to which no other American city can realistically aspire.

Approximately one of every five jobs in the central administrative offices and auxiliaries (CAOA) of American firms is located in New York. As Table 1-2 indicates, more CAOA employment is located in New York than in any other area, and this figure is more than twice that in the second largest concentration, Chicago.

Table 1-2
CAOA Employment in the United States, 1967

	Employment	Percent change, 1963–1967
New York	265,314	14.8
Chicago	115,505	15.6
Detroit	101,970	13.8
Los Angeles	52,654	16.0
Pittsburgh	48,342	13.0
Philadelphia	45,409	12.8
TOTAL United States	1,416,064	16.7

SOURCE: Planning and Development Department, Port of New York Authority, *Central Administrative Offices and Auxiliaries*, September 1969.

The larger a corporation, the more likely it is that its headquarters will be located in the New York region. Seven of the ten largest United States corporations are located there. Among the top 100, New York houses 40 percent, and among the top 500 approximately 30 percent are there.[3] The concentration in New York of the headquarters among the 50 largest corporations (1970) in each of six industrial sectors is presented in Table 1-3.

Table 1-3
Proportion of Corporate Activity in New York Region, 1970

	Percent of firms	Percent of business volume	Percent of assets	Percent of employment
Industrial	38	27.8	30.5	14.7
Retailers	30	30.1	29.2	37.0
Utilities	22	55.3	53.0	71.1
Commercial banks	20	40.3	40.0	33.8
Life insurance	18	47.9	53.8	37.8
Transportation	16	25.1	20.6	23.1

SOURCE: *Fortune*, May 1971, pp. 170–201.

The influence and control of these firms is even greater than the figures suggest, for in many cases they are the industry leaders. The decisions they make in New York affect communities all over the country.

Although firms in all sectors are represented in New York, most of the corporate offices in the city are the headquarters of manufacturers. Nearly two-thirds of all CAOA employment in New York is drawn from the manufacturing sector (Table 1-4).

Table 1-4
CAOA Employment in New York Region, 1967

	Actual employment	Percent distribution	Percent change, 1958-1967
Mineral	2,151	0.8	−6.0
Construction	893	0.3	NA
Manufacturing	174,904	65.9	28.0
Distribution (warehousing)	27,680	10.4	64.1
Retail trade	48,321	18.2	26.2
Selected services (other)	11,365	4.3	77.0
TOTAL New York	265,314	100.0	32.3

NA—Not available.
SOURCE: Planning and Development Department, Port of New York Authority, *Central Administrative Offices and Auxiliaries*, September 1969.

Expansion of CAOA employment in New York, which totaled 32 percent in a recent ten-year period, results in large part from growth of the nation's largest industrial firms. This process frequently involves reorganizations and mergers rather than an increase in the number of establishments.

The primary activity which draws to and retains corporate headquarters in New York is its financial community. As Table 1-5 indicates, New York is the nation's leading employer among its financial centers. Its rate of growth in FIRE employment was modest during the 1960s, but the enormous base upon which New York's financial community builds must be noted. The total number of FIRE jobs in New York is larger than that in the next five largest centers combined, and employment expansion in this sector in New York exceeded that in the next three largest centers combined.

Table 1-5
Employment in Finance, Insurance, and Real Estate in the 10
Largest Metropolitan Financial Centers

	1959	1969	Percent change
New York	470,150	581,196	23.6
Chicago	147,002	180,861	23.0
Los Angeles	105,733	154,628	46.2
Philadelphia	70,339	98,649	40.2
Boston	72,460	94,647	30.6
Hartford	28,253	38,860	37.5
Milwaukee	20,616	27,349	32.6
Cincinnati	19,654	24,801	26.1
Des Moines	10,975	14,766	34.5
Nashville	9,205	14,481	57.3

SOURCE: Planning and Development Department, Port of New York Authority, *Recent Employment Trends in the Finance, Insurance and Real Estate Industries in the New York Metropolitan Area*, April 1971.

A more detailed examination of FIRE employment in New York (Table 1-6) reveals that nearly half the jobs are in finance. Nine-tenths of the FIRE employment growth during the 1960s was in financial institutions. Brokerage institutions grew more rapidly than banks, although banking had the larger work force.

Table 1-6
FIRE Employment Trends in the New York Region

	Employment, 1969	Percent change, 1959–1969
Finance	254,346	73.2
Banking and savings	148,598	50.7
Brokerages	105,748	119.2
Insurance	159,000	7.2
Carriers	129,500	5.8
Agents and brokers	29,500	13.8
Real estate	131,200	1.3
Operators and lessors	101,700	−8.6
Agents and brokers	16,400	33.3
Miscellaneous	13,100	122.0

SOURCE: Planning and Development Department, Port of New York Authority, *Recent Employment Trends in the Finance, Insurance and Real Estate Industries in the New York Metropolitan Area*, April 1971.

Among the 45 commercial banking institutions in the New York area are 6 of the nation's 8 largest and 10 of the nation's 50 largest (Table 1-3). These 10 banks account for 40.3 percent of deposits, 40.0 percent of assets, and 33.8 percent of employment (of the top 50). Three-quarters of the banking and 95 percent of the regional brokerage work force are employed in New York City in close proximity to the major stock exchanges, Federal Reserve Board headquarters, and money markets.

Life insurance companies are also concentrated in the region; 9 of the 50 largest firms (including the 4 largest) with 47.9 percent of the insurance in force, 53.8 percent of the firm's assets, and 37.8 percent of their employment are in New York (Table 1-3).

The future of FIRE in New York depends on national growth in these activities and on the trends affecting geographic concentration. The shift to consumer loans and checking services suggests continued growth of banking employment. Factors which affect geographic concentration are difficult to evaluate. On the one hand, the need for knowledge in a hurry, the need to perform functions in close proximity to one another, and the possibilities for external economies suggest continued clustering of the major financial activities. And on the other hand, improved technology and the increasing size of regional markets may facilitate the passing on of certain functions to regional centers. Recent evidence of this trend is the floating of a $113 million municipal bond issue by a New Orleans bank after New York institutions refused to underwrite it.

In addition to its unrivaled financial center, New York provides corporate headquarters with an awesome concentration of specialized business services.[4] The region houses 35 of the 50 largest advertising agencies and accounts for 80 percent of their billings. Management and consulting services in New York do a volume of business more than 2½ times that of firms in the second largest concentration, Washington, D.C. Moreover, 27 percent of the nation's computer installations (5,900) are in the New York region, more than twice the number in Chicago (2,700) and Philadelphia (2,300). New York is the leader in the new industry of furnishing statistical and computer services. Regional receipts amounted to 17 percent of the nation's total; Los Angeles was second with 13.3 percent, and Washington, D.C. was third with 8.6 percent.

One new and important industry in which New York may be falling behind is commercial research and development (R&D). Recent growth in the industry has taken place outside of metropolitan areas; in 1958, the eight leading metropolitan areas accounted for 63 percent of sales, but their share had fallen to 38 percent by 1967. New York slipped from second place in volume (1963) to fourth (1967) after Boston, Washington, and Los Angeles–Long Beach.

The implications of the New York region's possible deficiencies in R&D are not yet fully apparent. In the past, new technologies and industries were incubated in the region precisely because of the externalities available. If externalized activities such as R&D become more independent as sponsorship broadens, communications and transportation improve, and competitive environments for personnel are developed, this may change. Climate, educational and recreational facilities, and environmental quality now play a role in the location of facilities employing professionals. However, for R&D firms whose clients are worldwide, New York still retains important competitive advantages because of its primacy in business functions and international transportation links.

New York's role as the nation's cultural and entertainment capital also reinforces its attractiveness as a headquarters city. In 1970, an estimated 16.5 million visitors spent $1.25 billion while attending conventions, doing business, and taking advantage of New York's myriad attractions—theaters, operas, concerts, galleries, museums, restaurants, nightclubs, libraries, department and specialty stores, trade associations, foundations, hospitals, universities, and friends (who doesn't have an associate or friend to visit in New York?).

The hotel-motel industry in New York is among the nation's largest. The occupancy rate (78 percent in 1967) of its more than 100,000 rooms indicates an average overnight visitor population which exceeds 120,000, more than the residents of many metropolitan areas. Hotels, which comprise the core of the industry, are concentrated in Manhattan. Motels are dispersed throughout the region. In recent years motel receipts have increased more rapidly than those of hotels. But even in motels, one-third of the increase occurred in Manhattan, where large units have opened.

New York and Los Angeles dominate the motion picture and amusement and recreation industries. These two areas accounted for 81.4 percent of the national growth in sales between 1958 and 1967. As the film industry has shifted to foreign productions, it has become concentrated in New York, the distribution center New York accounted for 36.2 percent of national motion picture receipts in 1967, compared to Los Angeles's 20.3 percent and Chicago's 3.4 percent, the next two largest concentrations. The television networks' headquarters in New York (NBC, CBS, ABC) are served by film production in the city as well as by its advertising and publications firms.

Another of the city's interdependent assets is its well-developed infrastructure of communications, transportation facilities, and public utilities. Almost ½ million people were employed in transportation, communications, and public utilities in the New York region. Two-thirds of these jobs are in New York City, and since many represent services utilized by nonresidents, they may be regarded as part of the city's export base. Ships and planes leaving the New York port system carry approximately 45 percent of United States ocean-bound cargo and two-thirds of the international air passengers.

The city's infrastructure is suited to the exchange of ideas and information as well as merchandise. There are 5.9 million telephones (74 per 100 population) hooked up to the one exchange that serves only New York City. The Greater New York region probably has twice the number, but data are not available. In comparison, London has 3.4 million phones (45 per 100), Tokyo, 3.5 million (40 per 100), Chicago, 2.3 million (64 per 100), and Paris, 1.7 million (60 per 100). In addition, Western Union is headquartered in New York City.

The printing and publishing industry is closely allied to New York's business, communications, and cultural functions. The two major "national" newspapers in the United States, *The New York Times* and the *Wall Street Journal,* are published in New York. National news services are headquartered there and half of the nation's books and 70 percent of the magazines with circulations of over 200,000 are published in New York City.

While publishing remains in the city, parts of the printing industry have moved to take advantage of improvements in printing technology. Moreover, postal rates for magazines have made Midwest locations attractive for the printing of periodicals. Printing which remains in the city generally requires close contact with the customer, varied inputs, specialized services, and short delivery times. Publishing thrives in New York because of external economies such as libraries, a supply of free-lance writers, artists, and literary agents, and the general concentration of talent which is drawn to New York City.

The international dimension of the city's activity is difficult to document. In many cases, the international operations which exist in New York represent one division of an organization. But no other city has such a convergence of international transport and communications routes as New York, and many activities locate there to take advantage of them. The United Nations headquarters, a prime example, located in New York to take advantage of the infrastructure and in turn became another comparative advantage of the city. Each delegation to the UN represents both a resource, since its expertise and information reinforce the growth pole functions, and an export activity, since each delegation is funded by its home country.

New York's apparel industry is also linked to the communications and transportation infrastructure. Although garment manufacture employment in the city declined by about 60,000 in the 1960s, New York retains the key design and sales functions. High-fashion goods made in New York require proximity to the originators and promoters of fashion and other taste-makers. The city has an agglomeration of sales functions that is large enough to attract buyers from all over the United States, and this asset is becoming more easily accessible to the major buyers scattered throughout the country. At one time Chicago was the apparel (fashion) center of the Midwest, but today it cannot compete with New York. The trip from Chicago to New York, which used to take sixteen hours by rail, now takes less than two hours by air. Moreover, retail outlets are now larger and can afford to send a buyer to New York.

CONCLUSION

New York's growth reflects the needs of the new industrial state, the increased dependence on capital, and centralized planning by the national and international organizations that dominate the economy. Its problems stem from the obsolescence of physical plant and social infrastructure that follows when those who achieve affluence move out rather than upgrade their community.

Despite its significant problems, there is little evidence that New York's crucial role suffers from serious competition from other cities. New York has successfully built up and maintained a set of related functions which provide outstanding advantages for corporate headquarters. It houses the world's foremost financial community, a sophisticated communications network, a panoply of specialized business services, and outstanding cultural and entertainment facilities, all of which are concentrated in an area with superior regional, national, and international transportation linkages.

Technological advances in communications and information systems may make feasible some decentralization of management functions. Certain corporate operations may be "spun off" in a manner similar to the displacement of certain manufacturing industries in the past. But New York is likely to retain its hold on major corporate offices and to replace lost functions with new ones developed at the core of the nation's growth pole.

2

A COMPARATIVE VIEW

Stanley Friedlander and Charles Brecher

NEW YORK'S PROBLEMS are frequently portrayed as the most serious in the nation; to many, the city epitomizes America's urban crisis. Yet a realistic look at New York indicates that its problems are part of national problems and that they are neither more acute nor worse managed than in other cities. For example, the crime rate in New York, the alleged crime capital of the nation, is less than that in Miami or San Francisco.[1] New York City's much publicized record of labor disputes is similarly deflated by the statistics, which show that the area's work force loses a smaller percentage of its total working time to strikes than that of any of the other four largest employment centers of the United States.[2] Its notoriety as a national welfare capital is also undeserved; Boston, Baltimore, and Newark each has a higher percentage of its population on the welfare rolls than does New York.[3]

An accurate description of the New York labor market and a realistic evaluation of its problems require perspective. In this chapter, New York's employment structure and growth, its unemployment record, its status with respect to the major barriers to successful labor market adjustment, and its response to new dimensions of the labor market are all considered in relation to the experience of other cities. The discussion is based on a large-scale study of employment problems in the 30 largest cities and the 16 major slum areas of the United States.[4] Parts of the analysis rely heavily upon data from the Department of Labor's Urban Employment Survey and special tabulations prepared by the Bureau of the Census from their Current Population Survey of 1967. These figures are the most recent detailed employment data gathered on a local level.

EMPLOYMENT STRUCTURE AND GROWTH

New York is the de facto capital of the United States. Although the federal government is centered in Washington, corporate head-quarters and key business services are concentrated in New York. Like Washington, its economy is rooted in the provision of services and in the fields of finance, insurance, and real estate (FIRE). New York has the second highest percentage (13.5 percent) of its private sector employment in FIRE activities of any of the other 29 largest American cities and ranks fourth in employment in services (Table 2-1). New York's highly diversified private sector, combining comparatively high proportions of FIRE and service activities with a relatively small proportion of manufacturing activity, makes it unique among American cities. Certain regional centers, such as San Francisco, Boston, New Orleans, Atlanta, and Denver, have similar structures, but none of these cities rivals New York as the business capital of the nation.

A second distinctive feature of the New York labor market is its enormous size. New York's total private sector employment (3,370,829) is almost 880,000 greater than that of the nation's second largest labor market, Los Angeles. The number of jobs in New York City's private sector is larger than the combined total for 10 of the 30 largest American cities, including 3 of the 10 largest.

The notion that New York's economic preeminence is rapidly declining is rooted in the numerous journalistic accounts of firms' leaving the city. Pessimistic views of the city's future are persistent. A 1971 *New York Times* article entitled, "But I Wouldn't Want to Work There," began with the following quote from *Fortune*, "By this autumn the management of nearly fifty companies with offices in New York City had acquired property in suburban Westchester County with the idea of moving most or all of their

Table 2-1
Private Sector Employment in the 30 Largest Cities by Industry, 1970*
(Percent distribution)

	Manufacturing	*Services*	*FIRE*
1. New York	25.6	23.5	13.5
2. Chicago	36.7	18.0	7.4
3. Los Angeles	34.2	20.7	6.7
4. Philadelphia	33.1	21.4	8.5
5. Detroit	40.9	17.8	6.0
6. Baltimore	28.6	21.7	8.6
7. Houston	23.1	19.4	6.4
8. Cleveland	41.1	17.7	5.4
9. Minneapolis–St. Paul	31.6	20.3	7.6
10. Washington, D.C.	7.3	40.7	11.1
11. St. Louis	35.2	21.2	7.5
12. Milwaukee	42.5	17.5	6.2
13. San Francisco	20.4	22.3	11.9
14. Boston	18.0	28.0	15.1
15. Dallas	29.1	17.1	9.2
16. New Orleans	14.2	23.7	8.6
17. Pittsburgh	34.7	20.4	6.2
18. San Antonio	17.4	23.0	8.9
19. San Diego	25.1	22.8	6.7
20. Seattle	27.5	19.4	8.9
21. Buffalo	38.4	17.8	5.5
22. Cincinatti	40.6	16.8	6.2
23. Memphis	27.2	21.0	6.6
24. Denver	18.8	22.3	9.8
25. Atlanta	19.2	19.6	9.8
26. Indianapolis	36.5	15.6	8.3
27. Kansas City	30.2	18.0	7.5
28. Columbus	30.1	20.1	8.6
29. Phoenix	26.8	20.8	8.3
30. Newark	32.6	18.4	10.8

* Cities selected and ranked on basis of 1960 population.
SOURCE: Bureau of the Census, *County Business Patterns*, 1970.

Retail trade	Wholesale trade	Transportation	Construction	Other private
13.7	9.4	10.5	3.2	0.6
16.7	9.2	7.2	4.1	0.7
17.7	7.8	6.6	4.6	1.7
15.6	8.1	7.7	4.5	1.1
16.5	7.4	6.6	4.1	0.7
17.7	7.7	9.6	5.5	0.6
17.2	9.7	9.1	10.7	4.4
16.3	8.2	6.0	4.3	1.0
18.7	9.1	6.9	5.1	0.7
19.0	6.2	9.2	5.6	0.9
13.4	10.0	8.5	3.4	0.8
17.6	6.5	5.8	3.4	0.5
16.9	9.7	11.3	6.0	1.5
15.1	8.6	10.2	4.3	0.7
17.9	10.2	7.9	6.5	2.1
17.2	10.4	15.9	5.9	4.1
18.1	7.8	6.4	5.3	1.1
26.4	8.7	5.7	8.1	1.8
25.4	4.7	6.6	6.8	1.9
19.3	8.9	8.7	6.1	1.2
19.6	7.0	6.8	4.2	0.7
15.9	8.5	6.6	4.6	0.8
19.3	12.0	6.9	5.9	1.1
18.3	11.7	10.7	5.8	2.6
19.0	13.6	12.1	5.7	1.0
17.4	9.4	6.4	5.7	0.7
18.5	9.9	9.5	5.2	1.2
21.6	7.2	6.2	5.3	0.9
21.8	7.1	5.5	8.0	1.7
14.8	8.0	10.6	4.0	0.8

general offices out of congested Manhattan." Ironically, the magazine article was written in December 1952.

The picture of New York as a decaying city is as erroneous today as it was in 1952. In both absolute and relative terms the city's growth compares favorably with that of other areas (Table 2-2). Despite the alleged exodus of firms from New York City, the labor market expanded by more than 380,000 jobs during the last decade. Net job growth was greater in New York than in any other American city but Los Angeles (662,586). The number of jobs *added* to the city's economy during the decade approximates the current *total* private sector employment in each of 16 of the 30 largest labor markets.

The rate of employment expansion in New York, however, is more modest. Each of the nation's 30 largest cities experienced some growth during the 1960s, but the growth rate varied from 5 percent in St. Louis to 107 percent in Phoenix. New York's 13 percent growth ranked twenty-fourth, exceeding that of Pittsburgh (12.3 percent), Newark (11.7 percent), Philadelphia (8.0 percent), and Baltimore (6.9 percent), as well as St. Louis. The fastest growing areas were concentrated in the Southwest and South, followed by Western cities and the smaller Midwestern cities. New York's growth rate was typical of the older Northeastern cities, all of which expanded by less than 20 percent during the decade.

If New York's modest rate of growth has continued throughout the decade and has generated over 380,000 new jobs, why is a pessimistic view of the city's future so accepted? The negativism is rooted in two trends: first, the declining position of the city relative to its suburban ring, and second, the decline in a key sector—manufacturing.

The implications of suburbanization for New York City's labor market are examined in detail by Thomas Stanback in the next chapter. Our purpose here is merely to place New York's experience in a comparative perspective. Between 1960 and 1970 employment in New York's suburban ring grew more than five times faster than in the five boroughs (67 versus 13 percent). However, the difference appears to have narrowed considerably during the decade, and in the last four years the rates were 19 and 6 percent, respectively.

Table 2-2

Private Sector Employment Growth in the 30 Largest Cities

	Employment in 1970	Employment change, 1959–1970	Percent change, 1959–1970
1. New York	3,370,829	381,996	12.7
2. Chicago	2,227,054	378,186	20.4
3. Los Angeles	2,491,889	662,586	36.2
4. Philadelphia	907,541	77,558	8.0
5. Detroit	922,705	107,307	13.1
6. Baltimore	367,249	23,859	6.9
7. Houston	630,227	280,143	80.0
8. Cleveland	684,864	125,334	22.3
9. Minneapolis–St. Paul	617,508	209,391	51.3
10. Washington, D.C.	326,584	67,152	25.8
11. St. Louis	376,113	18,954	5.3
12. Milwaukee	424,026	63,119	17.4
13. San Francisco	700,037	169,035	31.8
14. Boston	466,985	63,729	15.8
15. Dallas	586,139	261,962	80.8
16. New Orleans	226,161	43,764	23.9
17. Pittsburgh	554,125	60,311	12.3
18. San Antonio	183,468	63,262	52.6
19. San Diego	290,958	88,157	43.4
20. Seattle	371,691	83,442	28.9
21. Buffalo	338,568	46,660	15.9
22. Cincinnati	375,566	38,497	45.1
23. Memphis	221,767	74,315	50.3
24. Denver	253,696	75,386	42.2
25. Atlanta	372,692	138,381	59.0
26. Indianapolis	318,683	74,201	30.3
27. Kansas City	398,727	92,796	30.3
28. Columbus	281,414	88,609	45.9
29. Phoenix	276,182	142,990	107.3
30. Newark	362,092	38,216	11.7

SOURCE: Bureau of the Census, *County Business Patterns,* 1959, 1970.

The growth in New York's suburbs should be considered in relation to the growth of other cities' suburbs (Table 2-3). When the 30 largest cities are ranked according to the growth rate in their suburban ring, New York falls in the middle. Much faster suburban growth is found around cities such as Kansas City (197 percent) and Milwaukee (181 percent), while slower growth char-

Table 2-3
**Selected Characteristics of Employment Growth in
the Metropolitan Areas of the 30 Largest Cities**

	Employment growth in suburban ring, 1959–1970	Employment growth in central city manufacturing, 1959–1970	Employment growth in metropolitan government, 1960–1970
1. New York	66.7	−6.3	45.6
2. Chicago	84.4	7.4	50.9
3. Los Angeles	151.5	18.8	55.0
4. Philadelphia	59.8	−13.1	47.6
5. Detroit	93.9	−3.7	61.8
6. Baltimore	61.7	−2.4	83.8
7. Houston	50.2	60.4	54.5*
8. Cleveland	84.4	5.4	52.6
9. Minneapolis–St. Paul	80.6	51.5	53.7
10. Washington, D.C.	132.0	7.9	50.1
11. St. Louis	58.5	−6.0	60.3
12. Milwaukee	181.4	−0.5	61.5
13. San Francisco	72.2	9.4	50.0
14. Boston	38.7	−10.1	24.2
15. Dallas	38.3	73.1	90.2
16. New Orleans	109.2	10.4	48.7
17. Pittsburgh	7.7	−3.8	50.7
18. San Antonio	−44.7	55.6	50.6
19. San Diego	149.8	−4.1	72.6
20. Seattle	171.9	−11.5	66.1
21. Buffalo	7.2	0.2	55.6
22. Cincinnati	50.4	−1.0	66.2
23. Memphis	77.6	44.6	62.2
24. Denver	147.5	31.6	54.4
25. Atlanta	134.7	24.3	91.1
26. Indianapolis	59.7	16.6	40.6
27. Kansas City	196.8	18.7	58.6
28. Columbus	61.7	21.7	63.8
29. Phoenix	41.4	143.7	86.5
30. Newark	52.8	−9.4	54.9

* The 1960 figure is not available. Based on the period 1964–1970.

SOURCE: Data on employment in suburban ring and central city manufacturing are from the Bureau of the Census, *County Business Patterns*, 1959, 1970. Metropolitan government employment is based on annual averages reported in the Bureau of Labor Statistics, *Employment and Earnings*.

acterized areas such as Buffalo (7 percent) and Pittsburgh (8 percent). In only six cities (Houston, Dallas, Pittsburgh, San Antonio, Buffalo, Phoenix) did suburban growth lag behind central city expansion. Four of these cities are in the rapidly growing area of the Southwest, and their expansion includes annexation of surrounding areas, a process which masks suburban growth in the statistics. New York City is in the mainstream of a national process of suburbanization which typically generates more rapid employment growth in suburban areas than in central cities.

The drop in manufacturing activity is a second reason for concern among many observers of the New York scene. But a comparative view of the trend reveals that New York's loss is not unique, that its manufacturing sector is less significant than that in many other cities, and that it has several other important sectors where employment has grown more than enough to offset the losses in manufacturing.

An examination of changes in manufacturing employment in the 30 largest cities demonstrates that New York's experience is not unique (Table 2-3). Twelve of the cities lost manufacturing jobs over the last decade. New York's decline of 6 percent is modest compared to the declines in Philadelphia (13 percent), Seattle (12 percent), or Boston (10 percent), and is similar to losses in St. Louis (6 percent), San Diego (4 percent), and Detroit (4 percent). New York's manufacturing sector is indeed declining, but this fate is shared by at least a dozen other large cities, including most of the older East Coast areas.

New York's relatively modest loss of manufacturing jobs must also be placed in the context of the role of manufacturing in the city's economy. As noted earlier, New York's most important economic functions are in the service, and particularly the business service, sector. In comparison with other cities New York's labor market structure is more balanced and its employment is distributed more evenly among industrial sectors. Not only is its share of employment in manufacturing (26 percent) smaller than the national average, but its manufacturing sector is among the smallest of other large labor markets. In only 9 of the 30 largest cities and 2 of the 10 largest cities (Washington and Houston) does manufacturing account for a smaller share of employment,

(Table 2-1). Equally significant is the fact that in every large city except San Antonio there was a decline in employment in manufacturing as a proportion of total employment during the 1960s. This change in composition occurred despite absolute gains in manufacturing employment in two-thirds of the cities.

Finally, employment losses in manufacturing in New York must be weighed against the gains in its other sectors. Every other sector, except wholesale trade which dropped by less than one-half of 1 percent, expanded during the decade. The most rapid gains were in services (45.7 percent), government (39.4 percent), transportation (39 percent), and FIRE (21.1 percent), with smaller gains in retail trade (8.9 percent) and construction (3.8 percent). In the past ten years there were approximately 159,000 new jobs added in government and 428,000 jobs added in the three leading private sectors—services (249,095), transportation (99,467), and FIRE (79,866).[5]

The fact that a large number of the city's new jobs are in the public sector is sometimes pointed to as a weakness in the New York economy. But growth in government employment has been a national trend. Government employment, particularly at the state and local level, rose more rapidly than any other segment of the American economy in the 1960s. In fact, when the New York area is compared to other major employment centers, its growth rate in government employment appears among the lowest (Table 2-3). Among the 30 largest metropolitan areas 27 expanded government employment at a more rapid rate; among the 10 largest none had a lower rate of growth in this sector. Moreover, the New York area is not disproportionately dependent upon government employment. Of the five largest cities New York has a smaller share of total employment in government (11 percent) than San Francisco (15 percent), Detroit (12 percent), or Los Angeles (12 percent), and only a slightly higher share than the 10 percent in Philadelphia and Chicago.[6]

THE UNEMPLOYMENT RECORD

Employment growth, by itself, does not necessarily indicate a healthy labor market. A more direct measure of the capacity of a city to provide employment for its residents is the unemployment rate. The reported unemployment rate has important shortcomings; it does not indicate how many potential workers have given up looking for jobs nor does it tell how many workers are employed below their capacities. Yet despite these caveats, the unemployment rate warrants substantial attention because it is the best available measure of dysfunction in the labor market.

The most important point about unemployment in New York is that the city's diversified industrial structure protects its labor force from the abrupt shifts in employment opportunities which often characterize the national economy. While cyclical changes in the United States economy produced national unemployment rates varying from 5.5 percent in 1960 to 3.8 percent in 1966 to 5.8 percent in 1970, the variation in New York was limited to shifts from 5.2 to 4.1 to 4.8 percent in these years. The city's relatively small share of employment in cyclically sensitive industries, such as manufacturing and construction, provides greater employment stability in times of recession and relatively fewer opportunities in times of rapid national growth.

New York's unemployment record compares favorably with those of other cities in periods of prosperity and of recession (Table 2-4). In 1967 New York had a lower unemployment rate than 6 of the 10 largest cities; rates were lower only in Washington (2.1 percent), Minneapolis–St. Paul (2.6 percent), and Houston (3.7 percent). For 1970, unemployment data are available for only 15 major cities.[7] Of this group, five cities—Houston (3.8 percent), Dallas (3.9 percent), Chicago (4 percent), Boston (4.5 percent), and Baltimore (4.7 percent)—had rates below New York's 4.8 percent. Nine cities had higher unemployment rates, including three of the ten largest cities (Los Angeles, Detroit, and Cleveland), which had rates above 8 percent.

Unemployment has a differential impact on various segments of the population, and it is important to examine the experience of disadvantaged workers, particularly the nonwhite labor force and the residents of slum areas. Data for the slum areas of New York City (Harlem, East Harlem, and Bedford-Stuyvesant) indicate that a greater percentage of these areas' residents are unemployed than are the city's total residents. Unemployment rates in New York's slums were 7.5 percent in 1966 and 6.8 percent in

Table 2-4
Unemployment in the 30 Largest Cities, 1967

	Citywide unemploy- ment rate	Slum area unemploy- ment rate	Nonwhite unemploy- ment rate	Ratio of white to nonwhite unemploy- ment rate
1. New York	4.1	7.5	5.3	1.36
2. Chicago	4.3	5.4	8.2	2.83
3. Los Angeles	6.6	9.6	9.1	1.52
4. Philadelphia	4.4	11.1	7.5	2.42
5. Detroit	5.2	NA	9.8	3.38
6. Baltimore	5.5	NA	8.0	2.29
7. Houston	3.7	NA	6.3	2.25
8. Cleveland	5.8	11.5	10.1	3.48
9. Minneapolis–St. Paul	2.6	NA	*	*
10. Washington, D.C.	2.1	NA	2.8	3.50
11. St. Louis	6.6	12.9	11.3	3.77
12. Milwaukee	4.0	NA	7.8	2.17
13. San Francisco	6.3	12.5†	9.6	1.96
14. Boston	3.5	6.8	6.2	2.21
15. Dallas	2.5	NA	4.6	2.00
16. New Orleans	4.3	9.9	7.2	3.60
17. Pittsburgh	5.2	NA	13.2	4.40
18. San Antonio	2.0	8.1	7.8	4.33
19. San Diego	5.6	NA	4.3	0.75
20. Seattle	2.6	NA	3.4	1.42
21. Buffalo	6.4	NA	14.3	2.80
22. Cincinnati	3.1	NA	5.7	2.59
23. Memphis	4.0	NA	7.9	3.76
24. Denver	3.5	NA	4.2	1.20
25. Atlanta	3.8	NA	5.5	2.12
26. Indianapolis	2.7	NA	3.5	1.46
27. Kansas City	2.9	NA	4.7	1.96
28. Columbus	2.0	NA	3.5	2.33
29. Phoenix	3.3	13.2	1.9	0.56
30. Newark	10.2	NA	14.2	2.09

NA—Not available.
* Sample too small to produce significant figure.
†Includes Oakland.
SOURCE: Special tabulations from the Bureau of the Census. See Stanley Friedlander, assisted
by Robert Shick, *Unemployment in the Urban Core: An Analysis of Thirty Cities with Policy
Recommendations* (New York: Praeger, 1972).

1968 compared to citywide figures of 4.1 and 3 percent. Even in times of relative prosperity, slum residents live in conditions which resemble those of a serious national recession.

New York's slums have distressingly high unemployment rates, but they nonetheless compare favorably to similar areas in other cities (Table 2-4). Data for the slum areas in 11 cities indicate that New York's slum unemployment rate (7.5 percent) is lower than that of every other large city except Chicago (5.4 percent), and the figures for Chicago are subject to question. A more recent (1968) survey of slum areas in six major cities found that New York has a lower rate (6.8 percent) than those of five of the other largest cities—Houston (8.3 percent), Chicago (8.6 percent), Atlanta (8.6 percent), Los Angeles (10.3 percent), and Detroit (12.2 percent).[8]

In 1967 the unemployment rate for nonwhites was lower in New York (5.3 percent) than in any of the other 10 largest cities except Washington (2.8 percent). Among the 14 largest cities New York still ranked second, and among the 30 largest cities only 9 had a lower nonwhite unemployment rate (Table 2-4). Among the one dozen cities for which 1970 nonwhite unemployment rates are available, New York (5.4 percent) and Baltimore (5.4 percent) ranked behind Washington (5.1 percent) and Chicago (5.3 percent). Significantly higher nonwhite unemployment rates for 1970 were found in Cleveland (14.5 percent), Detroit (11.9 percent), St. Louis (9.9 percent), Los Angeles (9.8 percent), Dallas (8.6 percent), Houston (7.5 percent), San Francisco (7.3 percent), and Philadelphia (6.9 percent).[9]

When a ratio of nonwhite to white unemployment is computed, New York's experience compares favorably with that of other cities (Table 2-4). The ratio in New York (1.36) is the lowest among the 18 largest cities for which data are available and is less than half that for Chicago (2.83) and considerably below the ratios in Washington (3.50), Detroit (3.38), and Cleveland (3.48). Among the 30 largest cities New York provides better employment opportunities for blacks relative to employment of whites than any other city except Phoenix, San Diego, and Denver, in which there are small black populations.

EMPLOYMENT BARRIERS

Unemployment rates are a function of structural barriers to employment as well as inadequate aggregate (national) demand. Three of the most important of these structural barriers are: (1) the educational gap between the qualifications of workers and the requirements for available jobs; (2) the excessive geographic distance which separates workers' residences and potential jobs; and (3) the discriminatory practices of employers and labor market intermediaries, which prevent minority workers from securing satisfactory employment. A review of data specially compiled for the nation's 30 largest cities indicates the relative severity of these problems in New York.

The problem of inadequate educational preparation can be broken into three questions: What are the actual levels of educational attainment among the work force? Are nonwhite workers as well prepared as whites? Is the educational level of the labor force suited to the city's job requirements?

New York's labor force is not exceptionally well educated compared to other cities' (Table 2-5). The average level of education (10.3 years) was equaled or exceeded by 5 of the 10 largest and 20 of the 30 largest cities. Like their white counterparts, New York's minority citizens are not well educated. Their average educational attainment (9.7 years) was equal to or below that of the average of nonwhites in 5 of the 10 largest and 12 of the 30 largest cities.

Although New York does not have a comparatively well-educated labor force, its labor market does not suffer from sharp disparities between the educational achievements of blacks and whites. The ratio of white to nonwhite educational attainment in New York (1.07) is among the lowest of the 10 largest cities. Of the 30 largest cities only 7 had lower ratios, including Columbus and Minneapolis–St. Paul, where the average educational achievement of blacks exceeded that of whites (Table 2-5).

To assess how well the educational level of the city's labor force is suited to the needs of its employment structure, an educational gap index can be calculated by relating the educational achievement of the population to the educational requirements of

Table 2-5
Educational Barriers to Employment in the 30 Largest Cities, 1967

	Citywide average educational attainment (years completed)	Nonwhite average educational attainment (years completed)	White-nonwhite educational attainment ratio	Educational gap index
1. New York	10.3	9.7	1.07	1.89
2. Chicago	10.3	9.8	1.06	1.78
3. Los Angeles	11.4	10.4	1.12	0.71
4. Philadelphia	10.1	9.5	1.08	2.01
5. Detroit	9.9	9.6	1.04	2.15
6. Baltimore	9.3	8.4	1.20	2.83
7. Houston	11.2	10.1	1.15	0.89
8. Cleveland	9.5	9.0	1.08	2.56
9. Minneapolis–St. Paul	11.1	11.3	0.98	1.03
10. Washington, D.C.	10.8	10.0	1.22	1.58
11. St. Louis	9.3	8.8	1.09	2.81
12. Milwaukee	10.4	9.7	1.08	1.64
13. San Francisco	11.2	9.6	1.21	0.97
14. Boston	10.3	9.6	1.09	1.95
15. Dallas	11.4	9.8	1.20	0.70
16. New Orleans	9.6	8.5	1.22	2.55
17. Pittsburgh	10.5	10.2	1.04	1.61
18. San Antonio	9.7	9.1	1.07	2.50
19. San Diego	11.6	9.2	1.28	0.53
20. Seattle	11.9	10.7	1.13	0.17
21. Buffalo	9.9	8.6	1.19	2.15
22. Cincinnati	10.6	9.2	1.20	1.46
23. Memphis	10.4	7.8	1.53	1.72
24. Denver	11.1	11.0	1.01	1.09
25. Atlanta	10.5	9.2	1.23	1.64
26. Indianapolis	10.9	9.6	1.18	1.15
27. Kansas City	10.8	9.1	1.23	1.29
28. Columbus	11.4	11.8	0.96	0.70
29. Phoenix	11.3	10.1	1.13	0.82
30. Newark	8.8	8.8	1.01	3.31

SOURCE: Special tabulations from the Bureau of the Census. See Stanley Friedlander, *Unemployment in the Urban Core.*

a city's occupational distribution (Table 2-5). The education gap index in New York (1.89) is lower (i.e., a better match) than in 4 of the other 10 largest cities—Baltimore (2.83), Cleveland (2.56), Detroit (2.15), and Philadelphia (2.01)—but New York was still among those cities with a serious mismatch between supply and demand. Nineteen of the thirty largest labor markets appear to have a better balance.

The geographic barrier to employment is a function of the rapid growth in suburban employment. To assess the severity of the problem, a measure of job dispersal can be calculated by computing the percentage of total metropolitan area private sector employment which is located outside the central city. In New York this figure grew from 15 percent in 1959 to 21 percent in 1970. Despite this significant suburban growth, New York does not compare unfavorably with other metropolitan areas (Table 2-6). In each of 4 of the 10 largest labor markets (Philadelphia, Detroit, Baltimore, and Washington), there is a significantly higher share of metropolitan employment outside the central city, and in 13 of the 30 largest areas job dispersal to the suburbs appears to be a more serious problem than in the New York metropolitan area. Moreover, the problem does not seem to be increasing for New York. Comparative data about job dispersion in earlier years are hard to assemble because the boundaries of metropolitan areas have changed, but calculations using a variety of adjustments place New York in the middle range of the 30 largest areas in 1959 as well as in 1970.

Job dispersion is most serious when it affects manufacturing employment, for these are the jobs well suited for central city workers who do not have many skills or much education. The share of metropolitan area manufacturing employment located in the suburbs of New York (22.1 percent) is less than that in 4 of the 10 largest and in 15 of the 30 largest labor markets (Table 2-6). These figures confirm the earlier observation that New York is in the mainstream of a national process of suburbanization and is faring at least as well as a majority of large cities in retaining manufacturing employment.

Discrimination in the labor market is only one aspect of a cumulative, life-long process of discrimination which plagues

Table 2-6
Geographic Dispersion of Employment in Metropolitan Areas
of the 30 Largest Cities, 1970

	Percent of total employment in suburbs	Percent of manufacturing employment in suburbs
1. New York	20.6	22.1
2. Chicago	14.3	15.6
3. Los Angeles	15.6	14.2
4. Philadelphia	40.1	47.4
5. Detroit	30.0	33.0
6. Baltimore	39.4	47.3
7. Houston	6.2	8.2
8. Cleveland	8.6	10.3
9. Minneapolis–St. Paul	8.1	10.2
10. Washington, D.C.	53.7	57.2
11. St. Louis	51.2	55.5
12. Milwaukee	16.4	17.9
13. San Francisco	28.5	31.6
14. Boston	63.1	79.2
15. Dallas	5.4	6.6
16. New Orleans	27.0	40.9
17. Pittsburgh	26.2	33.7
18. San Antonio	2.5	3.1
19. San Diego	60.1	65.6
20. Seattle	14.2	25.6
21. Buffalo	17.2	24.3
22. Cincinnati	13.8	10.3
23. Memphis	3.2	3.6
24. Denver	33.2	45.6
25. Atlanta	29.4	43.6
26. Indianapolis	11.8	11.6
27. Kansas City	10.3	8.4
28. Columbus	6.1	8.4
29. Phoenix	11.4	6.3
30. Newark	46.8	55.6

SOURCE: Bureau of the Census, *County Business Patterns*, 1970.

America's minority groups. A family life hampered by low income, inferior schools and public services, and the other multiple inequities of American racism combine with subtle and overt prejudice on the part of employers to place minorities at a disadvantage in the labor market. The problem is difficult to measure, but a gross estimate of the severity of racial discrimination can be derived by comparing the occupational distributions of blacks and whites. An index of 1.00 indicates equality in occupational distribution; the higher the index, the more favorable the position of the whites (Table 2-7). New York's occupational discrimination index (1.81) is lower than that of the other 10 largest cities except Los Angeles (1.61). Among the 30 largest cities only 5 others had an index below that of New York. As might have been anticipated, cities in the South had the highest ratios—Memphis (6.19); Atlanta (4.69), Dallas (4.62), New Orleans (4.42).

It is impossible to isolate the effects of discrimination in the labor market from the effects of other aspects of racism. However, a rough gauge of labor market discrimination can be derived by adjusting the gross occupational discrimination index to allow for the educational levels of nonwhite workers. These figures show New York in a similarly favorable position (Table 2-7). Of the 10 largest cities, again only Los Angeles (1.46) has a lower adjusted index than New York (1.65). Among the 30 largest cities only the same additional 5 cities (San Diego, Boston, San Francisco, Seattle, and Phoenix) appear to have less discrimination than New York.

NEW DIMENSIONS: ALTERNATIVES TO THE LABOR MARKET

Two dimensions of urban life—crime and welfare—became increasingly significant during the 1960s. Between 1960 and 1970 New York City's public assistance case load increased by more than 200 percent, from 328,200 to 1,165,600. In the same period the area's crime rate rose from 1,391 to 5,220 per hundred thousand population. These trends are important because crime and welfare are now basic components of the urban labor market by operating as alternative or supplementary sources of income for a large segment of the population.

The rapid growth in the city's welfare rolls and the implica-

Table 2-7
Occupational Discrimination in the 30 Largest Cities

	Gross discrimination index	Adjusted discrimination index
1. New York	1.81	1.65
2. Chicago	2.28	2.00
3. Los Angeles	1.61	1.46
4. Philadelphia	2.09	1.82
5. Detroit	2.85	2.50
6. Baltimore	3.09	2.45
7. Houston	3.61	3.19
8. Cleveland	2.49	2.06
9. Minneapolis–St. Paul	1.83	1.83
10. Washington, D.C.	2.30	1.76
11. St. Louis	2.56	2.10
12. Milwaukee	2.41	2.13
13. San Francisco	1.70	1.43
14. Boston	1.67	1.38
15. Dallas	4.62	3.61
16. New Orleans	4.42	3.65
17. Pittsburgh	2.33	2.18
18. San Antonio	2.15	1.97
19. San Diego	1.54	1.32
20. Seattle	1.73	1.57
21. Buffalo	2.33	1.88
22. Cincinnati	2.34	1.95
23. Memphis	6.19	3.99
24. Denver	1.84	1.75
25. Atlanta	4.69	3.61
26. Indianapolis	2.70	2.33
27. Kansas City	2.84	2.27
28. Columbus	2.24	2.31
29. Phoenix	1.76	1.59
30. Newark	2.14	2.02

SOURCE: Special tabulations from the Bureau of the Census. See Stanley Friedlander, *Unemployment in the Urban Core.*

tions of this problem for the labor market are explored in Chapter 9. It will suffice here to place New York's situation in perspective. The two key facets of the welfare explosion are the size of the rolls relative to the city's population and the level of cash benefits. These two parameters can be combined to produce a welfare index for each of the 30 largest cities (Table 2-8). New York's index (637) ranks behind only those of Boston (792) and Baltimore (656). The lowest indices are in the Texas cities of Houston (23) and Dallas (34). It is interesting to note that New York's relative position is improving. In 1960 New York ranked second only to Boston. Since that year the welfare index has grown more rapidly in four cities (Boston, Baltimore, Cleveland, Newark) than in New York, although the indices for both Cleveland and Newark are still below New York's.

It is impossible to measure the employment effects of crime, but there is no doubt that many illegal activities produce income. One recent estimate is that over 10,000 people are employed in New York's illegal drug market. The significance of drug peddling is apparent when we note that the Urban Employment Survey found that 9,800 teen-agers and male adults in New York's slums were unemployed. Thus, it appears that there may be more people employed in the marketing of heroin in New York City than there are youth and men unemployed in slum areas. It has been estimated that 100,000 individuals in New York are employed either full or part time in the numbers and gambling "industry." The crucial role of gambling in the Harlem economy was brought to light in the recent protests by community groups which were seeking to close down the newly legalized municipal Off-Track Betting (OTB) offices in the neighborhood. Their aim is to legalize numbers and place control of this and other gambling operations in the hands of indigenous groups who, presumably, are anxious to retain the jobs for local residents. When the employment generated by drug traffic and gambling is added to that provided by other illegal endeavors such as prostitution, burglary, shoplifting and hijacking, it becomes apparent that crime is a major sector of the New York economy. It is possible that over 250,000 people are regularly deriving income from illegal sources.

The best comparative gauge of criminal activity in the largest American cities is the crime rate reported by the Federal Bureau of Investigation (Table 2-8). Despite the large number of people employed in its illicit economy, New York does not have the high-

Table 2-8
Welfare and Crime in the 30 Largest Cities

	Welfare index, 1966	Crime rate per 100,000 population, 1970
1. New York	637	5,220
2. Chicago	285	2,789
3. Los Angeles	365	5,064
4. Philadelphia	299	2,079
5. Detroit	253	5,149
6. Baltimore	656	4,370
7. Houston	23*	3,593
8. Cleveland	259	3,083
9. Minneapolis–St. Paul	304	3,246
10. Washington, D.C.	197	4,111
11. St. Louis	240	3,566
12. Milwaukee	179	1,999
13. San Francisco	419	5,329
14. Boston	792	3,098
15. Dallas	34	4,139
16. New Orleans	181	4,310
17. Pittsburgh	262	2,030
18. San Antonio	81	3,507
19. San Diego	246	2,923
20. Seattle	151	4,133
21. Buffalo	264	2,403
22. Cincinnati	224	2,367
23. Memphis	138	3,057
24. Denver	456	4,821
25. Atlanta	144	3,568
26. Indianapolis	68	3,085
27. Kansas City	127	3,690
28. Columbus	242	3,517
29. Phoenix	164	4,249
30. Newark	615	3,480

*1964.
SOURCE: Crime rates are from the Bureau of the Census, *Statistical Abstract of the United States, 1971*; Welfare index is from Stanley Friedlander, *Unemployment in the Urban Core.*

est crime rate. The crime rate per hundred thousand population in New York (5,220) was below that in San Francisco (5,329) and similar to the rates in Detroit (5,149) and Los Angeles (5,064).

However, New York is among those cities which have a serious crime problem and may be contrasted to other large cities such as Chicago (2,789), Philadelphia (2,079), Pittsburgh (2,030), and Milwaukee (1,999), where the rates are much lower.

The existence of a large illegal economy in cities like New York has conflicting implications for employment prospects. The negative impact is obvious: Firms leave the city because of thievery and the added costs of protective services; higher taxes are required to support additional public safety measures; fear drives the labor force to outlying areas. The positive effects are more subtle. For deprived citizens with limited job options a criminal career offers the possibility of glamour, status, and high income. It is possible that one of the reasons New York has a relatively low unemployment rate, and a comparatively low ratio of white to nonwhite unemployment, is the large number of job opportunities available in the criminal world. The problem presents a serious dilemma. If the estimates cited earlier are in range, it would require a large-scale job-creation program equivalent to almost a decade's private sector job growth to provide a replacement for illicit employment.

CONCLUSION

The New York labor market is unique in two respects. First, its enormous size places it in a class by itself. Second, its concentration of corporate office and business services makes New York the economic headquarters of the nation. Its industrial base combines manufacturing, services, government, and transportation in a better balance and more desirable mix than that of most other cities.

Predictions of rapid decay for New York's economy are likely to be proved wrong. The city's employment base grew substantially over the last decade and at a rate equivalent to that of most similar cities. Although the manufacturing sector has declined somewhat, this is true of manufacturing relative to total employment in every large city, and it is also true of the absolute level of manufacturing employment in a dozen other cities.

New York's problems are shared by the nation. Like almost

every other city, it is expanding more slowly than its suburbs. But suburbanization is not a particular threat to New York; the city retains a larger share of metropolitan employment than 15 of the 30 largest cities. Unemployment is not as serious a problem in New York as in other areas, and blacks and slum residents as well as whites share the jobs. New York compares favorably to other areas with respect to discrimination. Blacks and whites have closer unemployment rates, educational levels, and occupational distributions in New York than in most other American cities.

The problems which confront New York more seriously than most other cities are the educational mismatch between labor supply and demand, the rapidly rising welfare population, and the large illicit economy. In none of these areas is New York the most seriously affected city, but it is among the most affected. Raising the educational level of the work force to meet the demands of potential employers and developing methods for providing new alternative sources of income may be the most important challenges facing New York's policy-makers.

3

SUBURBANIZATION

Thomas M. Stanback, Jr.

THIS CHAPTER EXAMINES selective aspects of the development of
the suburban economy in the New York metropolitan region.[1]
It attempts to respond to three basic questions: What are the
unique characteristics of structure and growth in the suburban
economy and its labor markets? What are the central economic
problems facing suburbia and the prospects for its development?
What are the implications of suburbanization for the economic
development of the city?

GROWTH OF THE SUBURBAN ECONOMY

Population growth. Vigorous suburban growth in the New York
area began in the early 1900s, when rapid rail transportation became available between a number of outlying communities and
the city. It continued at relatively high rates until it was slowed
by the depression of the thirties and subsequently by World War II
(Table 3-1), but quickened once again as the postwar era unfold-
ed. In the most recent phase, however, suburban growth has not
been paralleled by significant growth within the core. Moreover,
the cumulative effect of earlier decades of suburban growth has
been that even slightly lower rates of change now represent substantial increases in population. Since at least the beginning of the
fifties suburban growth has dominated metropolitan regional

42

Table 3-1
Rates of Population Change by Decade and Share of Population,
New York Metropolitan Region, 1900–1970

	Core		Inner ring		Outer ring	
	Rate	Share	Rate	Share	Rate	Share
1900–1910	38.9	68.4	46.2	19.1	27.6	12.5
1910–1920	17.5	66.9	30.8	20.8	17.7	12.3
1920–1930	21.7	63.4	46.0	23.7	27.3	12.9
1930–1940	6.0	63.2	9.0	24.2	11.1	12.6
1940–1950	5.2	59.6	20.8	26.2	25.6	14.2
1950–1960	−2.1	50.3	34.7	30.4	57.4	19.3
1960–1970	−0.1	45.2	10.8	30.1	42.9	24.7
TOTAL population, 1970 (thousands)	8,181.6		5,441.7		4,472.5	

SOURCE: Censuses of Population.

growth and has resulted in an increase in the rings' (inner and outer) share of the region's population from 40.4 percent (1950) to 54.8 percent (1970).[2]

Migration. A sense of the revolutionary character of postwar suburbanization can be had only through an understanding of the major role played by migration in bringing about these population changes. From 1950 to 1970 migration accounted for a gain of almost 2,524,000 in the combined inner and outer ring areas, and at the same time there was an out-migration of over 1,547,100 from the core (Table 3-2).

This massive migration was made possible by the increase in automobile ownership and the rising affluence which made such ownership possible as well as by broad and effective governmental support for programs of highway building and insured single family home mortgages. Together, these factors made it feasible for workers to locate in the relatively low density areas outside the city and to commute daily to work places 15 to 40 miles away.

In general, this movement outward from the city was undertaken largely by middle- or upper-income families, and behind this shift lay a new set of values. Postwar middle-class parents wanted large families and considered the suburbs as the best location for raising and educating children.

Table 3-2
**Population Change and Migration in New York
Metropolitan Area, 1950–1970**
(Thousands)

	1950–1960		1960–1970	
	Population change	Migration	Population change	Migration
Core	−177.2	−933.9	+10.8	−613.2
Inner ring*	+1,275.5	+733.2	+495.9	+69.6
Outer ring	+1,141.3	+806.0	+1,341.9	+915.1

*If Essex County, New Jersey (which includes Newark), is excluded, population changes and migration estimates respectively are as follows: 1950–1960 are 1,257.9, 808.1; 1960–1970 are 489.5, 140.6.

SOURCE: U.S. Department of Commerce, *Current Population Reports,* ser. P23, no. 7 and ser. P25, no. 461.

Examination of the details reveals, however, a change in the importance and characteristics of suburban growth in the most recent decade. In the inner ring the rate of population growth declined sharply from the fifties to the sixties and the growth which did occur was due more to natural increase rather than to migration. In the outer ring, however, the rate of population growth declined only slightly during the sixties and migration continued to play the major role in this change, accounting for 68 percent of population change compared to 71 percent in the fifties.

A second observation is based on data which provide a racial classification of those who migrated. These data, which are available only for the most recent decade and for selected counties, show that a large percentage of the in-migrants to the inner ring were nonwhite, whereas most of those who migrated to the outer ring counties were white (Table 3-3). It should be noted that migration and natural increase together did not result in a sizable proportion of blacks and other nonwhites in the suburbs. In the main, blacks have been restricted to sharply segregated areas in the older suburban towns and cities such as Mt. Vernon in Westchester, and Hempstead in Nassau.

Employment expansion. Paralleling the migration was a vigorous expansion of suburban employment as plants and office activities

Table 3-3
Nonwhite In-migration and Share of Population, New York
Metropolitan Region, 1960–1970

	In-migration, 1960–1970 (thousands)		Percent population, nonwhite	
	Total	Nonwhite	1960	1970
Inner ring	69.6*	133.0	7.7	11.3
Inner ring (excluding Essex and Union Counties)	144.2	61.3	4.5	6.7
Outer ring (selected counties)†	809.8	42.6	5.7	6.4

* There was a net white out-migration of 63,400.
†Suffolk, Fairfield, Dutchess, Middlesex, Monmouth. Census data provide racial characteristics for migration in these counties only.
SOURCE: U.S. Department of Commerce, *Current Population Reports*, ser. P25, no. 461.

moved outward from the city to produce goods and services for the markets of the city, the nation, and for the local needs of the rapidly growing areas of suburbia itself. A comparison of employment growth rates of manufacturing and retailing with population growth rates in the inner and outer rings of the New York metropolitan region provides a quick sketch of growth in these suburban counties during the last three decades (Table 3-4).

In the first decade, which included the war years, manufacturing outpaced retailing in both rings. With the advent of the

Table 3-4
Average Annual Rates of Change in Population, Employment in
Manufacturing and Retailing, Inner and Outer Ring Counties,
New York Metropolitan Region

	1940–1950		1950–1960		1960–1970	
	Inner	Outer	Inner	Outer	Inner	Outer
Population	2.1	2.6	3.5	5.7	1.0	4.3
Manufacturing*	11.1	10.8	1.9	1.4	1.3	4.0
Retailing†	4.1	5.0	4.6	4.5	2.1	5.1

*Dates are 1937–1947, 1947–1958, 1958–1967.
†Dates are 1938–1948, 1948–1958, 1958–1967.
SOURCE: Censuses of Population, Manufacturing, Retailing.

postwar period and the onset of the more rapid increase in suburban population, however, retailing grew more rapidly and exceeded the rate of increase in manufacturing from 1948 to 1958 in both rings. During the most recent decade, rates of increase in retailing employment continued to be greater than those in manufacturing, but the differential has declined.

We also learn from Table 3-4 that retail employment has tended to grow more rapidly than population in both rings. This is an initial indication that the suburbs have grown and developed by providing more services for their own populace.

STRUCTURE OF THE SUBURBAN ECONOMY

This brief look at manufacturing and retailing serves to introduce one of the most useful concepts which economists have brought to the analysis of development: the notion that growth occurs through an interaction between export and local sectors. The former includes all activities associated directly or indirectly with production of goods and services which are exported from a given economy (e.g., manufacturing, wholesaling, headquarters activities) and which in turn provide the stream of income out of which goods and services can be purchased from outside economies. The latter sector includes all activities which are provided to meet the local requirements of the populace (e.g., retailing services, medical services, the local educational and governmental system).

Growth stems primarily from an enlargement of the export sector. With an increase in export activity there is an increase in income. If this income is spent for local goods and services, there is further stimulation of demand in the local sector and, consequently, further growth.[3]

The reciprocal influence of the local sector upon the export sector is somewhat different. As the economy grows and the local sector is enlarged, a fuller range of services is offered and an improvement in their quality is likely to occur. The availability of more abundant and improved services (e.g., better schools, shopping, and hospitals) acts, in turn, to increase the attractiveness of the economy for the location of additional export firms which in turn stimulate further expansion of the local sector.

Moreover, as growth continues, markets within the economy are broadened, resulting in an increased opportunity for firms to produce both consumer and business goods and services which previously had been imported. This process of *import substitution* is a vital part of economic development.

The local sector. One of the striking characteristics of the suburban industrial structure is the large proportion of employment accounted for by activities belonging principally to the local sector (e.g., retailing and other consumer services, and aspects of local and state governments). Table 3-5 reveals that employment in the combined "mainly consumer services" category comprised 31 percent of employment in the ring counties of the New York standard metropolitan statistical area (SMSA) in 1970 compared with 23 percent in New York City; state and local government accounted for another 19 percent.[4] Together, the mainly consumer services and government categories account for almost half of suburban employment.

How can we explain the large proportion of suburban employment in local services? The answer appears to lie in the unique nature of the suburban economy. In suburbia incomes derive exogenously not only from such activities as manufacturing and wholesaling but also from a large volume of employment that does not appear in the statistics shown in Table 3-5: the army of commuters who work in the city but who live in the suburbs. In 1960 this hidden suburban "export activity" accounted for the employment of almost ½ million persons, most of whom had incomes on the upper ranges of the scale. The extent to which the population of the suburbs is favored in this regard is readily seen in Table 3-6, where the labor force of the New York metropolitan region is classified by income, place of work, and place of residence.

As suburban markets have grown, a variety of personal services such as medical services and entertainment which were previously purchased in the city have been made available locally. Nowhere has this been of greater importance than in retailing.

Table 3-5

**Distribution of Total Employment and Job Increases/Job Decreases
in New York City and Suburban Ring of SMSA, 1965–1970**

Industry	*City*				
	Total employment (Percent dist.)		*Job increases*		*Job decreases*
	1965	*1970*	*Number (thousands)*	*Percent dist.*	*Number (thousands)*
Construction	3.0	2.8			0.1
Manufacturing	25.0	22.1	20.9	5.2	57.0
Utilities/sanit.	0.8	0.6			2.7
Mainly business services	*34.8*	*36.8*	*188.5*	*46.6*	
Transportation	5.7	6.0	29.8	7.4	
Communications	2.1	2.3	13.7	3.4	
Wholesale	8.7	8.1	3.3	0.8	
FIRE	10.9	11.7	65.0	16.0	
Repair service	0.8	0.8	3.2	0.8	
Bus., legal & other services	6.6	7.9	73.5	18.2	
Mainly consumer services	*23.3*	*23.3*	*91.9*	*22.7*	*14.5*
Retail	12.2	11.8	23.1	5.7	
Hotel & other personal services	3.0	2.4			14.5
Entertainment/ recreation	1.3	1.2	1.0	0.2	
Medical	3.1	3.8	39.7	9.8	
Education	3.7	4.1	28.1	7.8	
Government	*12.9*	*14.1*	*101.8*	*25.1*	*9.1*
Federal	3.2	2.6			9.1
State & local	9.7	11.5	101.8	25.1	
Unclassified	0.2	0.2	1.0	0.2	
TOTAL	100.0	100.0	404.1	100.0	83.4

* Ring consists of Westchester, Suffolk, Rockland, Nassau Counties.
SOURCE: Compiled from estimates in Department of Commerce, *County Business Patterns*, 1965, 1970, and New York State Department of Labor, *Employment Review*.

| Job decreases | Ring* | | | | | |
| | Total employment (Percent dist.) | | Job increases | | Job decreases | |
Percent dist.	1965	1970	Number (thousands)	Percent dist.	Number (thousands)	Percent dist.
0.1	5.9	4.9	3.3	1.4		
68.4	25.9	22.9	29.3	12.1	0.4	100.0
3.2	1.0	0.9	1.6	0.7		
	18.6	21.8	78.9	32.6		
	1.9	2.0	5.7	2.6		
	1.8	2.7	14.6	6.0		
	5.4	6.3	23.1	9.4		
	5.0	4.7	9.6	3.9		
	1.0	1.0	2.3	1.0		
	3.6	5.0	23.6	9.7		
17.4	30.3	30.8	78.7	32.5		
	19.1	19.2	47.1	19.5		
17.4	2.6	2.1	1.0	0.4		
	1.6	1.4	2.1	0.9		
	4.2	4.8	17.0	7.0		
	2.8	3.3	11.5	4.7		
10.9	18.0	18.6	50.0	20.7		
10.9	2.0	2.0	4.5	1.9		
	16.0	16.6	45.5	18.8		
	0.3	0.3	0.4	0.2		
100.0	100.0	100.0	241.9	100.0	0.4	100.0

Table 3-6
New York Metropolitan Population
by Place of Work, Place of Residence, and Income, 1960
(Percent distribution)

	Income	
	Under $10,000	$10,000 and over
Place of work		
Core	58.8	66.2
Inner ring	25.6	22.8
Outer ring	15.6	11.0
TOTAL	100.0	100.0
Place of residence		
Core	54.3	36.9
Inner ring	28.4	46.4
Outer ring	17.3	16.7
TOTAL	100.0	100.0

SOURCE: Regional Plan Association, *The Region's Growth*, p. 139.

The data below show branch store volume as a percent of total sales for the major New York stores:[5]

Abraham & Straus	52.9%
Alexander's	79.4%
Bloomingdale's	46.2%
S. Klein	83.5%
Lane Bryant	58.8%
Lord & Taylor	52.5%
Macy's (New York)	59.8%
Ohrbach's	53.6%

The Export Sector. Suburban growth in the export sector is not a result of a number of low-productivity activities. In the main, firms have moved to the suburbs not in search of low-wage employees, or even primarily for reduced taxes, but rather for more space and an opportunity to use modern and more capital intensive technology, to gain better access to regional and national markets, and to have a more attractive physical environment and, in some cases, a better-quality and more cooperative work force.

An additional distinguishing characteristic of the suburban economy is that its spatial organization departs from old locational arrangements and differs from that of the city. It is almost completely oriented to truck and auto transport and to the developing highway system. Moreover, growth has been superimposed on an already existing system of small towns and satellite cities which were established when modes of transportation and production were different from those of today. In outlying areas, space has often already been preempted by low-density housing and estates, or zoning has acted as a powerful deterrent to location. The result is that a new spatial organization has taken place which is extremely loose and in which economic and residential land use are poorly related. As we will see, jobs and homes are widely separated, with the result that commuting is typically lengthy and expensive.

Manufacturing. The most important type of export activity in the suburbs is manufacturing. Interviews with firms indicate that the need for land for plant expansion or to facilitate consolidation or modernization of facilities is the most important factor motivating manufacturing firms to move out of the city. Other important reasons relate to difficulties in the city of loading and unloading, making use of trucks, and parking both trucks and autos. Taxes, rents, and labor shortages did not appear as important causes for move-outs. Firms that have left the city have uniformly been found to have increased their employment and sharply increased their floor space per employee, and in most instances they have upgraded their facilities and improved their technology.

Migration of firms from the city is, however, no longer the major source of growth in suburban manufacturing. Many firms originate in the suburbs and many move from elsewhere or are branches of firms located in other areas. Our own analysis of new firms (largely manufacturing) in a seven-county area served by the New Jersey Public Service Electric and Gas Company indicated that fewer than 16 percent had migrated from New York City during the three-year period 1963–1966.

Relative to the city's economy, suburban manufacturing is more heavily weighted toward durable-goods production, where wages are higher than is the case for nondurable-goods production.

Moreover, suburban manufacturers typically operate on a larger scale and have a higher rate of capital formation and value added. As of 1967, the average number of employees per establishment, capital expenditures per employee, and value added per employee were significantly larger in the suburban ring than in the city's economy:[6]

	Average number of employees	Capital expenditures per employee	Value added per employee
New York City	31	319	$11,443
Ring counties, N.Y. SMSA	48	610	$14,113

Increasingly, plants are branches of major manufacturing corporations. Situated on or near high-speed thruways, they deliver their output not only to the city but to an even larger extent to the markets of the North Atlantic region, the nation, and the world. Because of the need to tie in to major highways and because of the stringency of zoning requirements these new manufacturing activities tend to locate at a considerable distance from the central city.

Finally, there has been a strong trend toward upgrading of product lines. In the older manufacturing areas lying outside the city (especially in New Jersey) there has been a movement toward diversification and refinement of product line. The traditional secondary processing activities have tended to stabilize. Growth has occurred through manufacture of a variety of new products. For example, in chemicals there has been a new emphasis on such lines as proprietary drugs, pharmaceuticals, plastics, and adhesives. Primary metals production has tended to give way to the manufacture of fabricated metal products.

Wholesaling. Wholesaling accounted for over 9 percent of all job increases from 1965 to 1970 in the ring counties of the New York SMSA (Table 3-5), and the share of total jobs accounted for by this activity increased from 5.4 to 6.3 percent.

The growth of wholesaling throughout the New York suburban area has been sparked by the revolution in truck transportation, by the transformation of the Atlantic seaboard into a mega-
lopolis requiring an enlarged and improved distribution system,
and by increased sophistication of production lines and of manufacturing techniques. Wholesaling firms have increasingly located
away from the city to avoid the high cost of operating in congested
areas and to tie into the network of highways. Along with this
movement to the outlying areas has come a trend toward modernization of facilities and an adaptation of new procedures and new
organization. Increasingly, manufacturers have combined smaller
warehousing operations into a single regional operation with a
consequent reduction in labor requirements, improved processing
of orders, and more efficient delivery.

Office activity.[7] The extent of office activity undertaken in
suburbia cannot be estimated by employment data, because such
data are classified by federal and state agencies according to the
principal product or service of the establishment rather than type
of work performed. Nevertheless, the Regional Plan Association,
by making use of special survey materials, was able to prepare
estimates of employment in office buildings in the New York
metropolitan region in 1965 by type of office activity. The data
show that the ring counties account for less than a third (27.1 percent) of office employment within the region, whereas Manhattan
alone accounts for 56.2 percent.

In discussing office activity, the Regional Plan Association's
three categories are useful: headquarters, middle-market, and
local office activities. Each differs from the others in the extent of
its export role and in locational characteristics.

The bulk of the New York metropolitan region's headquarters jobs (81.2 percent in 1965) are located in Manhattan. The ring
counties, with over 50 percent of the region's population, account
for only 15 percent. Their proportion of employment in middle-
market office activity is significantly larger, 24.6 percent; and
their share of local office employment, 47.3 percent, is roughly
proportional to their population.

In recent years there has been a sharp increase in office activity in the suburban areas. Once again we make use of Regional Plan Association estimates of office employment in office buildings.

Almost ¼ million office jobs in office buildings were added in the region during the period 1959 to 1965, of which roughly half were accounted for by the inner and outer ring counties. Nevertheless, Manhattan's position was left relatively unchanged, for at the end of the period it retained 56.2 percent of all office jobs compared to 58.3 percent in 1959. The significant loss of positions occurred in the rest of the core, which accounted for only 8 percent of new office building employment in this period even though over 18 percent of these jobs were located there in 1959.

Much has been said regarding the movement of corporate headquarters from the city. The shift began in the fifties but has accelerated sharply in recent years. In 1968 only seven of Fortune's "500" headquarters had moved from the city, but since that year approximately 50 major headquarters have been relocated in the suburbs.

It is intriguing that suburban locations have been increasingly favored in locating major headquarters since as noted above, it has been traditionally thought that the Central Business District (CBD) offers the special advantages of face-to-face contact and external economies which headquarters require. Interviews indicate several factors which go far to explain this seeming paradox. First, for many headquarters, the orientation of management in their day-to-day contacts, especially at the vice-president level, is toward the company itself rather than toward external business services, supplies, or customers. Executives relate chiefly to operating divisions located in the hinterland and in other areas of the country, to R & D activities located nearby, and to other officials within the company's headquarters. Second, many large companies "internalize" a number of business services (e.g., provide legal, accounting, financial, and engineering expertise within the company's own organization), with the result that it is not necessary to be close to these services in the city. Third, corporations headquartered in the suburbs typically maintain offices and other facilities in the city so that face-to-face contacts with customers, advertising agents, and other strategic persons are readily made by executives during once- or twice-weekly visits to the city.

When this obtains, the company is free to heed the preferences of its executives for a headquarters location which minimizes commuting and which features the amenities of a campus setting. Many officials claim that such an arrangement improves morale, increases effective work time, and significantly enhances their ability to recruit promising young executives.

This does not mean, of course, that suburban locations are satisfactory for all companies. For many, one or more of the conditions outlined above do not hold. A few firms have moved to the suburbs only to regret their decisions and to return. Others admit they have gained little.

When we consider middle-market and local office activities, we find a different situation. Such office activities are not found on campus-like sites but, most frequently, in urban concentrations such as White Plains or Central Nassau County. It is access to a supply of clerical labor and lower management personnel rather than to big city external economies that comprises their chief locational advantage. Modern data processing and communications technology permit efficient operation away from the central city, although a degree of proximity to headquarters, such as the suburban location affords, may be desirable.

Business services. Our discussion of suburban manufacturing, wholesaling, and office activities indicates that these functions are less dependent on the specialized business services which have traditionally been a major attraction of the large central city. The corollary to this finding is that business services do not comprise a major segment of the suburban economy. This may be noted in Table 3-5 which shows that only 5.0 percent of the work force in the suburban counties of the New York SMSA is employed in firms classified as performing business and legal services, whereas 7.9 percent are so employed in the city. The general classification, "Mainly business services," accounts for 36.8 percent of employment in the core and only 21.8 percent in the ring counties. Such estimates of proportions of the work force do not highlight the extreme specialization inherent in the city and which is not characteristic of the suburban business services sector. For example, among the 30,000 persons listed as employed in legal firms in New York City, there is clearly both a larger number and a higher percentage of persons with expertise in such fields as maritime, patent, and tax law than there is among the 3,500 persons so classified in the ring counties.

PROBLEMS OF THE SUBURBAN LABOR MARKET

The preceding discussion has pointed up a number of factors which have brought about the special character of the suburban economy: the massive middle-class migration, the importance of the local sector and of office employment, the strong orientation of the spatial organization to the automobile and the highway system. All these, in turn, affect the character of the suburban labor market.

This is especially true of the impact of the automobile and the highway system. Manufacturing plants locate to maximize access to major highways, retail shopping centers are built at or near high-traffic intersections, office activities tend to be organized around campus locations or office complexes. At the same time the location of housing has been influenced largely by zoning restrictions and by the ability of developers to put together sizable tracts of land to permit construction at acceptable prices. Such residential developments are rarely served by public transportation.

The result is a labor market for which the automobile is the major mode of transportation; for employees of many firms, it is the only mode. A recent (1968) study of Westchester County revealed that in the southern half, 77.3 percent of all workers traveled by auto, and in the northern half, 93.3 percent. Comparable percentages of workers who used public transportation were 15.8 and 6.0 percent.[8] Interestingly, in neither segment did the percentages of workers commuting by automobile vary significantly among office, manufacturing, or service organizations.

Suburban workers commute from distant points within their counties or from other counties. Rarely is one's job located near his residence. The commuting patterns revealed by the Westchester survey cited above are summarized in Table 3-7.

The implications of heavy reliance upon auto transport and the resulting extended journey to work are extremely important for any analysis of the suburban economy. The loose spatial or-

Table 3-7
Commuting Patterns of Employees in Westchester County, 1968
(Percent distribution of workers' residences)

Workers' residences	Function of employing establishment					
	Office		Manufacturing		Service	
	Medium	*Large*	*Medium*	*Large*	*Medium*	*Large*
Northern sector workers						
workers	4	1	3	1	11	—
Westchester	77	93	88	88	73	—
Other counties	19	6	9	11	16	—
TOTAL	100	100	100	100	100	—
Southern sector workers						
New York City	11	8	24	7	10	3
Westchester	68	65	70	80	76	74
Other counties	21	27	6	13	14	23
TOTAL	100	100	100	100	100	100

SOURCE: Westchester County Department of Planning, *Westchester's Economy*, White Plains, August 1970, p. 37.

ganization discriminates against the poor, the young, and the old, by increasing the cost and time required in searching for a job and reducing the effectiveness of the labor market information system. Surveys have shown that suburban employers rely heavily on referrals from their own employees and make little use of newspaper advertising or the state employment agencies. The individual qualified only for a low-paying job and without a car is likely to be ignorant of job opportunities and unable to seek them out. Moreover, he may be unable to take employment even if he is aware that it exists, because of his lack of transportation. Although car-pool arrangements are frequently used, they typically cannot be arranged until after employment begins.

In light of the inefficiency of the labor market information system and the heavy costs which must be borne by workers who search for and travel to work, we must ask how the suburban economy has been able to sustain high rates of growth without experiencing prohibitive labor shortages. The answer seems to lie in a combination of several factors. The first is that the potential labor market is large. Given the extensive network of highways and the willingness of persons to commute long distances, firms may draw from the suburbs, the city, and from outlying areas. For example, surveys have shown that manufacturing firms which move from the city to suburb are typically able to retain their production workers who are willing to travel the long distance daily rather than give up the seniority and fringe benefits which they have accumulated. These firms look, however, to the suburban labor supply for their clerical force.

The second is that the suburban labor force is generally well suited for the type of employment offered. On one hand the great migration to the suburbs of middle-class whites has created a large supply of labor, especially of educated housewifes, and in more recent years, a new generation of high school and college graduates. On the other, the structure of the suburban economy gives rise to a demand for labor which can be filled by the supply in the area.

There have, however, been some labor shortages at specific times and places. With the rapid growth of office activity, some clerical shortages have developed. Employment surveys indicate, however, that these have been much less serious than for the Manhattan labor market. More important, there has been an unfilled demand for certain critical skills, such as machinists, and a rather general lack of availability of workers for low-skill, low-wage jobs. None of these shortages appears to have been critical, however. Given the general abundance of the labor supply, accommodation has been made to specific deficiencies.

Characteristics of the work force. In the light of the above it is useful to examine some key characteristics of the work force (Table 3-8).

We see that the percentage of blacks and other nonwhites in the suburban work force is much smaller than in the city's, especially in the outer ring where the percentage is little more than half as large. With regard to the age distribution, again since the population in the suburbs tends to be younger, we find a larger proportion of the work force in the younger groups, especially in the outer ring.

Table 3-8
Characteristics of the Work Force,
New York City and Suburbs, 1966
(Percent)

Characteristic	New York City	Inner ring	Outer ring
Total Employment			
By race			
White	81.8	87.5	90.8
Nonwhites	18.2	12.5	9.2
By Age			
Less than 18 yr.	2.6	3.6	4.2
18 to 25 yr.	14.0	16.7	17.5
25 to 50 yr.	52.7	52.9	53.1
More than 50 yr.	30.7	26.8	25.2
By sex			
Male	59.2	61.6	58.7
Female	40.8	38.4	41.3
Percentage employed less than four quarters		*All suburbs*	
Male			
White	28.5	31.9	
Non-whites	44.0	45.8	
Female			
White	39.8	43.7	
Non-whites	48.6	55.8	

SOURCE: William A. Johnson, *Changing Patterns of Employment in the New York Metropolitan Area.* New York City Rand Institute, December 1971, tables 16, 17, C1, C2, C5, C6.

Female workers account for 38.4 percent of employment in the inner ring and 41.3 percent in the outer, compared with 40.8 percent for New York City. We must note here that the city's highly office-oriented economy employs an unusually high percentage of women (41 percent compared to 34 percent for the nation as a whole). Consequently, suburbia's proportion must be regarded as high. This conclusion is consistent, of course, with the factors which have been cited above—the relatively large role of the local sector in the suburban economy, with its emphasis on retail activities, and the importance of office activity.

The data for less-than-full-year employment require explanation. These percentages were derived from the social security files of workers who were employed for less than four quarters of the year 1966. Such data do not show part-time employment in the usual sense, but rather part-year employment. They give some indication of the extent to which individuals were out of the work force because of seasonal or other types of unemployment, voluntary or involuntary. In addition, they provide some indication of the extent to which employers have access to a flexible supply of labor, i.e., a supply upon which they may draw when their demand is heavy.

For every category the percentage is higher in the suburbs than in the city. Whether or not this implies a healthy functioning of the labor market depends on whether the less-than-full-year employment is voluntary. For many white suburban housewives this may be the case, but for the suburban white youth such a preference is less typical. For suburban blacks, male and female, the high percentages of workers with some employment in less than four quarters (45.8 and 55.8 percent, respectively), exceeding the comparable percentages in the ghetto-troubled city, can suggest only a labor market with imperfections from the workers' point of view. This market draws upon the supply only for peak load requirements and offers job opportunities which are unlikely to provide satisfactory annual earnings.

There is little evidence that suburban pay scales differ significantly from those of the city. New York State Department of Labor statistics indicate somewhat higher wages for jobs in suburban labor markets in durable-goods manufacture, and slightly lower in non-durable-goods manufacture (Table 3-9). Statistics for nonmanufacturing wages are not available, but interviews indicate that clerical wages in most suburban areas are only slightly below city wages, and in specific instances (e.g., experienced secretaries) wage levels are as high.

There is little evidence that serious labor shortages of office help have developed in the suburbs. During the prerecession year 1969 the New York Employment Service reported clerical vacancy rates as a percentage of estimated annual job openings in the combined suburban counties of Westchester, Rockland, Nassau, and Suffolk; these rates ranged between 5 and 9 percent for total clerical vacancies and 2 and 3 percent for long-term clerical vacancies (unfilled for 30 days or more), compared to rates rang-

Table 3-9
Average Hourly Earnings, Manufacturing, June 1971

	New York City	Nassau and Suffolk	Westchester
All manufacturing	$3.64	$3.71	$3.70
Durable goods	3.46	3.90	4.09
Nondurable goods	3.69	3.37	3.67

SOURCE: New York State Department of Labor, *Employment Review.*

ing from 12 to 26 percent and 3 to 10 percent respectively in New York City.

PROBLEMS AND PROSPECTS IN SUBURBIA

In the course of its growth suburbia has become a special kind of economy. In it there has been a vigorous process of adaptation and specialization. Firms which have found their way to the suburbs are those that found suburbia's markets or locational features important and which have been able to adjust to its special limitations.

From this vantage the suburban economy is viable and it will continue to grow and develop. Since spatially it is open-ended, which permits easy extension of firms and labor force on the periphery, there is no physical constraint which threatens its expansion. Moreover, since its population is relatively young and well educated, there appears to be no lack of human resources to supply it with the necessary labor force.

And yet suburbia faces problems. These arise out of its unplanned and highly inefficient spatial organization, coupled with a fragmented political structure. Individual communities, faced with the necessity of providing educational and other public services out of real estate tax revenues, attempt to prevent construction of housing for low- and lower-middle-income families. Residents faced with the prospects of losing the semirural quality of life which they sought in their migration to the suburbs attempt not only to prevent construction of the housing developments but also, more recently, to exclude additional firms. The result is a pattern of growth which is increasingly irrational in that the journey to work is longer and slower, the labor market communications network by which people find appropriate employment is poorer, and certain groups—especially nonwhites in both central city and suburban ghettos—are finding access to better-paying jobs with prospects for advancement increasingly more difficult to secure.

In sum, the problem of the suburb is that while its economy is vigorous and its modern and well-financed firms are adaptable, its spatial organization gives rise to extremely high social costs which are borne disproportionately by the nonwhite, the young, and the old.

IMPLICATIONS OF SUBURBANIZATION FOR NEW YORK CITY

Analysis of the suburban economy has implications for New York City and the prospects for its future health and vitality.

Losses and gains for the city. On the one hand, the city has lost many job opportunities to its outlying areas, while it has been faced with the task of providing productive and meaningful employment for the great mass of blacks and Puerto Ricans who have filled its ghettos. Past generations of immigrants have been assimilated into the city's economy via the route of a thriving manufacturing sector. This route recently has been almost closed. Moreover, the loss of a number of important headquarters and a host of smaller office operations has reduced employment opportunities and has raised questions about the city's attractiveness as a headquarters center.

Finally, the exodus of a large segment of the city's middle class has reduced the income base upon which the retailing sector is founded, and import substitution by retail stores in the suburbs has meant lost exports of retail services for the city. It is seldom noted that, if we exclude a restricted area in midtown, the city's retail sector has become old, unattractive, and undernourished. Here again, employment opportunities have been reduced in terms of both the number and the quality of the jobs.

At the same time the vigorous growth of the suburbs has

meant the continuous growth of the metropolitan area, and with this growth, new opportunities for the city itself. As long as New York grows *as a region,* its great markets thrive; manufacturing, wholesaling, and service corporations find it necessary and desirable to locate or to remain within the area; headquarters are still drawn to the city or its environs; and the whole economic and social process is underwritten by the continued attraction of the region as a place to live and work for a vast group of energetic, talented, and well-trained individuals.

Recently, there has been a tendency to speak of the increasing independence of the suburbs. This is incorrect. While there has been a process of adaptation by which many firms have exchanged big-city advantages for those of the suburbs, there is a strong symbiotic attachment. On one hand, suburban firms cluster around a great metropolis because they need not only its markets, but its financial, advertising, legal, and technical expertise, its universities, its medical centers, its cultural and entertainment resources. On the other, the city draws upon the great human resource base afforded by an affluent, aggressive, and well-educated suburban populace and finds increasing markets for its services and its own highly specialized manufactures.

The conclusion that must be drawn is that growth and development of the suburbs must be matched by reorganization and rejuvenation of the city's economy. In an attempt to seek this reorganization, much can be learned from the suburban experience. The strength of the suburban economy lies in its modern facilities, its abundant labor force, and its highly effective integration with the new highway transportation matrix which ties together the burgeoning economy of the nation and particularly the Atlantic seaboard. In seeking a new vitality, New York's leadership must reexamine the economy in the light of these criteria.

Need for continuous adjustment. It is apparent that the city must replenish its economy when firms die or find suburban or other locations more advantageous. Ideally, market processes bring about this adjustment automatically. With the growth of the metropolitan, national, and world economies, the city becomes more specialized. In those sectors in which it has greatest comparative advantages, old firms expand and new firms spring up. Under such circumstances there is no need for special assistance by government. To a considerable extent this has been the case in New York City. During the postwar period commercial and financial sectors have been engaged in an almost continuous process of rejuvenation. As a result New York has increased the scope of activities in these sectors and has reaffirmed its position as the world's first city in finance and trade.

But similar processes have not occurred in all its sectors. For example, there has been little rejuvenation in its manufacturing sector in spite of the fact that the city is richly endowed with skilled labor and resourceful, aggressive management. The problem here is the result of the fact that the city has inherited a highly specialized physical environment which is the product of an earlier technology, transportation network, and economic structure. Reorganization of economic function often requires a spatial reorganization which cannot be achieved through the decisions of individual firms. A recent study by the city revealed that the rapid growth of the commercial sector had displaced a large number of manufacturing firms which were unable to find new space with suitable physical layout or access to the mass transit system or to other parts of the transportation network.[9] Other firms had left the city because there was no appropriate way for them to expand their facilities, although there were large areas of the city which were underutilized—areas in which buildings were outmoded, rundown, and vacant. These vacant sites were typically too small or too far from transportation terminals and frequently required first rezoning and then demolition. As a result, large and virtually intractable problems of land accumulation have faced the individual firm and even the private developer. Such problems can be solved only by the intervention of the city. The city's industrial redevelopment plan, which has as its objective the rebuilding of industrial districts through staged renewal and the development of industrial parks, is an attempt to take the kind of initiative which is required. In light of the advantages of the suburbs, the possibilities for success in the city seem limited to a selected number of light industry activities.

The city must reorganize in another way. We have noted that

the suburban economy has not developed a sophisticated business service sector and must depend in large measure upon the city for those services not available within its own firms. To a significant extent this is true for consumer services as well. Although suburbia's local sector is large and its shopping centers offer a splendid assortment of goods, it does not offer the selection of restaurants, theaters, higher education, or medical services which are available within the city. While these services are being developed in the suburbs, the economic logic of mass market and centrality dictates that unique development will continue within the city.

It is the factor of access which has prevented the close integration of city and suburb in the delivery of these important services. Congestion of the highway arteries, inadequate parking facilities, and antiquated commuting railroads insulate city from suburb and bring increasing disaffection to suburbanites for the city as a place to either work or play.

A renascence of the city's role as a center of consumer services demands improved integration throughout the region via more efficient transportation ties. Perhaps a greater flow of auto traffic is not feasible. High-speed bus, jitney, and rail transportation, however, present appealing alternatives.

Need for improved tie-in to the transportation network. We have seen that New York City lacks one major economic advantage which is enjoyed by its suburbs: effective linkage to the interstate highway transportation system of the North Atlantic seaboard. In contrast to the highly effective access of the suburban counties, the city's economy is characterized by heavy congestion and inefficiency in loading and unloading at terminal points.

The inability to tie in to the highway network readily and inexpensively has been extremely damaging to the manufacturing and wholesaling sectors of the city. In a 1969 study by the City Planning Commission of industrial moveouts, firms repeatedly expressed dissatisfaction with delays in loading and unloading freight and with traffic congestion both in the vicinity of their plants and throughout the city. A study by the Tri-State Transportation Commission has revealed that Manhattan accounts for one-third of the city's truck tonnage, although it comprises only 7 percent of its land area. Productivity of the pickup operations has declined to such an extent that special rates are often assessed and surcharges for waiting time are levied.[10]

Moreover, two of the city's greatest transportation assets, its railway and shipping terminals, are obsolete, inefficient, and connected with the highway network only by inadequate and congested roads. New York City stands at the gateway to the world. Historically, its access to major markets everywhere provided the very basis of its growth and its ultimate primacy. These advantages exist today and can be exploited once again, although at the moment they have been shamefully eroded.

Here again, the initiative must come from the public sector. To capitalize upon its unique position, the city must depend on new technology, which will require extensive financing or subsidies as well as close integration with efforts to modernize and rehabilitate the industrial sector.

We have noted that the development of the suburban economy has enlarged the supply of talented and highly motivated individuals from which the city may draw. Once again, however, the need for a close physical integration between city and suburb is paramount. The ability of the city to draw upon the suburban labor force depends upon the willingness of these persons to commute into the city. As is required for selling the city's specialized consumer services, a dramatic improvement of high-speed transportation facilities is critical. The unreliable and demeaning arrangements by which the suburbanite must make his way into and out of the city have already driven many to other employment locations and have made recruitment of young executives and professionals difficult. Better access to the city is a sine qua non.

Prospects for employing the ghetto workers. One other important implication of suburbanization relates to the large ghetto population of blacks and Puerto Ricans. We have seen that the spatial looseness of the suburban economy is fundamental to its organization today and that it has given rise to a labor market which discriminates against the unskilled worker, particularly if he does not own an automobile.

"Reverse commuting" has been suggested as a method for making suburban jobs available to the city's poor. This concept is consistent with the need for closer integration of city and suburb through improved transportation facilities.

There is every reason to believe that reverse commuting would be useful. Many workers who live in Manhattan now commute across the George Washington Bridge to work in Bergen County. Surely others could find employment in the nearby areas of New Jersey, Westchester, and Nassau Counties if subsidized rail, bus, or auto transportation were made available. But this would be a limited step at best.

Recent suburban development almost excludes minority workers in either the city or suburbia from promising job opportunities. Often, the employment opportunities are simply too far away. Low-skilled jobs and workers can rarely be brought together when a long or expensive journey to work is required.

The answer then must lie to a large extent in making low-income housing available close to employment opportunities in the suburbs or in generating employment through development of the city's economy. The first suggestion is receiving attention and will probably be pushed aggressively in the future. This course of action involves long and difficult legal battles and huge investments in new housing. At best the result will probably be that newly located plants and offices will be built in tandem with housing developments. In actuality, housing for low-income families will probably develop only as a partial answer to the suburbs' need to house their own rapidly growing cohort of young people with families.

The city will solve the problem of its ghetto workers only after it meets the more general problem of revitalizing its economy and integrating it with the overall economy of the metropolitan region. It is in this task that the special lessons learned from the suburban experience can be of greatest value.

4

THE MANPOWER RECORD

Eli Ginzberg

THERE IS MUCH that is disturbing about New York City: the lack of personal safety on the streets, the abandonment of houses and the deterioration of neighborhoods, the small amount of new residential construction, the poor performance of the public educational system, the exacerbation of racial and ethnic conflicts.

In the economic arena, the disquieting evidence consists of the decline of manufacturing and wholesaling industries, with the corresponding shrinkage in jobs for the unskilled and semiskilled; the relocation of corporate headquarters out of the city; the deterioration of the port and the difficulty of finding a site for a fourth airport in the region; the mismatch between the output of the schools and the demands of employers for competence and skill; the removal of important retailing and related service functions to the suburbs, which has accompanied the relocation of the white middle class; the ever-mounting welfare rolls and the strain which they place on the tax structure and on the competitive position of the city; the difficulties that large employers, private and non-profit, face in obtaining land for expansion; the transportation bottlenecks that discourage the movement of people and goods into and out of the city.

Small wonder that those who are knowledgeable about these adverse conditions that characterize the city in general and its economy in particular foresee trouble: a weakening of the economy, a slippage in infrastructure, an erosion of jobs.

68

New York City has been the leading urban center in the United States since the early days of the Republic, whose first capital it was, and it stands today among the great metropolises of the world. The adverse trends and circumstances that have been delineated may point to a weakening in its foundations which spells slippage and decline, but there may be countervailing forces which will contain and reverse many, if not all, of these adverse trends. At least we must look at them. In seeking a realistic perspective, we will not consider the entire range of urban and metropolitan problems but will concentrate on specific economic and manpower dimensions of New York City. We will inspect a limited number of propositions that command widespread attention.

According to the chairman of the New York City Planning Commission, Donald H. Elliott, "The decline in the number of manufacturing jobs is serious."[1] He relates this proposition to the large proportion of low-skilled workers who need opportunities for increasing their skills and incomes. The facts are clear: New York City lost 174,000 jobs in manufacturing between 1960 and 1970, on the top of a net loss of 92,000 in the fifties, which came to a loss of 266,000 over the two decades. But during the same two decades jobs in the city's service industries increased from about 500,000 in 1950 to 790,000 in 1970, which more than compensated for the number of lost manufacturing jobs.

The presumption that manufacturing employment in New York City pays well is contrary to the facts. In 1970 the gross weekly earnings of factory production workers averaged $127. In terms of *real* spendable earnings, factory workers had actually suffered a decline from $78.50 in 1965 to $76.73 in 1970![2] Nevertheless, the question remains whether the earnings of service workers are not still lower, which would justify Chairman Elliott's concern that New York City is suffering because of the out-migration of manufacturing jobs.

Let us look at the facts. At the end of the 1960s the estimated straight-time hourly earnings of nonexempt workers in manufacturing amounted to $2.78; following is the range of earnings among service workers: hotels, $2.80; personal services, $2.23; business services, $2.68; auto rental, repair, and services, $2.85;

miscellaneous repair services, $3.00+; motion pictures, $3.00+; other amusement and recreation, $2.99; medical and health services, $2.85; legal services, $3.00+; museums and art galleries, $2.97; nonprofit organizations, $2.94; miscellaneous services, $3.00+.[3] We see that with the single exception of the approximately 55,000 persons in personal services, which include domestic workers, the hourly earnings among service workers are comparable with those paid to manufacturing workers.

It is often assumed that the worker with low skills in manufacturing will have an opportunity to advance through the "internal labor market" into better jobs. But of the more than 28,000 manufacturing establishments in New York City, about 19,000, or about 70 percent, have less than 20 workers, and only about 460, or less than 2 percent, have 250 or more employees. Of course, the size of service establishments is even more skewed in the direction of smallness: over 90 percent have less than 20 workers; under 1 percent have over 250. But the parallels between the two fields of manufacturing and services are greater than the differences. In both, a large internal labor market is the exception. Workers who seek opportunities to improve their skills and incomes must change employers, even industries. The conspicuous characteristic of New York City's more than 200,000 business establishments is the small size of the average unit: over 175,000 establishments have fewer than 20 workers![4]

A second commonly accepted proposition is that New York City's economy is shrinking—that its total payroll employment is declining. The facts, however, do not support this view of the local labor market. During each year between 1963 and 1969 there was a rise in total payroll employment: During this period there was a total increase of 266,000 on the payrolls, or approximately 44,000 a year. This trend was reversed in 1970 and 1971, however, when total payroll employment declined by 34,000 and 84,000 because of the recession that characterized the national and the city's economy.

Additional evidence of the strength of New York City's job market is adduced by the fact that throughout the 1960s, the private nonmanufacturing sector expanded at an annual rate of approximately 27,000 net additional jobs. And total government employment increased in every year by an annual average of about 15,000.[5]

Behind these generally expansionary trends in total employment during the decade of the 1960s, there was marked resilience in New York City's job market. From the beginning to the end of the decade, the city lost 63,600 jobs in apparel manufacturing; about 24,000 each in water transportation and food and kindred products; 15,000 in railroads; between 10,000 and 12,000 each in miscellaneous manufacturing, real estate, wholesale trade, and personal services; and about 6,000 each in hotels and lodging places and eating and drinking places, representing a total decline of 182,000 jobs in these 10 industries. But in the 10 leading sectors of job growth, there was a net gain of 460,000 jobs distributed as follows: local government, 145,000; miscellaneous business services, 67,000; medical and other health services, banking, and securities brokers, between 45,000 and 49,000 *each*; education (nongovernment), 28,000; air transportation, communications, miscellaneous services, between 20,000 and 22,000 *each*; and state government, 17,000.[6]

A third currently accepted proposition is that the unique role of New York City as a stronghold of corporate headquarters is being eroded and that it is only a matter of time before this trend will lead to the decline of the city's economy. Again, a look at the facts will help to set the record straight. In 1970, 118 of the 500 largest industrial firms in the nation and 44 of the 250 largest nonindustrial firms maintained headquarters in New York City. Since then approximately 20 industrial corporations have indicated their intention of moving their headquarters out of New York City. We do not know, however, how many corporations may decide to move in. In recent years only a few large corporations such as Norton Simon have decided in favor of New York City. A recent, as yet unpublished, study points out that the principal forces operating in favor of relocation out of the city are corporate efforts to minimize the commuting burden for executives, to escape from the negatives in the New York City environment— crime, dirty streets, etc. —and to eliminate the problem of persuading middle management to accept positions which require that they work in New York City. Certainly the city faces a challenge on this front. The critical question is how much of a challenge. The answer lies in the alternatives open to the major companies: If they opt to move out of New York City, to where will they move? One possibility is that they might relocate in the inner or outer ring of the metropolitan region; a second is to move to another major city such as Houston, as several of the oil companies have done; a third is to relocate in a medium-sized city such as Phoenix.

A recent report by the Regional Plan Association on the "Growth and Location of Office Jobs"[7] provides the following data about the New York region and particularly about New York City's role as the hub of corporate headquarters. Although the region has only one-tenth of the nation's nonagricultural employment, it accounts for one-fifth of headquarters jobs. Moreover, the report states, "Over the past decade or so, the Region maintained this position remarkably well. . . . With 28 percent of the Region's total employment, but 40 percent of its employment in the top eight percent income bracket . . . 82 percent of its top industrial headquarters, Manhattan's dominant position in the Region is clear."[8]

The report notes that one-half of the nation's 125 firms with the biggest advertising expenditures are located in the New York region and that 49 of these are in the Central Business District (CBD) of Manhattan. Another interesting point about the pull of the CBD is that, of the major companies with headquarters in the suburbs, two-thirds maintained branch offices in Manhattan in the mid 1960s.

If finance is the lifeblood of the economy, then the present role of New York City is again noteworthy: It serves as the banking headquarters, insurance headquarters, and the headquarters of the securities industry. In the mid-1960s, 80 percent of all headquarters jobs in the region were located in Manhattan, 86 percent in New York City. In 1963, when the only complete inventory was made, 50 percent of the region's office floor space was located in Manhattan's CBD, and this pattern has continued with "50 percent of the new construction since 1963 located there too. Thus there has been no decentralization of office buildings from the Manhattan CBD at all."[9] The 1967–1972 construction rate of 13 million gross square feet annually in Manhattan bespeaks the vitality of New York City's white-collar economy. During the 1960s total office construction in the region amounted to more than $2 billion, three-quarters of which was centered in New York City, primarily in Manhattan.[10] Nothing in these data suggests that New York City is likely to lose its preeminence as a headquarters community in the near future, although its relative position will probably be less dominant than in the recent past.

The fourth proposition holds that the root cause of all New York City's difficulties is the population shift that has taken place whereby middle-income whites have escaped to the suburbs and poor blacks and Puerto Ricans have taken their place in the city core. Certainly a major shift has taken place in the composition of the population. In 1950, in its total population of almost 7.9 million, New York City had approximately 800,000 blacks and 250,000 Puerto Ricans. In the twenty years thereafter the non-white population increased by about 1 million and the Puerto Rican, by about 700,000. Since the total population in 1970 had been maintained as it was in 1950, at just under 7.9 million, there was a drop in the non-Spanish-speaking white population from 6.8 to 5.1 million. Thus, within the two decades, the minority population (blacks and Puerto Ricans) in New York City increased from slightly over 1 million to nearly 2.8 million, and in 1970 accounted for approximately 35 percent of the city's total population.

From the vantage point of the city's labor market the critical questions relate to the extent to which the minority populations have been absorbed in productive employment and how well they are faring relative to the white population. In this connection we will want to look at the occupational distribution, unemployment rates, and income distribution of the subgroups.

One background point: It is important to note that after World War II minority groups came to New York City in large numbers because there were jobs available for them—jobs that the white population were no longer able or willing to perform, either because they had relocated to the suburbs or they had moved up the occupational hierarchy. New York City has a large minority population today because it attracted them in the past.

In the single decade 1960–1970 there were steady improvements in the occupational distribution of Negro and other races relative to the white majority. In 1960 less than one out of three (29 percent) minority workers were in white-collar occupations. In 1970 the corresponding proportion was about 42 percent, an increase of 13 percentage points. The proportion of white workers in white-collar employment increased only 8 percentage points from 55 to 63 percent. At the lower end of the scale, there was a drop in the proportion of minority workers in service jobs from 30 to 25 percent during the decade, while the proportion of whites in service jobs remained at a steady 10 percent. All the decline in service employment among minority workers occurred in private households, which declined from about 10 percent of total minority employment in 1960 to about 4 percent in 1970.[11] We see, then, that although discrepancies remain between the occupational distribution of whites and that of minorities, the gross differences are being reduced.

A critical measure of how well or poorly minorities fare in the labor market is the comparative unemployment rates—the rate for the city in which they live and work and the ratio of their rate to that of the white majority. In both comparisons New York City measures favorably. Both in 1969, a prosperous year, and 1970, a year of recession, the unemployment rate for Negroes and other races in New York City was considerably below those in most other large cities and in the country at large. In 1970, for instance, when the national nonwhite unemployment rate was 8.2 percent, the black unemployment rate in New York was 5.4 percent. Moreover, the ratio of Negro-white unemployment was 1 to 1.1 in New York City, compared to 1 to 1.8 for the nation. Clearly, discrimination in employment is less severe in New York City than in most large cities.[12]

The critical factors that determine whether or not a family can escape from poverty are whether it has one or more wage earners, the level of their occupational qualifications, and the number of dependents. Most minority group families which have more than one full-time worker are likely to earn more than the $7,200 which in 1970 the U.S. Bureau of Labor Statistics estimated was necessary to maintain a family of four.

With regard to income, we find that in 1968, 1 in every 10 families living in New York City reported incomes below the poverty line, and more than one-third of all four-person families reported incomes under $7,000. In the major poverty areas of the city where minorities are heavily overrepresented, nearly one-third of the Puerto Rican and more than a fifth of the Negro families were below the poverty line.

One measure of the failure of minority groups to make it economically in New York City is reflected in the steep rise in the relief rolls. This has led to another critical formulation. Welfare costs in New York City have risen to a point where they jeopardize the city's economic future. The high welfare and related costs have led to steep tax increases which act as a deterrent to businesses and families with high incomes which otherwise might remain in New York and deter more of both from relocating to the city. What are the facts?

Between 1960 and 1970 the total number of persons receiving public assistance in New York City increased from about 330,000 to 1,165,000. In both years, children under 18 years of age accounted for the majority of the case load; they accounted for 56 percent of the total in 1960 and 59 percent in 1970.[13]

The rising case load resulted primarily from increases in the Aid for Dependent Children (ADC) program. In 1960 ADC recipients accounted for 2.6 percent of New York's population; in 1970, for 10.9 percent. The public aid programs in August 1971 cost over $190 million *monthly.* It is not generally known, however, that medical assistance amounted to $81 million per month or about one-third more than ADC, which totaled $61 million.[14]

There is no question that the welfare situation, at least as reflected by ADC, worsened perceptively in New York City during the 1960s. At the beginning of the decade the ADC recipients in New York City accounted for 6.5 percent of the United States total; in December 1968 they had risen to 11.9 percent, and by December 1970 they had slipped back to 8.9 percent—a higher level than a decade earlier.[15]

As one might anticipate, the average monthly payment for ADC recipients—$67 per month—was higher in New York City than in most other large metropolitan centers. Minneapolis alone exceeded the New York scale; in Boston, it was $49; in Chicago, $54; in Philadelphia, $62.[16]

The budgetary impacts of the rising welfare costs can be estimated by looking at the increases in the city's expenditures in total and by major components between 1962 and 1972. Expenditures increased from $2.5 billion to over $8.5 billion, or by about 240 percent. Social service transfer payments, however, showed twice as rapid a rate of increase, about 500 percent, from $280 million to $1.670 billion. In 1962 welfare costs accounted for 11 percent of the city's expenditures; in 1972, for 19 percent.[17]

If the city had been forced to meet all or most of its rapidly rising expenditures out of its own resources, it probably would have failed. In point of fact, it had to double its tax yield from $2 billion to $4 billion, over the nine-year period from 1962 to 1971. The larger part of its revenue increase, about $3 billion, was covered by state and federal aid amounting to, respectively, $2.7 and $1.3 billion in 1971. In 1971 the city met 47.6 percent of its revenue needs from its own resources.[18]

One measure of the ease or difficulty with which the city doubled its revenue from local sources is the valuation of taxable property. In 1962 the full valuation was estimated at $33.6 billion; the revised figures for 1971 show $61.3 billion. Not quite a doubling, but almost.[19] While it would be foolish to deny that the city has found it difficult to meet its rising expenditures—including those precipitated by rising welfare costs—it has been assisted materially by the growth in its own economy and by state and federal aid.

Another related measure is total personal income, which in New York City increased from $23.4 billion in 1960 to $38 billion in 1969. While inflation exaggerates the extent of real growth, substantial gains did occur. Thus, the city's $2 billion welfare bill must be considered against its total personal income, which is in the $40 billion range.

The sixth and last proposition relates to the ability of the generation of young people, particularly the high proportion of minority youth, to fit into the job structure of New York City. Many contend that the city's economy is doomed and that its minorities are trapped because the new supply of job entrants will be unable to meet employers' demands. If this is true, and if the fact of this mismatch becomes known, many employers in New York City will seek to locate elsewhere and others will avoid expanding or locating here. This would further erode the city's economic base.

Once again we must look to the facts to see whether they support this prognostication. In the recent unpublished study referred to earlier which cites the factors propelling large employers to move out of New York City, an inadequate supply of clerical labor was mentioned by relatively few employers. Small wonder: In 1960 there were approximately 50 percent more whites than Negroes and others in clerical occupations; by 1970 the two groups were only 3 percentage points apart—28 and 25 percent respectively.[20] Also relevant in this connection is the substantial parity between the wage structures for office occupations of men and women in New York City and in Westchester and Rockland Counties. And where differentials exist, such as between New York City and the Nassau-Suffolk area, they are quite small.[21]

One principal thrust, however, must be to assess the young people who are coming through the school system. At the beginning of the 1960s, minority youth accounted for two out of every five on the public school register; at the end of the decade, they represented three out of every five of the approximately 1.140 million pupils. In 1969–1970 there were an additional 426,000 youngsters, predominantly white youth, on non-public school registers. Among public school pupils, about 10 percent had moderate language difficulty and an additional 5 percent had severe language difficulty. Youngsters from Puerto Rican backgrounds comprised the largest group of those with language handicaps.[22]

Clearly, young people with language difficulties face additional hurdles in moving through the educational system and in competing for the better jobs. But most of them should be able to overcome their language handicaps during their early years in school. Moreover, the majority of Spanish-speaking youngsters are no longer immigrants; they were born and are brought up in New York City, which points to a diminishing language barrier in the years ahead.

A more serious difficulty is the quantity and quality of education that is provided by the public educational system. The best current estimates point to a high school dropout rate of 40 percent in New York City, double the average for the nation. Another shortcoming is that approximately half of the students who do graduate receive a general diploma, which reflects more their ability to have negotiated the system than their competence in the use of language and quantitative skills.[23] These are not minor shortcomings, but neither should they be exaggerated.

First, the educational attainment of both whites and minorities continues to increase. By 1969 nearly one-third of both black and white adults had terminated their schooling with a high school diploma, compared to approximately one-fifth for each in 1960.[24] The new effort of open enrollment will increase the proportions of both groups who enter and complete higher education and holds promise of equalizing the percent of blacks and whites with college experience.

Equally important are the educational requirements for the jobs that are opening up. An estimate for New York State for the decade 1965–1975 suggests that only one in eight job openings will require a college degree or more, and only one in five requires education beyond the high school level. Even allowing for the fact that job openings in New York City are skewed in the direction of white-collar employment with higher educational requirements, the fact remains that a high school diploma which reflects achievement would suffice for about three out of every four jobs.[25] The public school system faces several challenges, none insurmountable: to reduce the language barriers affecting non-English-speaking populations; to increase their holding power; to narrow the gap between attainment and achievement.

The thrust of this analysis has not been to deny that the loss in manufacturing jobs, the slow growth in total employment, the relocation out of the city of corporate headquarters, the continued substantial rate of in-migration, the marked rise in the welfare population, and the shortcomings of the educational system represent, individually and collectively, a drag on the well-being and growth of New York City. But a closer inspection of each proposition has suggested the need to put the negatives into perspective. And in perspective, the impressive point is that New York is thriving as an economic center and is well on the way to absorbing effectively its vastly expanded minority population which now accounts for approximately one in three. The effective accommodation of newcomers is never easy, but over several centuries New York City has demonstrated a special capacity for effective accommodation. There is good reason to hope that the seventies will be an easier decade than the sixties.

5

OPPORTUNITY AND INCOME

Marcia Freedman

ENCOMIUM OR ELEGY—he who writes about New York City must first acknowledge its size and diversity, its dispersion of power, its lack of central tendencies. When considered as a labor market in which 4 million people were employed at the beginning of the seventies, the same difficulties of generalization arise. Is New York a white-collar town? Yes, but it has more factory jobs than any other American city. Is it a low-wage town? Yes, but it also provides the highest salaries. Is manufacturing activity declining in New York? Yes, but perhaps not as fast as elsewhere. Are corporate headquarters leaving the city? Yes, but some are also arriving.

Ultimately, a worker's question is: Can a living be made in New York City, and, if so, how? Answers to this question, of course, are relative. Compared with 31 of the world's largest cities, New York salaries are the highest. While automobiles, gasoline, and taxes are relatively cheap, all other consumer goods and services are among the most expensive, including astronomical rents for standard housing, which lead the way. Furthermore, the patchwork of available medical care services and payment methods never equals the coverage enjoyed by a citizen of, for example, Copenhagen, where all medical and dental services, including prescriptions, are provided without direct cost to the consumer.[1]

As a matter of policy, the United States has been reluctant to tamper with market mechanisms; and even with the expansion of social security, welfare, and health schemes, families require relatively high cash earnings to maintain themselves. This gives substance to an old joke, "Rich or poor, it's good to have money." In New York City, the Bureau of Labor Statistics (BLS) provides some convenient benchmarks as to just how much money is required for three different levels of living. For a precisely defined urban family of four in 1970, it took $7,183 to maintain a lower level of living; $12,134 to maintain an intermediate level; and $18,545 for a higher level.[2]

Meeting these budget standards requires a constant stream of earnings. The BLS implies as much in its "precise definition" of the family to whom the figures are meant to apply:

> ... a 38-year-old husband employed full time, his non-working wife, a boy of 13, and a girl of 8. After about 15 years of married life, *the family is well established,* and the husband is an experienced worker. . . . The family has, for each budget level, average inventories of clothing, house furnishings, major durables, and other equipment.[3]

Estimates are also furnished for other family constellations and for single individuals. While it may be possible for a single individual under 35 to earn $4,580 a year (the higher budget for individuals) through intermittent work, it is probably correct to assume that mature workers require a stable income flow. They must, in fact, be established in the labor market as well as in their marriages and family lives to achieve the BLS standards for families.

This usually means some form of occupational or organizational attachment that affords steady work at adequate wages and minimum protection against such hazards as unemployment, sickness, or old age. In a segmented labor market, not all workers achieve establishment. This is the phenomenon involved in concepts that dichotomize the labor market into such categories as primary and secondary,[4] preferred and transient,[5] or central and peripheral.[6]

The attributes of the job are critical for achieving work establishment. Very different kinds of work lend themselves to this degree of modest success, which in effect gives the worker a kind of property right in his job and keeps other possible claimants out.

For the purpose of minimizing both risk and competition, the most important work-related elements seem to be:

1. Professional or other highly specialized credentials
2. Substantial market power of the employing firm
3. Unionization

The strength of these elements and the nature of their inter-action depend in large measure on the product market to which the job is directed. To assess the opportunities available to work-ers in New York City, the first step is to look at the broad outlines of product markets as they are reflected in industrial composition (Table 5-1). The relative size of industry groupings for wage and salary workers in Table 5-1 is familiar to students of the New York labor market, who have drawn from the distribution quite divergent inferences about both the present and the future of the city. What it means to individuals and how they try to cope with it has also been analyzed. Inevitably, it turns out that the structure produces good jobs for some and bad jobs for others. The best we can do is to assess generally the probabilities, bearing in mind that an individual outcome may run counter to statistical predic-tions for the group.

PROFESSIONAL AND CREDENTIALED EMPLOYMENT

Cutting across the industrial distribution, to which we will return below, is a top stratum of workers whose market protection is in the form of distinct occupational activities usually requiring ex-tended preemployment training and specific credentials in the form of degrees and licenses. These workers are included in the census category, "professional, technical and kindred," which ag-gregates such disparate occupations as physician, entertainer, and engineering technician. The category as a whole constitutes 14 percent of New York City's total employment, about the same as the national proportion (Table 5-2), but the city has a dispro-portionate share of the higher-paid professionals.

Comparable detailed occupational figures for New York City are available only for 1960, but it is likely that the relationship persists. At that time, for example, physicians, lawyers, and ac-

Table 5-1
Wage and Salary Employees by Industry, New York
City, Annual Average, 1970

Industry	Number (thousands)	Percent distribution
Primary	*113.3*	*3.0*
Construction	108.9	2.9
Manufacturing	*772.8*	*20.2*
Durable goods	179.8	4.7
Nondurable goods	*593.0*	*15.5*
Apparel	203.8	5.3
Printing & publishing	122.2	3.2
Transportation	205.4	5.4
Communications	93.3	2.4
Utilities	25.7	0.7
Wholesale trade	304.4	8.0
Retail trade	317.0	8.3
Eating & drinking places	119.1	3.1
FIRE	463.9	12.2
Services	*841.1*	*22.0*
Producer & legal	293.4	7.7
Health	145.7	3.8
Private education & welfare	178.3	4.7
Hotels & motels	35.5	0.9
Personal & repair	130.7	3.4
Private household*	57.5	1.5
Government	*561.7*	*14.7*
Public education	157.2	4.1
TOTAL	3,817.7	100.0

* Estimate for 1969 from New York State Department of Labor, Special News Memorandum 141, *Private Household Workers, New York State, 1970*, June 1, 1971.
SOURCE: New York Department of Labor, Division of Employment, Research and Statistics Office, *Employment Review*, vol. 24, no. 5 (May 1971), pp. 7–21.

countants were a significantly greater share of total professional employment in the city than in the nation, while engineers and teachers (whose earnings are much lower) accounted for larger proportions nationally.[7]

Some idea of the incomes associated with these jobs may be gained from the BLS Annual Survey of Professional, Administrative and Technical Pay in New York.[8] In New York City in June 1970, monthly salaries for attorneys (excluding those in private

Table 5-2
Occupational Distribution of Jobs, New York City and
the United States, 1970

	N.Y.C.		U.S.
	Number	Percent	Percent
Occupation	*(thou-*	*distri-*	*distri-*
	sands)	*bution*	*bution*
Professional, technical, and kindred workers	571.5	14.0	14.5
Managers, officials, and proprietors	404.4	9.9	10.7
Clerical and kindred workers	1,013.5	24.8	17.3
Sales workers	321.5	7.9	6.2
Craftsmen, foremen, and kindred workers	421.9	10.3	13.0
Operatives and kindred workers	643.2	15.8	17.9
Service workers	568.6	13.9	12.6
Farmers and farm laborers	1.1	—	3.5
Laborers, except farm and mine	132.9	3.3	4.5
TOTAL All occupations	4,078.6	100.0	100.0

SOURCE: New York City figures are projections from New York State Department of Labor, Division of Research and Statistics, *Manpower Directions in New York State 1965–1975, Job Requirements and Labor Force,* vol. 2, March 1968, pp. 39–40. National figures are from U.S. Bureau of the Census, *Current Population Reports,* ser. P-60, no. 75, "Income in 1969 of Families and Persons in the United States," December 14, 1970, p. 109.

practice or employed by the government) ranged from $950 to $3,350 a month. The mean annual salaries for two levels surveyed, III and V, were $17,244 to $26,916. Accountants and auditors (excluding those employed in accounting and auditing firms) had mean annual salaries ranging from $8,328 for beginners with bachelor's degrees to $23,640 for the highest level among chief accountants. New York pay averages were 7 percent higher than the corresponding national figures, mainly because "49 percent of the accountants studied in New York were in the two top work levels surveyed for their occupation, as against 37 percent nationally."[9]

The three scientific occupations surveyed (chemists, engineers, and engineering technicians) were less numerous in the city, and their salaries compared unfavorably with comparable salaries in the rest of New York State as well as with the United States as a whole, probably because of the absence in the city of large durable goods manufacturing.

The outlook for professional and technical employment in New York City is mixed. On the one hand, the city's preeminence in producer services and in finance means that certain kinds of top professional jobs will continue to be important in the city's manpower picture. Many of these are protected not only by the level of credentials required but also by other kinds of control over the terms and conditions of employment. Physicians, dentists, lawyers, accountants, architects, and engineers all require some form of state license to practice, and to varying degrees they control the supply of the profession through their influence on training institutions and curricula. Public school teachers not only require licensing, but also have the added protections of civil service and a strong union. The same may be said of other professionals working for government in New York City.

These shelters will probably continue to yield high earnings for those who are employed, but, in some occupations, employment will not be as readily available in the seventies as in the sixties because of the pressure of increased supplies of well-educated workers. This effect is already apparent, most clearly among teachers. New York City teachers, who enjoy a high pay scale and other benefits, will doubtless continue to do so, but their ranks will not grow very much in the short run because of both demographic shifts in the school-age population and stringencies in the city budget. At the other extreme, the income of physicians will probably continue to increase as long as the profession is successful in limiting supply and in influencing the size of third-party payments in such schemes as Medicaid and Medicare.

In addition to the professionals, New York City has a sizable cohort of salaried managers. It is difficult to estimate their number, but the relative magnitude of high-salaried jobs in the city may be inferred from the proportion of exempt workers in various industries and their earnings. These workers by definition include salaried professionals, executives, administrators, and outside salesmen, who are ineligible for overtime pay and other benefits according to the federal and state minimum wage laws.

Table 5-3
Exempt Employment as a Percent of Industry
Employment and Median Weekly Earnings in Exempt
Employment, New York City and New York State outside New
York City, Selected Industries, 1966

Industry	Percent exempt		Median weekly earnings	
	New York City	Other New York State	New York City	Other New York State
All manufacturing	14.8	14.9	$226	$211
Durable goods	18.1	16.3	231	217
Nondurable goods	13.9	11.8	224	190
Wholesale	32.6	27.4	219	180
Finance & insurance	20.5	27.2	218	170
Business services	20.9	17.8	250	230
Legal services	23.5	12.1	206	163

SOURCE: New York State Department of Labor, Division of Research and Statistics, *The Structure of Earnings and Hours in New York State, The Over-all View,* vol. 1, May 1968, pp. 83–92, 113–122.

Figures available for 1966 show 507,000 exempt workers in private wage and salary employment in the city, with median weekly earnings of $208. The functions performed by exempt workers vary from industry to industry, and by no means do all have a favorable earnings picture. In hospitals, for example, 23,000 exempt workers had median earnings of $118;[10] however, the highest earners, physicians, are largely self-employed and thus underrepresented here.

Table 5-3 compares the proportion of exempt workers and their median weekly earnings in New York City with those in the rest of New York State. What is striking is not the differences in proportions of exempt workers, but the significantly higher earnings in the city. In durable goods manufacturing, part of the differential is due to headquarters operations. Among nonexempt workers, on the other hand, those outside the city earned $121 compared to $90 earned by those in the city.[11] Average wages outside the city are raised up by highly paid workers in such durable goods manufacturing industries as machinery, transportation equipment, photographic equipment, and steel and are lowered in the city by relatively low-paid female clericals.

In finance and insurance, the proportion of exempt workers is higher outside the city, probably because firms are smaller, but earnings are much higher in the city. In business and legal services, two areas where the city is predominant, both proportions and earnings are far greater than they are outside the city.

SELF-EMPLOYMENT

Even the casual observer is struck by the large number of small businesses in New York City, but data concerning them are few and unreliable. The figures presented in Table 5-4 were derived by the Internal Revenue Service from 1967 "business schedules filed by individuals who were proprietors of their own business organizations."[12] The term "proprietor" generally means a self-employed person, but the difficulties of definition and of geo-

Table 5-4
Number of Business Proprietorships and Average Net
Profits, Selected Industries, New York Standard Metropolitan
Statistical Area, 1967

Selected industry	Number of businesses	Average annual net profit
Agriculture, forestry, fisheries	7,524	$ 245
Contract construction	20,911	4,283
Manufacturing	8,388	7,562
Transportation	9,387	3,779
Wholesale trade	19,797	6,678
Retail trade	55,113	4,521
FIRE	20,079	5,751
Services	*171,190*	*6,657*
Personal services	29,074	3,290
Business services	41,534	4,431
Offices of physicians and surgeons	26,850	19,022
Other medical services	11,002	4,291
Legal services	17,581	10,006
Other services	45,149	2,793
TOTAL All industries	318,630	5,831

SOURCE: Internal Revenue Service, *Statistics of Income—1967, Business Income Tax Returns,* 1970, table 2.9.

graphical location make the data useful only to suggest the magnitude of self-employment in the New York City SMSA (the city plus Westchester, Rockland, Nassau, and Suffolk Counties) and the relative profitability of certain activities carried on by this heterogeneous group.

Table 5-4 indicates in a gross way the gap in earnings between professionals such as doctors, dentists, and lawyers, on the one hand, and the managers of small business enterprises on the other. This difference in profits corresponds with an analysis of aggregate national data on the self-employed by Irving Leveson.[13] He describes the long-term decline in nonfarm self-employment and relates it to a decrease in earnings opportunities relative to wage and salary employment. Given this conclusion, it is not surprising that the decline in numbers has been greater among nonprofessionals whose earnings potential is less in entrepreneurial competition than among professionals sheltered by the protective structures described above.

In New York City, there seems to be cause for concern about the continued existence of many small establishments in trade and service. Store rents have risen to levels that make continued operation uneconomic. Competition from larger units, undercapitalization, and managerial inadequacy probably have contributed to the problems of small business, but turnover is also adversely affected by the combination of inflation and recession that has slowed the rest of the economy in the recent past.

PRODUCT MARKET AND UNIONIZATION

One attribute of preferred employment that is usually taken for granted is its continuity. Jobs of the kind discussed above are structured in the expectation of full-time, year-round activity which, *ceteris paribus,* implies higher annual earnings than a part-time or intermittent work schedule. Data based on the Social Security Administration continuous work history file give a crude estimate of employment stability. In 1966 about two-thirds of the city's labor force had some employment in each of the four quarters of the year.[14] This is not the same as year-round work, nor does it indicate the proportion of part-time workers or new entrants to the labor force. The figure does, however, give some indication of the magnitude of the primary and secondary labor markets in the city.

Like the rest of the nation, New York generates a number of jobs in product markets with fluctuating demands—jobs that are best filled, from the employer's point of view, with a flexible work force. According to the product market, workers have more or less opportunity to stabilize the terms and conditions of employment or to bargain for a level of earnings that obviates some of the disadvantages of intermittency.

Unionization, or other forms of collective action, produce different results depending on two major industry variables, the degree of competition and the geographic scope of the market. Taking these into account, Martin Segal has made a convincing case that union wage policies have the best chance of success in relatively noncompetitive industries, whether the market be national (steel, auto) or local (transit, utilities). In competitive industries, unions have more influence where the market is local than where it is national, mainly because the geographically restricted character of demand makes successful organization and collective action more productive.[15] The apparel, construction, retailing, and public administration sectors provide contrasting examples of this thesis in New York City.

Apparel manufacturing. This industry accounted for 5.3 percent of average annual employment in 1970 in New York City. Total employment has declined steadily, but apparel is still the single largest source of factory jobs. It is probable that the job loss has been sustained mainly in contract shops, where the work is most routine and unstable and where the pay is lowest. Exempt workers, for example, are 9 percent of industry employment in the city, compared to 4.6 percent in the rest of New York State.[16] Furthermore, while women have 81 percent of jobs in this industry nationally,[17] in New York City they constitute two-thirds of the workers.[18] Since male occupations are by and large more stable and higher paid, the occupational structure of the industry is more favorable for establishment in New York City than elsewhere.

Nevertheless, employment in the industry exhibits wide seasonal fluctuations, especially among female sewing machine operators, the largest single occupational group. In the 2½-year period beginning in 1969, employment grew steadily in the winter months of each year from a low in December to a high in March. From March to July 1970, the work force decreased 12.1 percent. For women the decrease was 14.5 percent, and for men, 7.3 percent.[19]

In addition to seasonal instability, employment in the industry is adversely affected by cyclical movements in the economy, style confusions, and most of all, by competition, both domestic and foreign. The product market is, in effect, worldwide and intensely competitive, a combination that sharply constrains possible gains through unionization. Even though the industry is highly organized in New York and most of the concomitants of sweated labor have long since disappeared, wages in the industry remain low compared to those in other manufacturing. Nonexempt workers in 1966, for example, had median weekly earnings of $77.04, compared to $90.40 in all manufacturing.[20] Even with full-time, year-round employment, industry pay scales do not yield high earnings; in fact, however, the likelihood of an intermittent work pattern is greater for the lower paying occupations than for the higher paying ones.

Construction. The product market in construction, in contrast to apparel manufacturing, is geographically limited, even though construction workers are highly mobile. This fact, combined with a historically strong craft tradition, makes it possible for unions to offset some of the disadvantages that inhere in the industry pattern of activity.

Contract construction, which accounts for about 3 percent of employment in the city, is not as important in the city as it is nationally. It is more stable in the city, however, because the type of commercial construction which accounts for most building activity requires a larger proportion of electrical and mechanical craftsmen, whose work is relatively unaffected by seasonal patterns. These craftsmen have strong control over entry into their unions;

and they have negotiated high hourly rates and, in some cases, short workweeks that guarantee a steady stream of premium pay.

For other blue-collar workers, construction employment is a sometime thing. In 1970 summer employment represented a 16 percent increase over the 98,400 who were working in January. The big drop in both 1969–1970 and 1970–1971 occurred from December to January, a monthly reduction of 7.5 percent.[21] It is not clear how many people involved in seasonal declines are students who are employed during vacations, workers who find employment elsewhere when there are no construction jobs, or simply part-year workers attached to construction.

What is clear, however, is that high hourly rates and fringe benefits help ease the pain of intermittency.

> At $6.63 an hour in July 1970, the City's average scale for building trades workers was nearly double the hourly earnings average of $3.41 for factory production workers. . . .
>
> Pay scales for New York City building tradesmen were about seven percent above the national average of $6.19. New York City's $8.30-an-hour average for wages and benefits combined was 19 percent above the comparable national figure of $6.97. At $1.67 an hour, employer payments to funds of New York City building tradesmen were more than double the average payment nationally.[22]

Retailing. In this industry, the prevalence of jobs structured as part time represents a different kind of barrier to work establishment. Overall, one-third of those employed in retailing in New York City in 1966 worked less than thirty-two hours per week, although the proportion varied from 11.5 percent among automobile dealers and gas stations to 46.5 percent in drugstores.[23] This part-time work force is composed primarily of mature women and young workers of both sexes, augmented to some extent by moonlighters. Together they supply the flexibility required by the typically long hours of retail store operation. This flexibility, which is so integrally related to product market, is attained at the expense of an interstitial work force. That individuals may welcome the opportunity for part-time employment because of other demands on their time or even from purely personal preference does not alter the fact that such jobs offer neither high earnings, stability of employment, nor prospects for advancement.

Exempt workers in retailing (including eating and drinking establishments) numbered about 50,000 in 1966.[24] Among the rank and file, however, the two-thirds employed full time were in occupations with widely divergent prospects. In department stores, for example, salesmen who handle high-ticket items and receive commissions in addition to salary generally have high earnings. In large stores, not only unionization has raised wages, but for male personnel engaged in merchandise handling, contracts also provide several pay levels for internal promotions.[25] For the majority of retail workers, however, pay scales are low, and even though conventional styles of retailing retain a greater hold in the city than elsewhere, many of the new jobs in the industry are the same check-out cashiers and stock clerks one finds in self-service operations across the nation.

PUBLIC EMPLOYMENT

Another occupation where work activity is intermittent provides an interesting contrast to the typical manning schedules in retailing. On the theory that no one can predict when a fire will break out, staffing patterns for firemen are based on a twenty-four-hour cycle with the same number of men and pieces of equipment at all times. Since known statistical variations in the type and number of alarms are not taken into account, firemen spend about two-thirds of their time on nonwork activities. They are, nevertheless, paid at substantially the same rate as policemen, who spend 80 to 90 percent of their time in actual work.[26] This particular way of handling the flexibility question arises in part from traditional practice and insurance company requirements, but also—and not least—because of typical civil service staffing patterns and the advantages to organized workers of the local and monopolistic character of city government.

In addition to the protection afforded by civil service rules and regulations, public employees have made great strides through collective bargaining in the last decade. At the municipal level, the providers of essential services, teachers, police, firemen, transit and sanitation workers, have led the way. A major contribution to union success has been the emergence of strikes and slowdowns. Nationally, the number of strikes conducted by public employees was 411 in 1969 and 412 in 1970. "Man-days of idleness, however, increased substantially to 2,023,300 in 1970, compared with 745,700 in 1969."[27]

Postal workers in New York City, although federal employees, typify the militant behavior of locally based civil servants. Most of the tasks performed on the job are relatively unskilled, but postal workers claimed that only they could keep the system running, a claim borne out in the strike of 1970 when the National Guard proved incapable of even sorting the mail. The accustomed flow of work, the short cuts, the personal relationships that prevail in the work place, turn out to be a large part of system maintenance, and to these, only regular employees have access.

The ban on strikes by public employees in New York, written into the Taylor Law, has been ignored in several notable instances. Injunctions, large fines, and even the jailing of union leaders were not effective in restoring services. Once the ban was breached, the very fact that municipal services are essential and cannot be performed by a substitute work force lent strength to bargaining demands.

Meanwhile, public service was the fastest growing industrial sector in the sixties. Nationally, state and local government employment as a percent of the total nonagricultural employment increased from 11.2 to 14 percent. In New York City, the percentage increased from 8.2 to 11 in the decade.[28] The number of federal workers in the city remained stable at around 100,000, while employees of the state and city showed large increases, particularly in education (Table 5-5).

Budget stringencies, and demographic changes which level off or even reduce the school-age population, will probably result in at least a temporary halt to the rapid expansion of public em-

Table 5-5
Number of Government Employees in New York City, 1960–1970

	Employees (thousands)			Net change 1960–1970	
	1960	1969	1970	Thousands	Percent
Federal	116.4	105.5	107.8	−8.6	−7
State	23.6	38.2	40.3	16.7	71
Local	268.2	403.3	413.6	145.4	54
Education	79.5	149.4	153.8	74.3	93
Other functions	188.7	253.9	259.8	71.1	38
TOTAL	408.2	547.0	561.7	153.5	38

SOURCE: U.S. Department of Labor, Bureau of Labor Statistics, Regional Report no. 20, op. cit., table 1.

ployment in the seventies. Meanwhile, the more than ½ million government workers in the city enjoy wages and benefits that compare favorably with the private sector at most skill levels.

At the end of 1969, the largest city departments were in the main those that had showed the most muscle in collective bargaining in recent years. The salary scales in Table 5-6 apply to large numbers of workers. For example, there are about 60,000 day teachers in the public school system alone; firemen and sanitationmen account for over three-quarters of their respective department's employment, while patrolmen are about two-thirds of the police department.

Firemen, policemen, sanitationmen, and transit workers all share the additional benefit of eligibility to retire after twenty years' service at half pay without any age limitation, in contrast to all other city workers, who must be at least 55 years old with twenty years' service for the same retirement benefits.

By comparison, earnings are low among hospital workers in the private as well as the public sector, although great strides have been made in recent years. Both the city and the major voluntary hospitals in the city are unionized. Local 1199 in the nongovernmental sector has been particularly effective in raising the wages of the lowest-paid worker groups, but as of March 1969, nurse's aides, kitchen helpers, maids, and porters employed by the city were on balance somewhat ahead of the private sector (Table 5-7).

Table 5-6
Number of Employees and Pay Ranges, Selected City
Departments and Job Titles, New York City

Department	Number of Employees Dec. 31, 1969	Selected Titles	Pay Range, 1971
Education and higher education	130,141	Teacher	YEARLY RATE $ 9,400–16,950
Police	36,856	Patrolman	10,699–12,550
Fire	14,865	Fireman	10,699–12,550
Sanitation	14,192	Sanitationman	9,419–10,951
Transit Authority	39,009	Assistant station superintendent	10,648–12,463
		Bus operator	HOURLY RATE $4.32–4.93
		Porter	3.82–4.05
		Clerk	3.85–4.21
		Electronic equipment maintenanceman	5.50

SOURCE: City of New York, Department of Personnel, Civil Service Commission, *Annual Report 1969*, pp. 34–37; Research Division, Office of Labor Relations.

Table 5-7
Median Weekly Earnings in Selected Hospital Occupations,
New York City, 1969

Title	Median weekly earnings	
	State & local hospitals	Nongovernment hospitals
General duty nurses, RN	$152.50	$162.00
Medical technologists	141.00	152.00
Practical nurses, licensed	122.00	122.50
Nurse's aide (men)	121.00	92.50
Nurse's aide (women)	117.00	90.50
Kitchen helpers	108.40	94.80
Porters (men)	108.40	95.20
Switchboard operators	107.50	106.00
Maids	102.80	96.00

SOURCE: U.S. Department of Labor, Bureau of Labor Statistics, Industry Wage Survey, *Hospitals, March 1969*, Bulletin 1688, pp. 36, 58.

THE LABOR MARKET FOR WOMEN

The traditionally low wages for hospital workers are related to factors characterizing the labor market for women in the United States, a market whose segments are significantly less structured than those in which men predominate. Female-labeled occupations tend to be low paid and dead end, two attributes that weaken the opportunities to claim property rights in the job and to enhance pay, benefits, and security. At the lowest levels of the occupational structure, where many of them are concentrated, women workers are interchangeable, and it is becoming apparent that much of the turnover conventionally associated with women at work emanates to some extent from the nature of their jobs.

In pursuing this notion, it is important to distinguish the labor market behavior of young entry workers from that of mature returners. Job tenure is brief for both sexes up to the age of 25, when the figures begin to diverge. The median for women aged 25–29 is 1.4 years in the job, compared to 2.1 for men of the same age.[29] It is at this point, during the childbearing years, that the labor force participation of women shows a marked drop. It climbs back (to over 50 percent), however, in the 45–54 age cohort.[30] This interruption, which occurs in the work life of most women, has served as the rationale for keeping them in the flat parts of the occupational structure with limited mobility, even though their total work life expectancy may be quite long.

The result is a self-fulfilling prophecy in which the two major contributors to short job tenure, withdrawal from the labor force and turnover, are thoroughly confused. It is one thing to withdraw from the labor market and quite another to circulate at its lowest levels. The conclusions of a French study on absenteeism would seem to apply equally well to the causes of the turnover:

> . . . the comparatively high proportion of women at the lower levels of the occupational scale . . . goes a long way towards explaining their frequent irregularity at work.[31]

Clerical workers. The situation of clerical workers, the largest single female occupational group, illustrates women's position in the labor market. Nowhere is this as clear as among telephone operators. Operating divisions of AT&T, like the rest of the communications and utilities industries, operate in much the same fashion as government. Over the years, male employees in these industries have enjoyed the benefits of a quasi-civil service — adequate pay scales, promotional ladders built on seniority rights, and a wide range of fringe benefits. Telephone operators, in contrast, have no promotional opportunities, and pay scales and working conditions combine to create a revolving door. Recent reports indicate a complete turnover twice a year of new entrants in New York City.[32]

High turnover is also a feature of other low-level clerical jobs. A study by the City Planning Department of clerical workers in the banking, insurance, and securities industries reports that 54 percent of the 163,000 workers in 1969 were new hires.[33] The study estimated that industry expansion accounted for 17 percent; the rest were the result of turnover and particularly interfirm movement. Since employment in these industries is geographically concentrated in a limited downtown area, new entrants to the labor force quickly learn about differences in pay and working conditions.[34] And since mean starting salaries for the lowest job classifications range from $90 to $110 (in 1969) and promotional opportunity is limited, even small improvements constitute an incentive for job changing.

Although data from the City Planning Department study are incomplete, both earnings and promotional opportunities in these fields seem to be greater for men than for women. For all clerical positions, the percent which were held by female workers and the median earnings in 1970 were:

Insurance: 76 percent female $120 median weekly salary
Banking: 59 percent female $121 median weekly salary
Securities: 36 percent female $137 median weekly salary

From the entry level, clerks have access to promotion ladders in 33 percent of the insurance companies, 45 percent of the banks, and 50 percent of the securities firms. Typically, advancement is from a junior to a senior level of the same title. In insurance, however, the clerk-typist may in certain departments move up to underwriter.

About two-thirds of the typist jobs, the other main entry position, usually require a high school diploma but no previous experience. Earnings are similar to those of entry clerks, but promotion is limited to those who acquired stenographic skills. For the typical office clericals, advancement is minimal. Typists and stenographers can move to secretarial positions in only 8 to 12 percent of banking and insurance firms and not at all in securities. A secretary, can move to a nonclerical position in 12 percent of the insurance firms, but has no options in the other two industries.

In some firms, incumbents with senior clerical titles may advance to supervisory positions. In insurance companies, 55 percent of clerical supervisors are women; in banking and securities, the percentages are 28 and 16, respectively. In banking, opportunities for promotion to nonclerical titles are provided for tellers in 38 percent of the firms and for senior clerks in 20 percent. Apart from the possibility of becoming an underwriter, few insurance companies provide for internal movement among clerical titles or to nonclerical positions.

In securities, junior and senior grades exist for several titles. Maximum earnings for the senior grades range from $215 to $230. These jobs represent not only the top clerical grades in the securities industry but also, more generally, a type of industry-specific clerical activity where men are more likely to be employed than women.

Office occupations involving filing, typing, and secretarial duties are almost entirely female. Within this traditional pattern of occupational segregation, however, the New York area offers far more opportunity at the upper clerical levels, and average earnings for all grades are significantly ahead of other cities. The frequency distribution in Table 5-8 shows an increasing number of incumbents in the higher-ranking titles. Even though small establishments (less than 50 workers) are underrepresented in the BLS annual survey from which these data come, headquarters operations in the city and large firms in FIRE have pushed demand for female clerical workers to a point where wages for top jobs are now at respectable levels. At the very top, class A secretaries averaged $184 a week in May 1971, but the 4,000 women in these jobs occupy unique positions that are more nearly administrative than clerical. Class B and C secretaries, who make up the bulk of the $140-or-more class in Table 5-8 had average earnings of $164.50 and $149, respectively.

How one views the labor market for women clericals depends on what issue is being addressed. The expansion of demand and the removal of discriminatory barriers, for example, has resulted in increased clerical opportunities for young women who formerly would enter domestic work. During the sixties, the number of domestic workers in the city declined 27 percent. Earnings in 1971 for a full domestic workweek ranged from $70 to $110,[35] but preference for clerical jobs is not only a matter of pay; it reflects the fact that the labor market for domestic workers is still devoid of structure. In offices, unlike homes, working conditions are governed by established rules and regulations which fulfill the minimum criteria of a structured labor market and give the worker a degree of security. She usually does *not* have, however, a broad bond of promotional opportunity, that is, a well-articulated internal labor market. Furthermore, the customary development of necessary skills through preemployment training fits in with greater employer indifference about length of tenure. Work is organized in anticipation of turnover, and the work group as such has far less importance for clerical workers than for employees considered to be permanent.

Table 5-8
**Average Weekly Salaries for Selected Office Occupations,
New York Area, May 1971**

Average straight-time weekly earnings	*Number of occupations*	*Number of workers covered by survey*
Less than $100	2	12,585
$100–109	2	18,183
$110–119	6	20,430
$120–129	9	30,586
$130–139	6	33,997
$140 or more	5	40,645

SOURCE: U.S. Department of Labor, Bureau of Labor Statistics, Area Wage Survey, *New York, New York, Metropolitan Area, May 1971*, Advance Report.

FAMILY INCOMES

The distinct set of conditions in the female labor market is generally viewed as functional in the light of patterns of female participation in the work force. There also seems to be some feeling that current wages are appropriate for younger girls and married women. "Secondary" workers contribute about 25 percent to family income, a ratio that has varied only slightly since the turn of the century.[36] What has changed dramatically is the number of married women who work.

Wages and salaries account for 86 percent of all family incomes under $15,000. For incomes under $5,000, the contribution of earnings and transfer payments are equal at 48 percent.[37] These figures suggest the importance of two income sources in bringing the family up to the BLS standards described earlier. Moonlighting provides about 6 percent of the labor force with two incomes,[38] but by far the most common tandem is the working husband and wife. Nevertheless, among the low-wage, less-stable labor force, even two workers may not bring in enough for adequate family maintenance. Even more serious is the plight of female-headed families. Preliminary estimates show a 31 percent increase in such families in the last decade in both New York City and the nation as a whole, bringing the number in the city to 353,000, or 17 percent of all city families.[39] A *single* income from a typical female-labeled job might equal welfare payments, but it is likely to fall short of the standards suggested for families in general.

CONCLUSIONS

New York City has a large share of the nation's high-salaried jobs, many of them held by commuters. Its preeminence as a headquarters site and an exporter of services, which produces these jobs, also results in the proliferation of relatively low-wage clerical and service jobs (for an analysis of low-wage employment in the city, see Chapter 7). The big gap in opportunity is in well-paid structured employment for both men and women.

The creation of "male" jobs is generally linked to manufacturing under one of the following approaches: (1) to encourage factories to remain in, expand in, or move to the city; (2) to ease the agonies of the journey to work by improving transportation flows from and to the suburban ring; or (3) to plan for the long-run relocation of blue-collar workers to the suburbs where such jobs are locating. Attempts to implement these ideas have run into difficulties (see Chapter 3). In the meantime, factory jobs in New York City are concentrated in low-wage industries characterized by unusual amounts of intermittent employment. It is extremely improbable that high-wage mass production operations will ever move into the city. They were never there in the first place.

The typical steelworker in Pittsburgh can probably support his family through his own earnings, but the industrial mix of the city restricts the employment opportunities of his wife. In New York the typical factory worker may have an inadequate annual income, but the city's strong and accelerating growth in "female" jobs creates a demand for the labor of his wife. Given these *dramatis personae,* this appears to be nothing more than a tradeoff by which the family is supported. But the problems of other actors, particularly those who must make do with one low income for a family, remain acute.

Part II

PROBLEMS

6

MINORITIES

Dale L. Hiestand

THIS CHAPTER WILL ASSESS the changes in relative position in the labor market of minority groups in New York City and delineate the policies and programs which hold promise of removing the principal employment difficulties which members of minority groups face.

It is becoming increasingly difficult to deal with minority groups in New York City as if they were special groups whose labor market problems can be considered independently of the rest of the population. The employment problems of minority groups in New York City are increasingly related to the problems of the city's total labor force.

Therefore, the central issues are the improved development and utilization of the total human resources in New York City. It is now time to assess the programs geared to raise the quality of the city's total labor force and to remove the barriers preventing the more effective utilization of all the human resources in the city.

It is necessary, therefore, to consider various ethnic or racial groups as more than competitors with the older residents for jobs. These groups are complementary to each other, and each is an integral part of the city's human resources. Increasingly, the strength of the city's economy depends on the strengths of its minority-group members. More and more employers are finding that the effectiveness of many of their operations depends on the skills and continued development of their minority-group employees. Many firms can remain prosperous and competitive with the firms located elsewhere only if those of their employees who happen to be black, Puerto Rican, women, or members of other minorities are effectively educated, trained, and given an opportunity to develop and advance in their work.

Nevertheless, most members of minority groups have distinct problems. In many fields, members of minority groups are treated as outsiders and are systematically denied opportunity for employment and advancement. In many other fields, however, members of minority groups are increasingly integrated. Today blacks, Puerto Ricans, and women are slowly being introduced into the economic mainstream, just as were other minorities in the past, such as the Irish, Jews, and Italians. This invites a consideration of the newer minority groups—the Chinese, Cubans, Dominicans, Haitians, Hasidic Jews, and Filipinos—to determine how they depend upon and contribute to the local economy, in order to assess whether their problems are so distinctive as to put them outside the mainstream or whether, despite their distinctiveness, they can be treated within the broad rubric of the city's economy.

THE CHANGING DEMOGRAPHY OF THE LABOR MARKET

The demographic structure of New York City is changing.[1] Between 1960 and 1970, the total population of the city remained essentially stable; it increased from 7.8 to 8.1 million between 1960 and 1968, but decreased to 7.9 million by 1970. Between 1960 and 1970, however, the number of nonwhites increased from over 1.1 to over 1.8 million.

These aggregates do not reveal the changes within the minority groups. The number of blacks increased from nearly 1.1 million to 1.7 million. While most of the new members in this group are American-born, there were significant increases in the number of Haitian, West Indian, and Cuban blacks. The number of Puerto Ricans increased from about 600,000 to over 800,000. Most Puerto Ricans are classified by the census as white, but in fact some are black. There are, in addition, a minimum of 400,000 in other Spanish-speaking groups, including both white and black Cubans and Dominicans. The Haitians are French-speaking. During the past decade the number of nonwhites other than blacks (Chinese, Filipinos, Asiatic Indians, etc.) increased from 53,000 to 178,000. The increases in all these minority groups reflected not only migration into the city, but also high birth rates, particularly among blacks and Puerto Ricans.

The other side of the coin was the decline in the white population from 6.6 million to 6 million; the non-Spanish-speaking, white population declined from 6.1 million to 4.8 million. Perhaps even more significant is that the average age of the white population has been increasing, while the minority-group population tends to be relatively young. The reduction in the number of whites reflected the departure of many for the suburbs and other parts of the country, the expected higher death rate and lower birth rate of the older white population, and the decreasing numbers of white in-migrants who settle in New York City.

The result is, as Table 6-1 shows, that while blacks, Puerto Ricans, and other nonwhites comprise about one-third of the city's total population and about 40 percent of those between 15 and 44, the proportion represented by these minority groups is 20 percent

Table 6-1
Percent Distribution of New York City Population by Race and Ethnic Background and Age, 1970

Age group	White*	Black*	Puerto Rican	Other nonwhite
0–4	53	27	17	3
5–14	54	28	16	2
15–24	63	22	12	3
25–34	62	23	12	3
35–44	63	23	11	3
45–54	75	17	6	2
55–64	83	12	4	1
65 or over	88	9	2	1
Total	68	20	10	2

*Other than Puerto Rican.
SOURCE: U.S. Bureau of the Census.

or less of those aged 55 or over, but over 45 percent of those who are less than 15 years old.

The white population is by no means homogeneous. The complex composition of the Spanish-speaking population has been noted. Jews comprise perhaps one-fourth of the city's population. This group may have declined somewhat during the past decade, although the number of strongly Orthodox and Hasidic Jews, who comprise small and relatively distinct subgroups, may not have declined. The Italian community comprises perhaps one-sixth of the city's population. This relatively younger and less affluent group has probably remained more or less stable; it is likely that births offset out-migration and deaths. There has been a significant in-migration of Greeks as well as a growing Arab population.

Large numbers of the minority populations do not show up in the census data, and the importance of this fact is apparently increasing in New York City. One reason is that census enumerators often fail to find and identify persons whose lives, families, and neighborhoods are most disorganized and poverty stricken, or those who are engaged in illegal or illicit activities. Moreover, since New York has direct overseas air and ship connections, it includes many aliens who have jumped ship, who have overstayed tourist, visitor, or student visas, or who are employed in violation of their entry permits.

The shifts in the city's population are only partially reflected in its labor force. In 1970, of a total labor force of 3.4 million residing in the city, 650,000 were nonwhites other than Puerto Rican, 230,000 were white and nonwhite Puerto Ricans, and 2.5 million were whites other than Puerto Rican. Between 1960 and 1970, there was a reported small increase in the number of Puerto Ricans, an increase of about 140,000 in nonwhites, and a decrease about 280,000 in whites, which resulted in a net decrease in the resident labor force of about 140,000.

Other data indicate that men accounted for nearly all the decrease in white employment. Among both blacks and other nonwhites, the employment of both men and women increased.[2] The data also suggest that practically all the increase in the black and other nonwhite labor force reflected resident youth who reached working age, although there was a net in-migration of black men.

During the same time many black men and women previously employed in the city found jobs in the suburbs, and a significant number of white women shifted to jobs outside the metropolitan area.

The number of people who work in New York City is considerably larger than its resident labor force. About 500,000 persons commute into the city; these are primarily whites, but included are an increasing number of middle-class blacks, perhaps about 15,000. On the other hand, about 200,000 persons who live in the city commute to work in the surrounding areas, and about one-third of them are black or Puerto Rican.

Blacks and Puerto Ricans will soon become almost as important as whites among the new entrants to the labor force. In 1970, whites comprised over 80 percent of those in the labor force who were aged 55 or older, about 70 percent of those aged 25 to 54, but only 60 percent of those under 25.

These differentials are reflected in the ethnic composition of those who will retire in the near future and those who will be new entrants to the labor force. During the 1970s, those who will retire will be overwhelmingly white, while blacks and Puerto Ricans will comprise over 40 percent of the residents who will enter the labor force for the first time. By 1980, unless the demography of the city undergoes unforeseen changes, over 45 percent of all new entrants will be black or Puerto Rican.

New York City is distinctive in that its minority populations are not confined to one or two ghettos. New York City has a series of neighboring, overlapping, and isolated minority neighborhoods in Harlem and East Harlem, large parts of the upper, middle, and lower West Side, and lower East Side in Manhattan; the South and North Bronx; Bedford-Stuyvesant, Brownsville, Williamsburg, and many other neighborhoods in Brooklyn; and South Jamaica, North Corona, Long Island City, and other areas in Queens. There are many other neighborhoods which are confined primarily to one or another ethnic group, including a Chinatown which has recently doubled in size; the Arab and Mohawk Indian communities in Brooklyn; and the many Italian, Jewish, and Eastern European communities throughout the city. Of course, many Negroes, Puerto Ricans, and others live in essentially integrated neighborhoods and some in integrated apartment buildings.

The essential demographic characteristics of New York City, then, are its many distinct minority groups spread throughout the city, the likely fact that blacks and Puerto Ricans will account for nearly half of the additions to the work force in the decade ahead, and the increase in the minority labor force as a result of both the large number of young minority children living in the city who will soon be of working age and the continuing in-migration of diverse racial and ethnic groups.

THE CHANGING RELATIVE POSITION OF MINORITY GROUPS

Concern for minorities, particularly for blacks and Puerto Ricans, is now a central issue in the city's affairs. The occupational position of blacks relative to whites in New York City improved significantly during the 1960s. In 1960, blacks and other nonwhites were disproportionately represented among operatives, laborers, and service workers. This pattern still prevailed in 1970, although blacks were still underrepresented among some occupations in these groups, such as firemen and policemen.

However, they made significant relative gains in the craftsmen and foremen, clerical, and professional and technical occupational groups. By 1970, as Table 6-2 shows, blacks and other nonwhites had achieved 64 percent of parity in the broad range of professional and technical occupations, 79 percent of parity among craftsmen and foremen, and 88 percent of parity among clerical workers. They had undoubtedly achieved more than parity in such occupations as social worker, auto mechanic, or telephone operator, while they were far below parity among most jobs in the skilled building trades, executive secretaries, engineers, and college professors.

The major areas in which blacks and Puerto Ricans have not yet achieved significant opportunity is among sales workers and managers, officials, and proprietors. According to data collected by the Equal Employment Opportunity Commission (EEOC) and other evidence, a significant number of blacks and Puerto Ricans are sales clerks in low-priced variety and department stores. With few exceptions, however, blacks and Puerto Ricans have not been

Table 6-2
Ratio of Blacks and Other Nonwhites to Whites (with
Parity at 100), by Occupational Groups, 1960 and 1970

	1960	1970
White-collar workers	53	66
Professional and technical	53	64
Managers, officials and proprietors	33	36
Clerical workers	68	88
Sales workers	34	32
Blue-collar workers	119	126
Craftsmen and foremen	59	79
Operatives	141	157
Nonfarm laborers	200	133
Service workers	288	244
Private household	1,089	733
Other	212	213

SOURCE: U.S. Bureau of the Census.

able to obtain sales positions involving high-priced merchandise, industrial equipment, raw materials, supplies, and securities; that is, few blacks and Puerto Ricans are employed in businesses where the size of sale is significant and/or the customer is a business, government, institution, or middle-class consumer. Similarly, black and Puerto Rican managers, officials, and proprietors usually work in small or insignificant enterprises, primarily where the minority community is the customer or client. Even in these situations blacks rarely comprise the majority of managers, officials, and proprietors.

In general, the occupational positions of Puerto Ricans and other Spanish-speaking people are below those of blacks. This reflects at least three somewhat contradictory factors. Puerto Ricans are, on the average, less well educated than blacks. However, among blacks and Puerto Ricans with high school educations, Puerto Ricans are more likely to be in white-collar occupations. The distinctive language and culture of the Spanish-speaking people seem to be reflected in the fact that a relatively large number of them are proprietors of stores and other businesses which serve a Spanish-speaking clientele. Wherever the English language is used as a criterion for employment, either legitimately or arbitrarily, relatively few Spanish-speaking are employed. Tests in English are used by the civil service and the telephone company, and for many other types of white-collar and blue-collar work, even when the Spanish-speaking population comprises a large part of the clientele. Another factor is that Spanish-speaking women avoid domestic service. Finally, we must distinguish among the various Spanish-speaking groups. Cubans, for instance, are more likely to be in business. Dominicans and others who are not citizens are even less likely than Puerto Ricans to be in civil service. Filipinos include many physicians and nurses who have been attracted by the manpower shortages in these fields in the United States.

EEOC data reveal that many small firms do not employ even one minority group member. This is particularly significant since New York is primarily a city of small employing units. Many national businesses have a relatively small number of personnel in their New York offices and employ few, if any, minority group members. The EEOC data further reveal relatively few blacks in such prestige operations as the large law firms, management consulting businesses, and other elite organizations.

Membership of minority groups in unions varies greatly. According to 1969 EEOC data on unions in the New York area that provide workers to employers, Spanish-Americans comprised 15.8 percent of their membership, blacks 12.2 percent, and Orientals 0.2 percent.[3] These minority groups were heavily concentrated in the Ladies Garment Workers', the Teamsters', and the Laborers' Unions. Relatively few minority workers were members of the Electrical Workers', Plumbers and Pipe Fitters', Bricklayers', Clothing Workers', or Stage and Moving Picture Operators' Unions. There were a significant number of blacks but few Spanish-speaking members in the Carpenters', Operating Engineers', Plasterers and Cement Masons', and the Meat Cutters and Butchers' Unions. These are incomplete data, particularly for the building trades, and the true picture is probably even worse than these data suggest.

Members of minority groups continue to be unemployed more than other workers, but the disparity is and has been less sharp in New York City than in the rest of the country. This is because Negroes in New York City have markedly lower unemployment rates than Negroes elsewhere, although New York's white unemployment rates are the same or over the national average. In 1970, New York City had the fourth highest unemployment rate for whites of the 12 largest cities, but among the 12, it has the ninth highest unemployment rate for nonwhites.[4]

Other cities have been more hurt by cutbacks in defense spending and industrial purchases. New York City's troubles have been reflected more in difficulties experienced by the finance and advertising sectors, business services, and hotels. This is a more indirect and diffuse effect of the national recession. New York's economic troubles have also reflected recent limitations in the growth of federal and state grants-in-aid, due in part to shifts in political philosophy as well as lower-than-anticipated tax collections by local, state, and federal government, which were used to justify limitations on spending for health, education, welfare, and other programs.

Although it has been stated that black and Puerto Rican men are outside the labor force in larger proportions than whites, this is not generally true in New York City, even among the poorest and least educated in the poverty areas. Older black men are somewhat more likely to continue to work than older white men, apparently because of the inadequate pensions and social security available to black men. Poor health and disability bear more heavily on blacks and Puerto Ricans at all ages, but blacks are about twice as likely as Puerto Ricans to report bad health as a reason for being out of the labor force.

Black women are more likely than white women to be in the labor force, while Puerto Rican women are much less likely than black or even white women to be employed. This is reflected in the larger proportion of black women but the relatively few Puerto Rican women in domestic service. Apparently, black women will accept such employment, but Puerto Rican women will not.

A new element in the employment situation has been the rapid increase in concern, action, program, and legal procedures with respect to expanding the range and level of employment opportunities for women, particularly educated women. New York has long been a mecca for young educated women from the rest of the

United States because they believed it afforded them better opportunities in business, professions, and the arts. The legend outran the fact, of course, but a list of the fields in which some women found unusual opportunity would include publishing, theater, retailing, fashion design, popular entertainment, advertising, and the dance. It is perhaps indicative of the extent to which attitudes and expectations have changed, and perhaps nowhere more so than in New York, that these formerly significant breakthrough fields are now under direct attack on the ground that they severely discriminate against women. The characteristic charge in nearly every instance is that women are restricted to certain functions and positions which are popularly dubbed feminine and that they are rarely permitted to advance beyond the position of assistant or associate of the men who wield the real leadership and power.

THE CHANGING SIGNIFICANCE OF MINORITY-GROUP STATUS

The previous two sections suggest that the typical concept of what is involved in expanding employment opportunities for minorities needs to be revised. In the first place, those in the conventional minority group, i.e., blacks and Puerto Ricans, are becoming a central and essential part of the labor force. They will account for nearly half of all additions to New York City's labor force in the decade ahead. Employers have little choice but to utilize the entire pool of human resources in the city more effectively. Otherwise, they will not have the workers they need, and their operations will be less productive than they might be.

Secondly, it is no longer possible to assume that practically all members of identifiable minority groups are subject to significant and consistently hostile employment discrimination. It is probably fair to say that most blacks are discriminated against by most employers. However, a significant group of blacks have achieved high levels of occupational attainment. A significant number of employers, faced with a choice between a white and a black of equal skill and promise, now tend to choose the black over the white. A similar argument could be made, although with less force, that qualified women are beginning to be hired over equally qualified men by some employers. Significant numbers of persons of Spanish-speaking or Oriental background have for all practical purposes merged into the mainstream of American life in terms of employment, education, residence, etc. Either as managers in public or private enterprises or as entrepreneurs, a slowly increasing number of blacks, Spanish-speaking people, Orientals, and even women are in positions in which they make significant hiring and promotion decisions.

As a result of these changes, many members of minority groups now find enough employers who will hire them, and they are not markedly constrained by the fact that many other employers continue to follow biased practices. Indeed, discrimination is increasingly subtle and complex, for employers and supervisors consciously or unconsciously tend to favor or to limit those from their own ethnic backgrounds or from other ethnic groups. Thus Jews, Christians, Catholics, WASPs, Irish, Italians, Greeks, whites, blacks, homosexuals, heterosexuals, and others may variously find themselves on the receiving or the giving end of biases in employment.

Many members of minority groups which do not face significant discrimination in employment encounter difficulties because they refuse to accommodate to the customs and expectations of the larger community. The latent hostility of the larger community seems to erupt against those who openly dare to be different. Black or Puerto Rican nationalists, women's and gay liberationists often encounter discrimination from employers who think of themselves as nondiscriminatory. Hasidic Jews often encounter job problems because employers refuse to make relatively simple adjustments to meet their religious needs.

Finally there are those who might suffer from discrimination, but who create no situation for it to occur. Some blacks, Chinese, and others simply remain within their communities and refuse to deal with the hostile world outside. On the other hand, many women and some members of racial minorities seem clearly to bear the brunt of discrimination but, for a variety of reasons, they accept their treatment.

Increasingly, the problem of expanding opportunities for minority groups in New York City must be approached through general policies and programs as well as those directed toward specific population groups. The rest of this chapter, therefore, will consider economic policies to improve employment opportunities, and educational and manpower policies to improve the quality of the city's human resources and to meet the special problems of those whose opportunities are limited.

THE GOALS OF LOCAL ECONOMIC POLICY

A dynamic local economy is essential to promote improved employment opportunities, but this does not necessarily mean a rapidly growing local economy. A dynamic local economy may be one in which new and better opportunities continually appear, producing a continuous upgrading in the local industrial and occupational structure.

Optimally, employment in the city should be somewhat above its present level. There should be at least enough additional jobs to provide employment opportunities for those who are unemployed, or underemployed, or out of the labor force because of a lack of jobs. Some of these last two groups are now engaged in illegal activities; others are institutionalized, whereas the availability of a job might have forestalled their confinement or would create the opportunity for their release.

In fact, total employment in New York City did grow during each of the last two decades, although the population remained essentially stable. Indeed, as employment growth in the national economy accelerated during the 1960s, New York City employment also grew, although less rapidly. New York City employment declined after 1969, as the national economy failed to grow. The economy of the city thus seems to be geared to trends in the national economy.

Despite pervasive concern about the local economy, employment has increased during the past decade in the New York metropolitan area, in New York City alone, in all boroughs but Brooklyn, and in the Central Business District (i.e., Manhattan below 61st Street). The larger part of this growth has been an increase in public employment, especially in the educational and health functions. The growth in the private sector has been concentrated in profit-making and nonprofit health and educational enterprises, in finance, in business services, and in the headquarters of national corporations. This growth has been in the rewarding, high-quality, white-collar, managerial, and professional jobs, while the number of poor-paying, unpleasant, and demeaning jobs has declined.

Much of the growth in the profit, nonprofit, and governmental sectors has been based on increased flows of federal and state grants, contracts, and welfare spending. Federal and state employment in the city, always quite low on a per capita basis compared to the rest of the state or country, did not change substantially during the past decade.

The increases in public and private employment have added to congestion, overcrowding, and competition for space. This competition tends to be won by those activities which benefit most from being located in the city, that is, those willing to pay higher rents, wages and salaries, the costs of inconvenience, and, in the case of profit-seeking enterprises, taxes. These activities also tend to be the most attractive from the point of view of the city's economic welfare, precisely because they are able and willing to pay higher salaries and rents and taxes.

Unemployment in the city is concentrated at the lower end of the occupational, educational, and income scale. This has sometimes been used as an argument for subsidies and other incentives to encourage firms which employ relatively unskilled, undereducated, low-wage employees to remain in or to move to the city. The opposite concern is that subsidies and the like for this purpose may be disastrously counterproductive to the city and its inhabitants in the long run. Directly or indirectly, the preservation or expansion of enterprises which pay low wages, taxes, and rents may inhibit the growth of firms which can pay higher wages, taxes, and rents.

To encourage the retention or expansion or location in the city of low-productivity industries may simply compound the problem of unemployment. By their very instability and the kind of a labor force they utilize and attract, such industries tend to have a penumbra of unemployed, poverty-stricken persons and families with severe social problems. The supply of undereducated persons in other nearby cities, in the South and Puerto Rico, and indeed in other countries is essentially unlimited. Too generous promotion of such industries may simply lead to a larger penumbra of individuals and families attended by social difficulties. New York City compares favorably with other cities in terms of its relationship between wage rates and prices for goods and services purchased by low-income families, while it is at a disadvantage in relation to other cities in terms of salaries compared to prices paid for goods and services by middle- and higher-income groups.

There are, in fact, many unfilled lower-skilled jobs in the city at the present time. This reflects a host of factors: transportation costs and lack of propinquity of housing to the jobs; inadequate child-care facilities; wage levels which are too low in the light of welfare benefits; opportunities for illegal trafficking in gambling, narcotics, and stolen goods; and a strong aversion on the part of increasing numbers of minority men and women to any employment which they consider servile and demeaning. These unfilled low-paying jobs have opened up opportunities for illegal aliens. They find the interior of the city especially attractive, since the police and immigration and employment officials tend to ignore these areas or fail fully to enforce the law because of aversion, indifference, fear, or corruption. Among the illegal aliens are many Chinese, Greeks, Italians, Haitians, Dominicans, and others from Asia, the Mediterranean, and Latin America.

At the same time, many of the productive, rapidly growing industries and occupations have been unable to find the range of qualified personnel they need. As a result of these manpower shortages, some operations, firms, and industries have failed to grow as rapidly as they might while others have relocated to more favorable locations. In both cases, the city has not realized its potential in incomes and employment. The city has also lost the employment which would have been generated in firms supplying materials, waste disposal, transportation, trade, services, space rental, and construction.

The most promising economic goal for the city seems to be that of simultaneously upgrading the industrial, occupational, and pay scale of its employment structure. This would have to be

combined with an educational and manpower policy to upgrade
the educational skill and productivity level of the work force. Optimally, the city might evolve a set of economic forces and policies
which would produce a structure of manpower demands designed
to fully employ the local labor force, whose members would develop higher-level skills and work attitudes as rapidly as possible.
Only in the absence of a demand which fully employs the members of the present labor force at their existing or potential levels
of skill should economic policies seek to ensure that the number of
jobs in the lower occupations and skills does not decline.

It is not possible within this chapter to appraise the range and
effectiveness of local policies and programs which influence the
establishment, growth, and retention of different types of private,
nonprofit, and public enterprises. They include zoning, land use
and assembly, transportation, traffic, police, fire, labor relations,
education, training, manpower, recreation, housing, taxation, information, and industrial promotion. They include the quality and
responsiveness of government, and its influence on the quality of
business operations and life in general. Each of these has a bearing
on the structure of local employment opportunities which emerge,
survive, and grow, and therefore on the types of employment opportunities to which members of minority groups have access.

In a larger, more fundamental sense, the economic future of
the city depends on national and state economic and spending policies. As noted earlier, the extent of growth and change
in the city's private economy depends on the rate of growth
of the national economy, which has been sluggish since 1969.
The fiscal situation of the state and local governments also
depends on the level of national prosperity. In the last few
years this has been reflected in sluggish tax collections, increased
welfare and unemployment benefits, and slow growth in the expenditures of the federal, state, and local governments. Local
governments, nonprofit enterprises, and businesses have all suffered from such governmental expenditure policies, and recipro-
cally they in turn have limited their expenditures. A return to national full employment and a strengthening of the financial flows
among the various levels of government, the nonprofit sector, and
the profit-seeking sector are essential for the economic future of

the city. This in turn is the principal determinant of access to opportunity of members of various minority groups. The ways in which different industrial, occupational, and minority-group labor markets will be affected will be determined largely by the complex pattern of spending and production by consumers, businesses, nonprofit enterprises, and governments which will emerge. For example, federal expenditures for defense and space seem to have little effect on minorities in New York City. On the other hand, expenditures for hospitals or for public service employment tend to create jobs for large numbers of blacks, Puerto Ricans, and other minority groups, whether they are relatively well educated or are undereducated.

EDUCATIONAL AND MANPOWER POLICIES

The logical corollary of the economic goals set forth above is a set of educational, training, manpower, and related policies which will accelerate the development of skills and potential for work performance. These general policies have special relevance to members of minority groups, including women.

Indeed, the opportunities for employment in a broad range of white-collar and professional occupations, particularly in the health fields, promise to continue to grow, particularly if the national and the local economies revive. Of course, local and short-run imbalances will continue and will depend on the directions of governmental and other spending programs. But over the long run, it will be necessary to stimulate members of minority groups and others to higher ambitions and expectations.

If supplies of manpower with acceptable skills are found deficient, both employers and students will be pressing for better education and training. The primary brunt of this pressure will fall upon the schools. Employers will also have to continue or initiate internal training programs, or undertake programs jointly with other employers. An example is the American Institute of Banking, which over the decade has been engaged in a large-scale industry-upgrading program.

A major dimension of manpower waste in the city is the inadequate education and training which schools and employers have provided for members of minority groups in the past. Just how to provide remedial or catch-up programs will be a major challenge in the future. This will involve more than pedagogical and training innovations; it may also involve continued development of selection, supervision, and incentive systems.

The open enrollment policies of the city's universities are an essential part of this need for and drive toward higher educational and occupational achievements. While many admitted under this policy will find higher education unrewarding or uninteresting, many others who otherwise would have been excluded from college will grow in response to these new opportunities.

It may be helpful to note here that the employment and related policies developed during the last decade to improve the position of members of minority groups reveal that most of them are applicable to every group, not just to those minorities which have suffered from discrimination.

The experience of the past decade has demonstrated that the major problem is not so much direct bias against members of minority groups, although that surely exists. But conventional employment and manpower policies tend to operate in such a way as to recruit, select, train, and promote members of the majority rather than the minority, even when the latter are qualified or potentially able to fill available jobs.

In an attempt to deal with this problem, the concept of the "affirmative action program" has been developed. Essentially, this represents the establishment by employers, unions, and other groups of goals and programs with the specific purpose of opening up opportunities to minorities. The first step is to identify jobs and job groups in which an unusually low proportion of an identifiable population group is found. The second step is to estimate the total number of job openings that are likely to occur during the next year and for several years ahead through expansion, retirements, promotions, and employee turnover. The third step is to set specific goals with respect to the number and proportion of such job openings for which members of the identifiable population groups will be sought. The fourth step is to analyze and reorganize various personnel policies and programs to ensure that these goals are met.

The reexaminàtion and reorganization of personnel policies may take several forms. It is usually necessary to devise new systems whereby information about job openings can be conveyed to particular groups who otherwise would not learn about them. In addition, recruitment processes must be reexamined to ensure that adequate numbers of different groups of workers apply. Hiring standards and procedures must be reexamined or revised to ensure that they are not explicitly, implicitly, or unnecessarily stringent with respect to particular minority groups. Training programs should be reexamined in order to assure that they are effective for people with different backgrounds. Personnel officials, foremen, lead workers, and coworkers usually need training, education, and indoctrination to help them to create a more open social environment to maximize the development of the latent potential of diverse individuals and groups. Internal mobility and promotion systems must also be reexamined to ensure that members of minority groups are not shunted into dead-end, minority-identified, or otherwise unpromising jobs and job ladder systems. Finally, it is necessary to constantly reexamine each of the above systems to quickly identify newly emerging situations which tend to impede the continued acquisition and development of skills by identifiable population groups and individuals.

Such an affirmative action program is not simply a matter of goodwill toward minorities or a matter of justice. It is essential to the more effective operation of individual enterprises and consequently the local economy. Constant vigilance to uncover and remove barriers to the development of human potential is necessary as a matter of general human resources policy, not just with respect to identifiable minority groups.

No matter how well organized, education, training, manpower, and affirmative action programs will not be effective unless job openings and promotions occur in individual enterprises and the total economy. General economic improvement and upgrading of the industrial and occupational structure are thus the primary policy goals.

The city's manpower-training programs are directed toward approximately 750,000 residents who are poor, including some who are employed the year around, some who are unemployed during some part of the year, and some who are not in the labor force but have some employment potential.[5] In attempting to increase skills, productivity, and income-earning potential, the manpower programs provide remedial, basic, and other education; institutional and on-the-job training and upgrading; job and career ladder development; and such supportive services as health care, child care, and vocational and other rehabilitation services.

However, during any year less than 10 percent of the target population receives significant education and training from these programs. Perhaps half of these do not find or stay in work corresponding to their training. To some extent, this poor showing reflects recent economic difficulties in the city. However, such meager results indicate that the development of effective educational, training, and employment programs for the poor is one of the most pressing issues facing the city.

CONCLUSION

The thrust of this chapter is that in New York City minority groups are rapidly becoming an integral part of the local labor force, qualitatively as well as numerically. Employment opportunities for minority groups have greatly improved in many white-collar, professional, and technical occupations and in many large firms. However, in a number of industries, occupations, and types of situations members of minority groups, particularly women, have limited opportunities for jobs and promotions. Among these are management and high-level sales positions, many building trades, and many small enterprises. Often discrimination is more severe against subgroups within the conventional minority groups, such as Hasidic Jews, black Haitians, or Puerto Ricans who have difficulty speaking and understanding English. For all these people, continued aggressive action by human rights groups and agencies, employers, and others are necessary. But in the larger sense, New York City is entering a situation in which the expansion of opportunity for all becomes a matter of general human resources policy. In this context, the principal issues of public policy become a matter of the general and specific policies which bear on the evolving economic structure, the complex structure of educational and training programs and policies, and the way in which the urban labor market and the internal labor markets of different employers deal with people of many different backgrounds, attitudes, skills, and potentials. In this light, ethnic and racial conflicts in the early 1970s reflect primarily the difficulties of a new pluralism in a temporarily stagnant local and national economy. A return to a more dynamic economy should create more opportunities in which all can share.

7

UPGRADING

Charles Brecher

THE PROBLEM OF UNDEREMPLOYMENT

The perception of a phenomenon as a problem requires some normative judgment. Unemployment is considered a problem because most Americans feel that individuals who are willing and able to work ought to be at work. Underemployment is a problem because most citizens feel that those who are working ought to be earning enough to support their families at a standard of living which is at least above the level defined as poverty. Few would disagree with the proposition that a man who works forty hours a week, fifty weeks a year, ought not to live in poverty.

That this is not always the case is well documented in national census figures. An estimated 5,214,000 families in the United States, about 10 percent of the total, had incomes which placed them below the poverty level, which was set slightly under $4,000 for a family of four in 1970. Of this group more than half, or 2,865,000 families, were headed by an individual who worked during the year. A large portion of this subgroup, 1,068,000 families, were headed by individuals who worked full time for fifty or more weeks during the year.[1] About one-fifth of these full-time working poor live on farms. There are presently, then, over 1 million family heads who work year round but do not earn enough to support their families at a level above poverty.

There are no similar data defining the problem of underemployment in New York City. However, analysts concerned with the issue generally agree that the income yardstick of $3,968 for a family of four as a demarcation between poverty and better is an inadequate indicator because of the higher living costs which characterize the New York metropolitan area. Suggested alternative income levels are the eligibility line for supplementary assistance under the Home Relief program, which is now slightly higher than $5,000 for a family of four with a working head, and the Bureau of Labor Statistics' lower-level standard budget for the New York area, which is slightly over $7,000. Equivalent weekly incomes for these measures are: $75, which is the Social Security Administration's national poverty measure; $95, which is the Home Relief cutoff level; and $135, which is the Bureau of Labor Statistics' lower standard budget. [2]

The New York City Cooperative Area Manpower Planning System (CAMPS) Committee, using data provided by the New York State Department of Labor, has specified a target population for the city's manpower programs which includes 263,500 family heads employed full time whose incomes are below a level set one-third above the Social Security Administration poverty figure. This is slightly less than the Home Relief cutoff line. The target population also includes 128,700 single individuals who work full time but have less than poverty-level incomes. As Table 7-1 suggests, the underemployed are the largest segment of the work force who require special manpower services.

Some indication of the kinds of jobs the underemployed are likely to hold is available from a survey of private firms in New York City, conducted by the New York State Department of Labor. The state agency estimated that in October 1969 more than 400,000 workers covered by minimum wage laws earned less than $2.00 per hour. We should quickly note that these low-wage jobs cannot be directly equated with underemployment. Low-wage jobs may be filled by teen-agers or married women whose supplementary earnings are an important part of the city's economy and of family income. Moreover, many of New York's middle-income families rely upon these secondary sources of income to maintain their status. In addition, there may be under-

Table 7-1
New York City CAMPS Committee Population
Estimates, Fiscal Year 1971

1. *Poor individuals, employed year-round*	444,200
a. Family heads, employed full time	263,500
b. Unrelated individuals, employed full time	128,700
c. Individuals employed part time	52,000
2. Poor individuals with unemployment during the year	130,000
3. Poor individuals not in the labor force, but with employment potential	171,200
TOTAL target population	745,400

SOURCE:*New York City CAMPS Plan, Fiscal Year 1971*, p. 26.

employed individuals in low-wage jobs in sectors not covered by the survey.

It should be noted that data dealing with wage rates are inaccurate indicators of underemployment because the hourly or weekly rates cannot be translated directly into annual incomes. Some jobs paying over $2.00 per hour are only available on a part-time basis. Many others are seasonal in nature and do not provide year-round employment. Nationally, it has been estimated that 43 percent of all individuals employed during the year are "peripheral workers"; that is, they do not work full time full year.[3]

Despite these limitations, the New York State Department of Labor Survey is a useful guide to the industries in which underemployment is prevalent. As the data in Table 7-2 demonstrate, low-wage jobs are not evenly distributed among all industries. Nearly one-third are located in the manufacture of nondurable goods, but this sector accounts for only about 15 percent of total employment in the city. Within this group, the major specific sources of low-wage jobs are apparel manufacture and the production of leather and other miscellaneous goods such as toys and jewelry. Ten percent of the jobs paying less than $2.00 per hour are in retail eating and drinking places, an industry with only about 3 percent of all employment. One of every five low-wage jobs is in a retail store, primarily food and apparel. The remainder are scattered among all other industries.

Table 7-2
Estimated Employment in Nonagricultural Industries
in New York City
(Thousands)

Industry	1960 total	1970 total	Less than $2.00/hour
Total—nonagricultural	3,538.4	3,763.8	405.3
Manufacturing	946.8	772.8	162.6
Durable goods	228.5	179.8	34.4
Nondurable goods	718.3	593.0	128.2
Apparel	267.4	203.8	48.4
Printing	127.2	122.2	7.9
Leather & miscellaneous	106.7	90.4	43.0
All others	217.0	176.6	28.9
Nonmanufacturing	2,591.6	2,991.0	242.7
Mining	1.9	1.9	—
Construction	125.3	108.9	1.8
Transport & utilities	318.1	324.4	4.4
Wholesale trade	311.4	304.4	19.4
Retail trade	308.6	317.0	82.0
Eating & drinking places	124.8	119.1	40.9
FIRE	386.0	463.9	18.6
Services	607.3	789.5	75.6
Hotels	42.0	35.5	2.4
Personal services	62.7	52.8	20.7
Business services	135.0	202.3	31.2
Medical services	97.1	145.7	3.5
Private education	51.5	79.4	NA
Other services and misc.	219.0	273.8	17.8
Government	408.2	561.7	NA

NA—Not available.
SOURCE: The 1960 annual average employment figures are from New York State Department of Labor, *Annual Manpower Planning Report, 1971*, p. 47 and Bureau of Labor Statistics, *Changing Patterns of Prices, Pay, Workers and Work on the New York Scene*, Regional Report no. 20, p. 11; the 1970 figures are from *Employment Review*, May 1971, pp. 17–21; the low-wage employment figures are from New York State Department of Labor, *Estimated Structure of Earnings in 1969 in New York State and New York City Industries*, Special Labor News Memorandum no. 132, table 4.

LONG-RUN TRENDS

Three basic factors affect the extent and nature of low-wage employment in New York City. First, because low-wage jobs are unevenly divided among industries, the shifting industrial composition of the city's economy can significantly alter the total number of low-wage jobs. Second, changing patterns of manpower utilization within an industry can increase or decrease reliance upon less-skilled, lower-wage labor. Finally, increased collective bargaining power may significantly raise salary levels of low earners. Each of these trends deserves discussion.

The industrial composition of the city's economy has shifted significantly in the past decade (Table 7-2). Total nonagricultural employment increased by about 225,000, from 3,538,400 in 1960 to 3,763,800 in 1970. But the aggregate figures conceal a mixture of growth and decline. Manufacturing employment actually dropped by 174,000, from 946,800 to 772,800. Much of this decline has been in industries with large proportions of low-wage workers. Over the decade the apparel industry lost nearly 64,000 jobs. Other key low-wage industries also experienced significant declines; the leather goods and miscellaneous manufacturers lost over 16,000 jobs. While some firms in virtually all manufacturing industries have been leaving the city, the exodus has been most pronounced in the low-wage sector.

Nonmanufacturing employment rose from 2,591,600 to 2,991,000 in 1970. Here again we must look at the detailed figures to assess the impact on low-wage employment. Employment in eating and drinking places declined by 5,700 while other retail stores added about 8,400 jobs. Together, the three largest sources of low-income jobs—nondurable manufacturing, retail trade, and restaurants—showed a decline of about 128,000 jobs, while total nonagricultural employment demonstrated a net gain of 225,000. To a large extent the city's economy has grown by trading jobs in predominantly low-wage industries for a greater number of positions in higher-wage fields. While the past cannot be projected, it does appear that the long-run industrial shifts which have characterized New York's economy in the past will continue to reduce the supply of low-wage jobs while expanding the supply of better positions.

Changing occupational requirements within an industry can also affect the incidence of underemployment. Regardless of the size of an industry, shifts may occur in the proportion of low-wage manpower which it utilizes. These changes generally result from technological advances or transformations in the organizational basis of the industry. For example, the introduction of electronic data processing equipment reduces the need for low-wage clerical help in many business offices, and this alters the nature of the industry's occupational structure.

Intraindustry occupational shifts are having only minor effects upon the supply of low-wage jobs in New York City. Industries with a large number of low-wage jobs have relatively stable occupational structures. In the garment industry, over half the workers are engaged in sewing operations and there are no developments on the horizon which will significantly alter this proportion. The sewing machine has been and is likely to continue to be the basic instrument in the industry. Rapid fashion changes and small production lots often prevent the introduction of mass production techniques, particularly in women's wear. Automated processes may be feasible in cutting and sizing operations, but these are presently among the highest-paid jobs in the industry. Organizational trends are toward an increased separation of design, production and marketing. Many of the firms leaving the city are contractors, who perform only sewing operations. The more-skilled and better-paying jobs in design, layout, and sales have remained in New York City showrooms, while lower-wage operative jobs have been moved elsewhere. To a limited extent this trend may alter the structure of employment in a local segment of the industry in favor of higher-wage positions in design and marketing functions.

The food service industry, consisting largely of eating and drinking places, also has a relatively stable occupational structure. About 40 percent of the workers are waiters, waitresses, or others engaged in serving food, and another third work in the kitchen preparing food. Wages in many of these jobs are near the statutory minimum. Because of the increased use of prepared and frozen foods and sauces, fewer of the personnel are skilled chefs or cooks. The substitution of less-skilled workers for skilled craftsmen has also been accelerated by the tendency of restaurants to limit the scope of their menu. Organizational shifts favoring franchise and chain operations have similar effects. Because these changes make possible greater productivity, as measured in sales per employee, it is likely that fewer workers will be needed in the city's food establishments and that of those employed a slightly smaller proportion will be in positions requiring extensive skills.

Retail trade is undergoing gradual changes that may have a limited effect upon manpower requirements. The trend has been toward the dominance of large department stores. Employment in these enterprises has grown by about 10,000 in the past five years, while other retail facilities have remained stable. No precise occupational data are available, but large stores probably have a larger managerial and administrative component than do smaller outlets. This would indicate an increase in the number of better-paying job opportunities in retailing. However, a simultaneous trend has been toward self-service in retail sales. This means less reliance upon skilled sales personnel and cashiers. Because there are few studies of the changing occupational structure of local industries, it is difficult to assess the impact of this factor on low-wage employment. However, it does not seem that intraindustry shifts in skill requirements are significantly changing the nature of employment in key low-wage industries.

Low-wage jobs can become better-paying positions through wage gains achieved through collective bargaining. In the 1960s unionization proved to be an effective way of raising the pay of workers in previously low-wage industries. Hospital workers are a notable example. Largely as a result of union activity, accompanied by increased government financing of health services, the wages of many of the nonprofessional employees in the industry were raised above poverty levels. For example, the average weekly earnings of nurse's aides in nongovernment hospitals rose from $46.50 in 1960 to $104.50 in 1970. In the same period x-ray technicians' salaries rose from $78.50 to $158.50.[4] The wages of many municipal employees in a variety of low-wage titles, both inside and outside of hospitals, were increased substantially as a result of the unionization of city workers which took place during the past decade.

However, the major remaining low-wage industries in New York City are also unionized. The garment industry was one of the first in the nation to be unionized. The International Ladies Garment Workers Union (ILGWU) and the Amalgamated Clothing Workers are two strong national unions. Yet wages remain low because of the highly competitive nature of the industry. Many restaurant workers and retail sales employees are also represented by unions.

The New York Urban Coalition has charged that "Some unions—many of them independent, unaffiliated bargaining agents—have been willing to enter into collusive or 'sweetheart' contracts with low-wage employers. These contracts usually call for a wage settlement of only a few cents an hour above the legally required minimum wage, and this is then checked off at payroll time as union dues for the benefit of the union 'leaders.'"[5] However, even the most critical estimates indicate that alleged racket unions cover only a small part of the working poor. Law enforcement efforts should be devoted to eliminating collusive practices where they exist, but only a small number of those in low-wage jobs will be affected. The difficulties of the low-wage earner lie primarily in the basic conditions of the industry, such as inadequate capital investment or the absence of market concentration.

MINIMUM-WAGE LEGISLATION

One measure which has been proposed to alleviate the problem of underemployment is a higher statutory minimum wage. At present New York State has a law which stipulates that the minimum wage is $1.85 per hour for covered workers; federal legislation requires only $1.60.

The proponents of minimum-wage legislation allege the following benefits: Workers at the lowest pay levels, as well as those slightly above the minimum, usually have their wages increased when the minimum is raised. Their absolute earnings rise and the differentials between high and low earners tend to be reduced slightly.

But a higher minimum wage is not likely to eliminate underemployment. A stipulated wage far above that which can realistically be expected would be required to yield an income above the poverty level, even for a full-time year-round worker. To produce a $95 weekly income, which is the Home Relief supplement cutoff point, the minimum wage would have to be raised to $2.37 per hour for a forty-hour week or $2.71 per hour for a thirty-five-hour week. This would still not be sufficient for the large number of low-wage workers who can obtain only part-time employment or who work in seasonal industries.

In addition, classical economics provides an argument against minimum-wage legislation. The theory predicts that a decline in the demand for labor will follow upon a wage increase, with a consequent increase in unemployment among formerly low-wage workers. It is believed that many of those whose jobs might be eliminated are teen-agers, and economists have engaged in a continuing debate over the employment effects of earlier minimum-wage increases, particularly on teen-age employment.[6] The issue to be decided by policy-makers is whether the income gains for those whose jobs are not eliminated, especially heads of households, which result from a higher minimum wage would outweigh the possible adverse employment effects for (primarily) secondary workers. Since teen-age employment rates are at levels few consider acceptable, officials have been reluctant to undertake action that might further aggravate the problems of youngsters. In fact, proposals have been made for a lower minimum wage for teen-agers in order to stimulate their employment, but this in turn also might provide an incentive to employers to replace other workers with teen-agers. The result could be a substitution of unemployed adults for unemployed teen-agers. The actual employment effects of minimum-wage laws have not been measured to anyone's satisfaction, so rational calculations of the costs and benefits of any given increase are impossible at present.

Further difficulties arise in discussing the relative merits of a higher minimum wage if one considers the issue in terms of New York State (or New York City). If New York State were to enact a higher minimum wage without corresponding action by neighboring states or at the national level, the employment effects would take on an added dimension. Some workers would undoubtedly benefit. However, employers would have a further incentive to relocate to take advantage of cheaper labor costs in other states. The movement of low-wage industries from the city would likely be given added stimulus. Whether or not this is desirable depends upon the possibilities for replacing them with higher-wage jobs. As noted earlier, the past trend has been for the city to offset the decline in low-wage industries with growth in other white-collar and service fields. However, it is impossible to predict if future growth could offset the decline which would be generated by an increased differential between state and national minimum wages. In addition, firms which cannot relocate, such as local restaurants or retail stores, may suffer a decline in employment because the effect of a state minimum is similar to that of a national one for local service employers.

Assessing the consequences for the city's economy of a higher minimum wage imposed by either the state or federal government is a complex matter. As with most difficult issues, expert testimony is available to support a variety of points of view. There is no agreement about the magnitude of the favorable effects on the incomes of the underemployed or on the degree to which employment, particularly among teen-agers, would be adversely affected. Even if both sides of this equation could be filled in, some value judgments would have to be made about the relative importance of unemployment among secondary earners and underemployment among primary earners.

UPGRADING

Upgrading programs are another approach which have been proposed to alleviate the problem of underemployment. The programs are designed to provide skill training to low-wage workers so they can advance into better positions. This approach has some potential, but it also has serious limitations.

First and foremost, the potential of upgrading efforts is restricted by the lack of better jobs into which low-wage workers might move. There are simply not enough higher-level jobs currently available for all, or even a significant proportion of, the low-wage workers. There is no reason to believe that if a substantial number of underemployed workers were trained for better jobs in their industry, they would actually find such jobs.

The shortage of better jobs is especially acute in the industries which account for much of the city's low-wage employment. These industries have relatively flat occupational structures. Figure 7-1 uses income data from the New York City Rand Institute's Metropolitan Area Subsample of the Social Security Administration's Continuous Work History File to show that the structure of employment varies among industries.[7] In apparel manufacture and retail eating and drinking places, employment is not evenly distributed along the income scale, but is concentrated at the lower levels. These industries have "flat" employment structures with few opportunities for advancement. In contrast, the construction industry has a large number of workers at high-income levels and many others distributed fairly evenly in other categories. Medical services provide many jobs at the lower end of the income scale, and also have a significant number of workers in the middle levels.

The potential for new upgrading efforts is further limited by the fact that often promotion from within an industry is presently used to fill those better positions which do exist. Studies of several blue-collar and service industries, both high wage and low wage, indicate that the better jobs are often reserved for experienced lower-level workers.[8] For example, practically all intermediate and upper-level maintenance and operations positions in the New York City Transit Authority are filled from the ranks of entry-level workers such as conductors and maintainer's helpers. The few higher-wage positions in the food service industry, such as cooks and bakers, are also usually filled by men who have worked their way up by serving as kitchen helpers in different restaurants. In the steel industry, the higher-paying production jobs are filled by workers who have advanced along a clearly defined progression of jobs. The better jobs in both high- and low-wage fields are most often filled by workers from lower-level positions; upgrading is an ongoing practice in many industries.

In most cases upgrading workers does not require formal training. A cutter in the garment industry, a bricklayer in the construction industry, and a foreman for the Transit Authority will learn the skills that are required primarily through observation and on-the-job instruction. Most jobs are prepared for in this manner. A national survey of workers found that only about 30 percent had ever had any formal training and only about 12 percent indi-

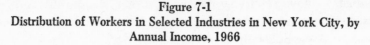

Figure 7-1
Distribution of Workers in Selected Industries in New York City, by
Annual Income, 1966

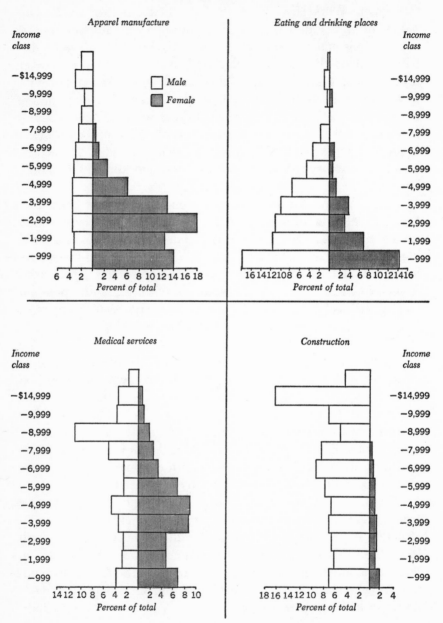

cated that formal training had been the most helpful way in which they learned about their trade.[9] A major exception to the general rule that upgrading provides most of the upper-level manpower are occupations which do require formal schooling. The fields in which workers require formal training are the professions and other specific occupations where custom, and frequently licensure laws, mandate institutional preparation. These jobs usually are not filled through upgrading, but are staffed by new entrants or reentrants to the labor force who begin in higher-level positions. Generally, the extended preparation which is required prevents workers employed at lower levels from entering these fields. However, there are occupations with formal entry requirements that are less extensive than those of the professions, and these jobs might be suited to upgrading efforts. The health services industry provides several examples. The jobs of nurse, x-ray technician, medical laboratory technician, and dental hygienist are licensed occupations requiring formal preparation of about two years. In fields such as these, upgrading could become an important source of manpower. Other than the health services industry, there are few occupations which require some formal training which are not presently being filled from within, so this field may be a rare example of an industry with significant potential for expanding upgrading practices.

What kinds of programs are needed to facilitate the movement of employed workers into suitable occupations? Under present arrangements the new entrant shares the cost of his training through tuition payments and bears the additional cost of forgone earnings during the training period. Workers employed in low-wage jobs are often not able to meet these costs. Even if money were available for tuition, or training were provided on a tuition-free basis, workers often cannot afford to forgo earnings for an extended period. Many have family obligations and depend on their small incomes to support their dependents. Others in lower-level jobs may not have the basic reading and arithmetic skills to successfully undertake further training. The upgrading of workers into positions requiring formal preparation is likely to require remedial education, compensation (or loans) to cover earnings forgone, and low tuition for training.

A demonstration upgrading program to qualify nurse's aides in New York City municipal hospitals for licensed practical nurse positions, which provided these three basic components, has worked successfully. Remedial education was provided for those who tested below the eighth-grade level in reading and mathematics. Occupational training was provided free in a fourteen-month program. Trainees were granted released time from work and were given stipends by the U.S. Department of Labor to make up for lost income. Of the 463 trainees who began the program, 422 completed training. The cost of training and stipends amounted to $5,638 per enrollee, or $6,185 per graduate.[10] Another program with a similar format is now being undertaken to train practical nurses to become registered nurses.

The demonstration project shows that upgrading can become an important source of manpower for occupations which have traditionally relied primarily upon new entrants. But federal grants cannot be relied upon as a permanent source of funding. To continue upgrading efforts, hospital unions have negotiated training funds to pay tuition for workers attending formal programs and to finance remedial training for those who require it. Paid released time for study has not been institutionalized, so most workers seeking to advance will probably have to attend classes after working hours at a sacrifice of leisure rather than income.

Another demonstration project in New York City intended to promote the upgrading concept is the Training Incentive Payments Program (TIPP), a federally subsidized experimental manpower program administered by the Institute for Public Administration. Rather than directly financing training services and stipends for workers, the program provides incentive payments to employers who promote their workers. The program has been operating for about one year and has signed contracts with 15 firms covering 92 enrolled workers.[11] The limited experience and the design of the program make evaluation difficult. One cannot determine if the occupations involved are normally staffed through upgrading and whether the program is reaching workers who would not have otherwise advanced. The program's administrators are aware of the pitfalls of upgrading efforts as well as their potentials and are planning modifications. A final evaluation of this novel approach to stimulating upgrading must await further experience.

In a broad sense the largest upgrading program in New York City is the evening courses provided by the City University. Community colleges have over 5,800 part-time evening students who are working toward a degree, and there are over 7,300 part-time students in evening programs working toward a baccalaureate degree in City University senior colleges.[12] Many individuals who cannot afford to sacrifice earnings in order to attend school work during the day and study in the evening in order to qualify for a better job. Often completion of an associate or baccalaureate degree is related to a shift in both industry and occupation. The large-scale availability of low-tuition, part-time, college-level training is an important source of occupational mobility in New York City.

In sum, there are a limited number of intermediate-level jobs which cannot presently be filled through upgrading because lower-level workers in the industry lack the requisite skills. In these instances part-time training opportunities suited to the needs of employed workers can help expand upgrading practices. However, most of the low-wage workers in New York City are trapped in industries with few better jobs and little potential for advancement.

Although in most industries the few better positions are filled primarily from the ranks of experienced workers, this does not mean that there is no room for improving the upgrading process. Government programs can have little impact on the shape of occupational structures, that is, on the relative number of better jobs available to low-wage workers in the industry. However, public action can help ensure that these jobs are filled equitably from among the eligible lower-level workers. In many industries the higher-level positions are filled from within, but this process works in a discriminatory fashion. For example, in the New York City labor market, blacks constitute over 20 percent of the construction laborers but only about 2 percent of the pipetrades craftsmen, 2 percent of the electricians, and 7 percent of the carpenters in the industry. Females constitute over 95 percent of the sewing machine operators in the women's apparel industry, but only 8 percent of the pressers and less than 1 percent of the cutters and markers. Similar examples showing an underrepresentation of blacks and/or females in upper-level occupations could be cited for most industries. Better jobs may be filled from within, but this does not necessarily mean the process is not discriminatory.

A wide range of action is possible to help make the upgrading process more equitable. A recent Supreme Court decision should force changes in testing procedures frequently used by large employers in making promotional and hiring decisions. In the case of *Willie S. Griggs v. Duke Power Company,* the Court declared unconstitutional practices which disqualified a disproportionate number of blacks because the tests were designed to gauge general aptitude rather than measure job performance. The Court said, "If an employment practice which operates to exclude Negroes cannot be shown to be related to job performance, the practice is prohibited." Tests must "measure the person for job and not the person in the abstract." The Court noted that there need not be a discriminatory intent, only discriminatory results. "Under the (Civil Rights) Act (of 1964), practices, procedures, or tests neutral on their face, even neutral in terms of content, cannot be maintained if they operate to 'freeze' the status quo of prior discriminatory employment practices."[13]

This decision may have important consequences for many industries in New York City. Local court cases have resulted in challenging tests for selecting apprentices for construction trades and for making promotional decisions in the public school system. A federal district court judge has granted a preliminary injunction preventing the city's Board of Examiners from using its tests to select school principals. While apparently neutral in intent, the tests were found to produce de facto discrimination against minority candidates and not to be a direct measure of job performance. The court declared that a review of the exams "reveals that the questions appear to be aimed at testing the candidate's ability to memorize rather than the qualities normally associated with a school administrator."[14] It can be hoped that legal efforts will be devoted to securing reviews of procedures for making promotional decisions in other settings, since they are likely to produce similar findings.

Affirmative action requirements for contract compliance under federal, state, and municipal regulations can also be used to ensure that minorities have a fair chance to be advanced to better positions within an industry. Outreach and training principles established for compliance with these requirements in the construction industry could be applied to other industries with an underrepresentation of minorities at the higher levels. In the past, public agencies with contract compliance responsibilities have been gravely understaffed in light of the volume of work they have to cover and the complexity of the issues involved. This appears to be one area where increased manpower expenditures could yield substantial payoff.

Upgrading, or the advancing of low-wage personnel into related higher-level positions, is an ongoing process in all industries. The most serious limitation of the process is the number of better jobs which the industry provides rather than the lack of qualified workers. In a limited number of cases the provision of part-time training opportunities could make possible a shift in recruiting practices from external to internal sources. But the greatest potential for improving upgrading practices lies in preventing discrimination from influencing the choice of who from among the eligible workers shall be selected for advancement. Public action to achieve this end includes legal efforts aimed at eliminating testing practices which are not job-validated and strict contract compliance procedures supplemented by training programs when they are needed to ensure an available supply of qualified minority workers.

8

CAREER GUIDANCE

Alice M. Yohalem

EVERYONE IS CONFRONTED with the necessity of making educational and occupational decisions at various times in life. While some people are able to resolve their career problems with the advice and aid of relatives and friends, many persons need assistance in perceiving and exploring available opportunities.

Career guidance can be a critical intervention for residents of large cities like New York where the network of educational, training, and employing institutions is too complex and differentiated to be readily understood. Without informed help during the decision-making process, many city dwellers find it difficult to plan courses of action that will enable them to make the most of their career options. As New Yorkers attempt to negotiate the interlocking educational, training, and employment structures, the mediation of guidance counselors may ease their progress into and through the labor market and help them to surmount institutional barriers that restrict their range of choice. Since career decisions are made by both youths and adults, an effective guidance system must aim to serve people of all ages.

A person's career options are affected not only by his personal attributes, but also, to a significant degree, by the availability of family and community resources which can be devoted to the development of his potential and to the pursuit of his goals. "Guidance specialists share with most Americans, the belief that a man is largely in control of his own fate. However, guidance has paid

142

relatively little attention to the ways in which the economic and social status of some families restricts the opportunities for education and work available to their children."[1]

In New York, for example, at one extreme we find people with sufficient resources to select and realize any of a large number of career possibilities. At the other extreme are those whose circumstances drastically restrict their opportunities. In the first instance, while guidance may provide a measure of reinforcement to the decision-making process, the determinants for successful outcomes preexist. In the latter instance, socioeconomic barriers to the realization of choice severely limit the potential contribution of guidance to effective decision making.

Most New York residents fall between these two extremes. Few are so well situated that they never require or seek formal help in decision making. On the other hand, few are so unalterably disadvantaged that they cannot derive some benefit from guidance, especially if it is combined with supporting services. Guidance cannot produce major social transformations, but skillful intervention can contribute to decisions that may improve an individual's prospects.

Certain aspects of the New York labor market which bear upon the provision of guidance services in the city are set forth below. Many of these are discussed in other chapters in this volume.

—New York has a heterogeneous population with a substantial component of poor minorities, many of whom are recent in-migrants from rural areas. These migrants have little or no access to informal sources of aid and support (successful relatives and friends) in planning courses of action which will enable them or their children to make secure attachments to work.

—The job market has less visibility for those engaged in work-related decision making in a large city than in communities where there are either a small number of business establishments or where employment is concentrated in a few industries. While New Yorkers may get a bird's-eye view of many different occupations, neighborhood and social isolation prevents large numbers from gaining familiarity with local employment opportunities, including those that offer the most attractive conditions of work and advancement.

—New York high schools provide various courses of study which are divided broadly into academic and vocational curricula. Many students are enrolled in the general program, which is a modified version of the academic curriculum with significantly lower requirements that provide limited skills and credentials for college or employment. Students who did not learn to read adequately in elementary and junior high school are usually assigned to the general track. In May 1969, an estimated quarter of all twelfth-grade pupils in New York high schools were enrolled in a general program, 62 percent were in a college preparatory curriculum, and the remainder were in vocationally oriented courses.[2]

—In 1970 nonwhites and students with Spanish surnames comprised 62 percent of the total New York public school population, 52 percent of the students in all senior high schools, and 69 percent of vocational high school pupils.[3] This last figure suggests "some justification for the complaints of many minority group students (and particularly Puerto Rican students) that they are disproportionately counseled out of the academic high schools and into vocationally oriented programs."[4] However, since the vocational schools enroll only a small fraction of the city's total high school population, more than 80 percent of minority students are in academic high schools, where they represent a significant proportion of those pursuing the general curriculum.

—Attrition rates during the high school years are high. For example, of the public high school students who were originally admitted to the class of June 1968, only three out of five were graduated. Blacks and Puerto Ricans account for most of the dropouts.[5]

—In 1970, the City University of New York (CUNY) instituted a system of open admissions which enabled all graduates of New York high schools, regardless of type of diploma or academic average, to enter a two- or four-year public college. During the first year of operation, 19 percent more New York high school graduates were enrolled as full-time students in a postsecondary institution than in the previous year. The proportion of all the city's high school graduates who enrolled in college in September 1970 was 76 percent, compared with national attendance estimates of 55–60 percent of high school graduates.[6] The difference can be attributed to the open admissions policy, which provided opportunities for full-time college attendance for groups who until that time had attended college part time or not at all. Black and Puerto Rican students comprised 29.1 percent of the 1971 CUNY entrance class, compared to 19.7 percent in 1969.[7] However, the chancellor of CUNY has stated that the overwhelming majority of those admitted under the open admissions program were white high school graduates whom he described as "the sons and daughters (of the) 'working poor' of our city."[8] Many of these pupils would otherwise have entered the labor force or vocational training after high school graduation. There were higher college-attendance rates for students who had received vocational diplomas from vocationally oriented high schools than for general diploma students who had attended academically oriented high schools, possibly because of the selective nature of admission to preferred vocational programs.[9]

—The attrition rate during 1970–1971 of freshmen in CUNY who would not have qualified for matriculation prior to the open admissions policy was 16 percent higher than among students whose high school performance met regular admissions standards. At the senior college level, attrition was more than twice as high among open admissions freshmen; at the community college level, it was less than 6 percent higher.[10] Since few if any freshmen were forced to leave college for academic reasons, it is presumed that students dropped out voluntarily.

—The city's occupational structure is complex and diverse, and employment requirements have shifted upward; large numbers of occupations now specify educational credentials as prerequisites for entrance and advancement. There are few of the unskilled factory jobs that formerly served as primary points of job entry. For example, of the 16- and 17-year-olds, who are required to obtain working papers, only 6 percent obtained papers specifying factory worker in 1968, compared to 17 percent in 1952.[11] Today's entrance point for those with minimal skills is in the service sector where many jobs offer neither the security nor income potential of blue-collar work, nor do they satisfy the rising aspirations of minority youth. The decline in jobs in manufacturing, wholesale trade, and personal services and the growth of the white-collar sector have serious implications for many young people and adults who have no business or technical skills.[12]

—Publicly sponsored vocational training programs have proliferated in recent years, both on and off the job. In addition, New York has many profit-making institutions which provide training in technical and business skills. The constantly changing number and range of training opportunities make it difficult for any one individual to obtain an overview of their requirements, costs, and benefits.

—The unemployment rate in New York during 1969–1970 for black teen-agers living in poverty areas was 28.2 percent, and for Puerto Rican teen-agers, 34 percent. During the same period the rate for white teen-agers was 9.4 percent.[13] It is probable that the majority of unemployed youth are high school dropouts, since data in the Birnbaum and Goldman study of New York high school graduates of 1970 suggest an unemployment rate of about 6 percent among those who completed secondary school.[14]

—New York's 1970 adult unemployment rate was 4.1 percent, which included higher percentages of blacks and Puerto Ricans than whites.[15]

—Many middle-aged workers seek to change careers, and large numbers of housewives contemplate returning to the labor force. In New York, the board of education, local universities, and other institutions have inaugurated programs designed to provide basic education as well as specialized training for adults.

Other aspects of the New York labor market have implications for guidance; the foregoing are noted primarily because they represent circumstances that are distinctive to New York. Using them as guideposts, one can develop a hierarchy of need for career guidance in terms of clientele, settings, and types of assistance. A list of priorities must start with the recognition that the number of qualified personnel and the amount of funds allocated by the governmental bodies which provide the bulk of support for guidance are limited. Therefore, counselors should be allocated with the aim of enabling them to make a significant input into the career decision-making process.

Special attention should be paid to providing an adequate number of guidance counselors at the junior and senior high school levels. It is in junior high and intermediate school that students make their first critical decisions as they select courses and curricula, and it is in senior high school that they decide about their plans after high school.

Since career guidance is concerned with individual educational and vocational decision making, it serves no relevant purpose at the elementary school level. Admittedly, the New York public elementary schools have been malfunctioning for a large proportion of their pupils. Consequently, many students enter high school without the skills necessary to master additional education. This undoubtedly affects their self-image and their approach to career planning.

The New York public school system has tried many different expedients to solve its problems, including employing guidance counselors in elementary schools in the hope of improving pupil performance.

A New York principal of an elementary school composed primarily of black and Puerto Rican pupils recently publicly expressed his dismay at the assignment of several guidance counselors to his school. He saw a great need for pupil personnel workers who could provide concrete assistance to children who were ill clothed, ill fed, and troubled by language difficulties. And he was committed even more to improving teaching. But he could define no role for guidance in his school. Even if one could define such a role, it is questionable whether in the face of financial stringencies this is the proper locale for expansion.

Students at the secondary school level may be divided broadly into three groups: those from middle-class families for whom higher education has become conventional; those from working-class backgrounds whose orientation is toward jobs or job training rather than further academic pursuits; and those from poor homes whose scholastic experiences and environmental disadvantages have prematurely closed out many options available to their more fortunate classmates.

For the first group, the counselor's task is relatively simple. In the junior high and intermediate schools, it consists primarily of discussing high school options, including admission to schools which have special entrance requirements, such as the Bronx High School of Science, Stuyvesant and Brooklyn Technical High Schools, and the High Schools of Music and Art and of the Performing Arts. It is unlikely that many children from middle-class homes will choose to attend vocational high schools, but this option should be explored since some vocational schools provide technical training that is oriented toward higher education and others, such as the High Schools of Art and Design and Fashion Industries, present alternatives that can satisfy middle-class aspirations.

At the high school level, the primary concern of guidance counselors with respect to middle-class students is college entrance. Various investigations have shown that an inordinate amount of attention is paid by high school guidance counselors to the middle-class college-bound student. However, as Eli Ginzberg has noted, "There is considerable evidence that indicates the preference of educated parents to be operative with respect to their children's choice of college."[16] The more time that counselors spend in attending to questions about the college choice of middle-class students, the less time they have to devote to the problems of young people from lower-income homes who are more sorely in need of their help.

However, there is growing evidence that many middle-class children are questioning the value of college, both as a goal immediately after high school and as a long-range goal. It is important to provide counseling to these pupils in order to explore alternatives to college.

The second group of high school students is composed of children of blue-collar or low-level white-collar workers who tend to consider high school as preparation for a job, not for college. These students grow up in a milieu which often serves as an informal job placement channel. It provides entrée to apprenticeships and can assist youths to obtain employment in firms which welcome applicants recommended by present employees, and which provide favorable conditions of work and opportunities for advancement.

We have noted that large numbers of working-class youths enrolled in CUNY as open admissions students. This suggests that many young people from blue-collar families have sought jobs after high school not by choice but by necessity, either because of parental disinclination to approve and support higher education or because their high school course of study precluded admission to college. Of course, the general state of the economy may have played a role in their decision to go to college; fewer jobs were available to high school graduates in 1970 than in preceding years. In any event, the new college option places upon guidance the responsibility for helping this group of youngsters to weigh the relative value of the vocational and academic curricula.

Guidance counselors should also have a wide range of labor market information to assist job-oriented youth, an undertaking that points to greater reliance on close contacts with the New York State Employment Service and the employer community, and to the utilization of work/study programs and summer jobs as occupational exploratory devices.

Another challenge to high school guidance is presented by the large number of open admissions students who are entering college, only to drop out after a short stay. Counselors should help high school seniors to understand the differential demands and missions of senior and community colleges and should encourage them to choose that setting which best meets their needs and goals.

Girls in all income groups are often steered toward commercial training, since they and their families believe that business skills are easily marketable in New York and will provide attractive temporary employment prior to marriage and childbearing. Counselors should make every effort to disabuse them and their parents of the notion that females are likely to be only short-term members of the labor force and to encourage them to prepare for congenial long-range career opportunities.

The most difficult high school guidance task involves the large number of students, usually from poor minority families, who have not been taught to read adequately in elementary school and who are shunted to the general curriculum as a holding operation rather than a learning experience. Students are usually required to remain in school until they are 17 years old, but the schools do not have a reciprocal requirement to ensure that the period of compulsory education is personally rewarding. Hence, many students with scholastic difficulty come to realize that their schooling can result at best in jobs with low status and low pay.

As noted earlier, a clientele with such a limited range of options places a heavy burden upon guidance counselors. It is far easier to deal with middle-class students on the academic track, whose primary interest is in college selection, than with poor blacks and Puerto Ricans whose options have been prematurely closed. Some counselors may decide that the best help they can offer the disaffected student is to hasten his school leaving by expediting his acquisition of working papers. Others, however, may hope that special efforts for these students such as arrangements for remedial help and for part-time jobs, as well as advocacy on their behalf when they are in conflict with school and other authorities, may encourage them to remain in school long enough to acquire credentials that will stand them in good stead in the job market.

There appears to be no statistically significant difference in the employment experiences of dropouts and terminal high school graduates.[17] Thus, rather than attempting to persuade potential dropouts to remain in school until graduation, guidance counselors could help many of them by facilitating their admission to appropriate public job-training programs when they reach school-leaving age. Terminal high school graduates also need help in locking into the job market via entrance into desirable apprenticeship programs or into preferred corporate employment. High schools with a preponderance of poor minority students should try to keep in touch with those graduates who have made a successful transition to the world of work and to seek their help as models for decision making.

While there is a positive relation between income and college attendance, about two-thirds of New York high school graduates with family incomes of less than $3,700 were attending college full time in 1970.[18] The following year nearly 9 percent of the freshmen in CUNY were welfare recipients; in three community colleges, the proportion was over 20 percent.[19] Higher proportions of low-income blacks with medium or low school grades entered college than did whites with similar incomes and grades. This confirms the findings of several investigations into the aspirations of blacks and indicates that there are many poor minority students who have not been forced into an early departure from the educational system. It is important that high school counselors identify those students who have not been completely discouraged from continuing their schooling and that they stimulate and support them in their efforts to graduate and to continue their education at either public or private institutions. In general, because of discriminatory hiring practices, a high school diploma has relatively less value for blacks in terms of earnings and employment opportunities than for whites. Counselors must explore all alternatives with minority students and seek to keep abreast of changes in local labor market conditions that may open new possibilities for those who prefer jobs to further education.

The high attrition rate of open admissions students attests to the need for improved guidance in CUNY. The University's dean for community college affairs has testified to this need: "We have less concrete knowledge of reasons why students leave or drop out than we have had in years past. Obviously, more extensive counseling is required, with an emphasis on a final interview for the student who is definitely leaving, so that the student may be counseled in realistic alternative courses of action within CUNY or elsewhere."[20] However, earlier counseling is often indicated. Dean McGrath acknowledged that "counselors . . . have been waiting in their offices for the arrival of clients," and he remarked that they have been "advised to adopt more aggressive outreach procedures in order that they may have more direct contact with the newly arrived students."[21]

Of course, open admissions students are not the only ones who need improved guidance at the college level. "There is irony in the fact that guidance services for the college-bound student are the central concern of the high school advisory system, but when he gets to college, the student is largely on his own."[22] Many college graduates flounder in the labor market even in the best of times, because they chose their fields of concentration unwisely or because they had no help in learning where their skills could be put to use, or how to engage in the job search. Since so many CUNY students, as well as graduates of other New York colleges, expect to enter the local labor market, it would be mutually beneficial for guidance staffs and local employers to have ongoing relationships that would provide colleges with information about employer demands and apprise employers of the availability of graduates who have the skills they seek.

We have referred to the large number of unemployed ghetto youth in New York; the question here is whether guidance can reach and help them. The fact that so many have failed to acquire even modest skills means that the traditional guidance approach whereby the counselee engages in self-assessment and in a review of options can be a futile endeavor. These young people need jobs or job training. Since so many of them do not know about the channels of communication of job opportunities or they mistrust conventional public or private employment offices, outreach and outstations in poverty areas are needed. Each borough has a Youth Opportunity Center of the Employment Service which is designed to counsel and make referrals to jobs or job training. But these are not neighborhood facilities, and many youngsters have neither the initiative nor know-how to make use of them.

Guidance may be able to assist this group after they have been placed in jobs or in training programs. Preemployment counseling can be counterproductive since these youth want and need work, not words. After a youth is placed in a job, follow-up counseling may be of help in assisting him to cope with the demands of the work setting and to prepare for advancement. There is much that improved counseling can do if jobs are available but, regrettably, the absence of jobs, especially desirable jobs, continues to characterize the labor market, particularly with respect to positions open to young people.

In addition to unemployed youths, New York has a significant component of out-of-work adults with varying skills and diverse work experience. At present, veterans constitute an important segment of this group. Many of the adult unemployed have had little urban work experience and have few skills that can be readily utilized in the city. They require assessment and training that will better fit them for employment in the local labor market. Experimental programs that simulate a variety of work settings and tasks have proved to be a successful method of assessing this group prior to Employment Service counseling and placement in training or jobs. Like their younger counterparts, many adults have so limited a range of alternatives that they are best served by imaginative job matching and postplacement counseling.

Consideration should be given to a slow redirection of guidance away from students and toward the nonschool population. The assumption that formal education sets the parameters of a person's lifetime career opportunities is no longer valid, if it ever was. Second chances abound, and they are increasing, for people at all levels of skill and work experience. In addition to unemployed youths and adults, the potential guidance clients range from present and former prisoners and mental patients to dissatisfied executives and unfulfilled housewives, most of whom need help in planning and taking their next steps.

A strengthening of the counseling services of the New York State Employment Service is one line of action. There also should be increasing experimentation with new structures and locales to meet the needs of different adult groups, such as prerelease counseling in institutions, improved guidance in neighborhood facilities, and career information at community centers where large numbers of housewives assemble. In all settings more effort should be expended in improving and disseminating occupational information in a form that meets the needs of large client groups (see Chapter 12).

The thrust of this chapter has been to call attention to the population groups in New York City who might benefit from skilled guidance in negotiating the preparatory system and in finding satisfactory places in the job market. The difficulties that the city's poor, its minorities, and its undereducated residents confront are formidable, and it would be unrealistic to place too much reliance on strengthened guidance efforts to solve their problems. Yet we have pointed out a number of settings and a number of ways in which career guidance can respond to certain needs of New York's population that are presently being neglected. Guidance personnel must deepen their understanding of their clients, of the New York labor market, and of the diverse institutions that they can call on for assistance. There are margins for improvement despite the fact that the key to individual progress is a dynamic economy with nondiscriminatory employment practices. If guidance counselors are committed to helping all their clients to optimize their opportunities and if they have sufficient skill and adequate tools to permit them to intervene with confidence, they can often make a positive contribution to individual development.

9

WORK AND WELFARE

Miriam Ostow and Charles Brecher

IT IS ONE OF THE IRONIES of American social history that the theory and assumptions of our income-maintenance programs, elaborated in the aftermath of the depression of the 1930s when unemployment rates rose above 25 percent, were questioned in a period of prosperity. Yet it was not until the late 1960s that analysts focused their attention on the relationship between work and welfare, and consideration was given to the hypothesis that earnings from employment together with public assistance grants interweave in complex structural and temporal patterns to produce income for large segments of the poverty population, and are not independent, mutually exclusive streams. A review of the development of the welfare dilemma, with particular reference to New York City, and of the experience with alterations in the assistance programs that have been initiated during the past few years should sharpen our understanding of the nexus between work and welfare and our thinking about the relationships between income transfers and general economic planning.

NATURE AND DEVELOPMENT OF THE WELFARE CRISIS

The social welfare system serving the nation today is rooted in the Social Security Act of 1935 and has persisted for over three decades without fundamental reform in structure, assumptions, or

objectives. Under the social security legislation two distinct income-maintenance programs have evolved which differ in financing, eligibility, and administration.

Old age, survivors, and disability insurance (OASDI), commonly referred to as "social security," was designed as a federally
administered program for the employed worker and his dependents. It is a social insurance system for labor force participants
who make mandatory contributions throughout their working
careers. Benefits are thus earned as a right through employment
in covered industries, whose originally narrow range has expanded over time. These benefits range within statutory limits, and are
roughly proportional to the individual's contributions. On the assumption that a normal economy should provide full employment
with adequate income for the needs of the labor force, it was expected that this model would eventually encompass the full
range of vicissitudes which might threaten a worker's income.

Categorical assistance programs, or "welfare," are a set of
income-transfer programs for unemployable groups, administered
by state and local agencies and financed by general federal revenues matched with state and local tax funds. Unlike the "insurance" benefits, eligibility for these programs is established
through a means test. "Welfare" was conceptualized not as an
earned right but as discretionary assistance subject to eligibility
criteria which varied by administrative jurisdiction, usually the
state. The categories of unemployables eligible for federally reim-
bursed assistance were the aged (OAA), the disabled (AD), the
blind (AB), and children in one-parent families who have been
deprived of normal support as the result of a working parent's
death, desertion, or some other tragedy (ADC). The wholesale
classification of the heads of single parent families — almost univer-
sally the mother — as unemployable was in accord with conceptions of the 1930s. The assumed beneficial effects for children of
their mother's presence in the home, the exigencies of the de-
pressed labor market of the 1930s, and the traditional low labor
force participation rates of married women (about 15 percent in
the thirties compared to approximately 40 percent in 1970)[1] all
combined to make women with children "unemployable" by definition.

Employable adults other than mothers of young children have consistently been omitted from federally reimbursable assistance, and their treatment left completely to the discretion of the individual states. It is significant that to this day there is no mandatory assistance program for the able-bodied adult male. Aid to families with dependent children–unemployed parent (ADC-U), legislated in 1961 to extend reimbursable assistance to two-parent families in which the father is unemployed, has remained a voluntary program which was adopted by 25 states, rejected by the rest (1971). The sole mandatory protective program for the employable unemployed adult today, as in 1936, is unemployment insurance, temporary income based on earnings which does *not yet* include all the nation's labor force. With limited benefits and exempted employment, unemployment insurance either excludes or is minimally effective with regard to the most deprived segment of the population. Except for state-supported general assistance (Home Relief), there are no public programs to support families with underemployed primary wage earners.

The much-publicized "welfare crisis" of recent years is the result of the sizable and rapid rise in the number of families and individuals receiving assistance through the categorical programs, particularly ADC. Table 9-1 presents the relevant data for New York City. From 1960 to 1970 the total number of public-assistance recipients rose from 328,000 to near 1.2 million. The proportion of the city's population receiving assistance rose from approximately 4 percent to about 15 percent during this period. The growth was concentrated in the ADC (and ADC-U) category, which expanded by over 400 percent—from 200,000 to over 860,000 during the decade. The largest gains in these categories, over 100,000 annually, occurred during the relatively prosperous years of 1967 and 1968. In fact, throughout the decade the public-assistance rolls expanded regardless of trends in the national economy and the local unemployment rate.

The explosion in the welfare rolls had fiscal consequences for local taxpayers. New York City's expenditures for welfare grants and for administration of the public-assistance programs rose from $242 million in 1961 to nearly $1.3 billion in 1970 and, by the end of the decade, welfare had replaced education as the

Table 9-1

Beneficiaries of Income Transfer Programs, New York City, 1960–1970

(Thousands)

	1960	1961	1962	1963	1964
Total—public assistance	328.2	351.6	364.7	414.8	471.9
ADC	200.1	212.8	228.3	260.6	298.9
ADC-U	—	22.9	22.8	33.8	39.6
HR	59.6	42.7	44.4	50.6	63.4
OAA	41.5	47.9	44.7	45.8	46.0
AD	24.5	23.2	22.4	21.9	21.9
AB	2.5	2.1	2.1	2.1	2.1
Total—OASDI	727.4	789.6	847.6	884.7	912.6
Retired workers	433.0	471.1	505.3	529.6	548.2
Dependents of retired workers	158.3	163.1	171.1	173.0	174.5
Disabled workers	22.5	29.9	35.1	38.6	40.6
Dependents of disabled workers	6.1	11.4	14.6	17.2	17.7
Survivers	107.5	114.2	121.6	126.4	131.5
Special age 72 beneficiaries	—	—	—	—	—
Unemployment insurance beneficiaries	NA	NA	NA	NA	NA
Unemployment rate	5.0	5.6	5.0	5.3	4.9

NOTE: Figures may not add due to rounding.
NA—Not available.
SOURCE: 1. Public Assistance data are from the New York City Department of Social Services, *Monthly Statistical Report.* All figures are as of December of the year indicated. The OAA figures include MAA (Medical Assistance for the Aged) recipients for the years 1961–1965. 2.

largest single item in the municipal budget. The reasons for concern with welfare policy in New York City are neatly summarized in these two figures—15 percent of the population and 20 percent of the budget.

In contrast to welfare, the OASDI program grew slowly and steadily throughout the decade, from 727,400 beneficiaries in 1960 to slightly over 1 million in 1970. Because the program is financed through contributions from the current work force, is administered nationally, and has benefits which average well below public assistance grants, the expansion has not been interpreted as a "crisis." It should be noted, moreover, that OASDI and

1965	1966	1967	1968	1969	1970
531.3	616.2	787.3	978.4	1039.6	1165.6
345.2	413.9	525.3	660.6	728.2	818.1
43.3	44.2	57.6	62.2	41.1	45.6
70.6	91.0	128.1	166.7	153.4	155.1
48.6	42.2	48.4	54.2	62.9	72.8
21.5	22.9	25.8	32.4	51.6	68.0
2.1	2.1	2.1	2.2	2.4	2.6
945.7	1029.5	1071.9	1077.8	1085.1	1096.7
565.6	622.4	646.0	613.9	620.7	632.7
178.3	188.2	193.6	114.4	111.4	110.5
44.5	49.9	54.6	56.6	58.5	59.5
20.0	23.8	27.1	28.9	29.8	30.7
137.4	145.2	150.6	231.3	236.0	239.2
—	—	—	32.6	28.6	24.1
94.3	90.7	65.4	51.4	67.4	96.1
4.6	4.2	3.7	3.2	3.1	3.9

OASDI figures are from data supplied by the Social Security Administration. All figures are for December of the year indicated, except 1967 which is as of February 1968. 3. UIB data is from New York State Department of Labor, *Employment Review*. All figures are for December of year indicated. 4. Unemployment rates are annual averages supplied by the Research and Statistics Office, Division of Employment, New York State Department of Labor.

public-assistance beneficiaries are not mutually exclusive groups. Because of the low OASDI grant levels many beneficiaries also receive public assistance. In a recent month (May 1969) for which data are available, over 10 percent of all public assistance cases were also receiving OASDI, including more than half the OAA case load.

Underlying the significant increase in the dependent population are fundamental demographic, economic, political, and administrative changes. Since 1950 the city's population has remained at a fairly stable 7.9 million persons. However, the movement of middle-class whites to the suburbs and the simultaneous in-migration of blacks and Puerto Ricans have combined to alter the racial and economic composition of the city. Blacks and Puerto Ricans constituted an estimated 35 percent of the population in 1970, compared to 13 percent in 1950. Most of the city's new citizens came in search of employment opportunities more favorable than those available in their birthplace, and most found them. They filled jobs in the growing health services industry, in the large garment industry, in the numerous hotels and restaurants, and recently in local government and office clerical positions. Without the influx of new labor it is possible that New York could not have maintained services essential to its population and to its central economic function as corporate headquarters. Many of those who came to the city in search of greater opportunity faced serious problems, including language barriers and racial discrimination, but most found a place for themselves in the local labor market. Few went directly on welfare, a fact revealed by recent studies of ADC recipients in New York City which indicate that while approximately 80 percent of the mothers were born outside the city, only 14 percent obtained assistance for the first time within two years of coming to New York. [2]

While most migrants have made an adjustment to the city, the process is difficult because of long-run shifts in the local economy. Many industries in which unskilled workers could readily secure jobs have sustained a reduction in their level of employment. For example, the apparel industry lost over 60,000 jobs in the 1960s, other nondurable-goods manufacturing jobs declined by another 60,000, and restaurant and hotel employment each dropped by several thousand (see Chapter 7). Job growth has been concentrated in the white-collar categories, which frequently require specialized skills. These basic transformations in the labor market have made successful adjustment more difficult for unskilled workers, who frequently have rural backgrounds.

These underlying demographic and economic shifts provide a background against which to view the development of the welfare crisis. However, they have been at work for almost a generation and therefore do not explain the dramatic changes which took place in the last five years. Several more immediate causes have been suggested for the rapid rise in New York City's welfare population. David Gordon's calculations with the limited data available for the period 1964 to 1968 led him to conclude that the principal source of increase was a rise in the income level at which families may be eligible for assistance, which extended coverage to a larger proportion of the population, rather than shifts in the composition of the population. Specifically, he found that "the largest source of the increase in welfare stemmed from the increase in real grant levels, that changes in the income distribution accounted for a smaller share, and that those eligible for welfare showed no greater propensity to join the rolls."[3]

Gordon's calculations have been challenged on several grounds, including his assumption of declining *real* income for nonwhites and Puerto Ricans and improvements in income for whites which do not exceed cost-of-living hikes.[4] Blanche Bernstein has analyzed specially prepared tabulations of New York City income data for 1968 taken from the Bureau of the Census, and concluded that Gordon's estimate that approximately 60 percent of all eligibles actually received assistance throughout the period 1964–1968 was erroneous. Her finding is that virtually all eligibles are on the welfare rolls.[5]

Nevertheless, the level of welfare benefits has risen substantially during the decade (Table 9-2). The ADC allowance for a family of four rose from $2,218 annually in 1960 to $4,212 in 1970. Higher grant levels not only have the effect of including a larger percentage of the population within the criteria of eligibility, but also make public assistance increasingly competitive with low-wage employment. Tables 9-2 and 9-3 present minimum wages and average earnings in selected industries and occupations and relate these data to the weekly ADC allowance for a family of four in New York City. Earnings at the minimum wage have remained close to the welfare allowance throughout the decade, rising from slightly below (93.8 percent) in 1960 to slightly above from 1962 to 1965, then dropping to a relative low of 80.8 percent in 1966 and slowly increasing in subsequent years, but remaining below welfare allowances. Earnings in low-level office occupations have dropped relative to welfare allowances from 30 to 40 percent above in the early part of the decade to 1 to 5 percent above in 1968 and have remained only slightly higher since. Over

Table 9-2

Wages and Welfare Allowances in New York City, 1960–1970

	1960	*1961*	*1962*	*1963*	*1964*
Weekly equivalent of welfare allowance for specified family of four	$42.65	$43.72	$43.72	$43.72	$47.12
Weekly earnings at minimum wage	40.00	40.00	46.00	46.00	50.00
Weekly earnings—selected office jobs					
Office boy	NA	57.50	59.00	62.00	63.50
Office girl	NA	57.00	59.50	62.00	63.00
File clerk—class C	NA	NA	58.50	60.50	62.50
Average weekly earnings in selected industries					
Apparel manufacture	68.50	75.45	75.88	77.51	81.40
Leather manufacture	62.19	69.96	70.91	73.14	75.17
Retail trade	71.03	75.18	76.85	80.59	83.13
Hotels	64.86	68.28	70.33	71.46	73.59

NA—Not available.

SOURCE: Welfare allowance and minimum wage figures for 1960–1967 are from Elizabeth Durbin, *Welfare, Income and Employment,* tables 12 and 13; for 1968–1970 the figures are from data supplied by the New York City Department of Social Services and New York State

the decade average weekly earnings in selected industries, which reflect earnings of skilled as well as unskilled workers, declined relative to welfare allowances from approximately 60 to 70 percent above to 20 to 40 percent. The data provide evidence that welfare allowances have risen much faster than wage rates for unskilled jobs, and consequently the income differences between the two have declined significantly.

Other observers have questioned whether the rising eligibility limits are actually responsible for the increased case load. Pointing to the fact that the state of California experienced over a 50 percent rise in welfare population without any increases in benefits, Edward Banfield has asserted: "In my opinion, the principal underlying causes of the increase in welfare caseload have been these political ones—first, the general ideological change produced by the civil rights movement and the war on poverty and, second, the effort of militant organizations created under OEO and other auspices to encourage the poor to demand all that they are legally entitled to."[6]

1965	1966	1967	1968	1969	1970
$47.12	$61.86	$63.22	$ 72.98	$ 75.69	$ 81.00
50.00	50.00	60.00	60.00	64.00	74.00
65.50	69.00	72.00	77.00	83.50	91.50
65.00	66.50	70.00	74.00	79.00	86.50
64.00	66.00	70.00	74.00	79.50	87.00
83.11	87.88	95.12	100.16	106.70	112.78
78.66	79.61	86.30	88.80	89.79	98.74
84.02	88.15	90.22	95.82	102.51	107.76
79.80	81.31	85.78	91.08	103.53	104.96

Department of Labor. The selected office occupations data are from the annual Bureau of Labor Statistics, *Area Wage Survey*. Bulletins 1285-65, 1303-58, 1345-79, 1385-72, 1430-80, 1465-82, 1530-83, 1575-78, 1625-58, and 1660-89. The wage data for selected industries are as of December of the year indicated, as reported in monthly issues of *Employment Review*.

The political explanation of the welfare crisis has been presented with considerable historical documentation by Richard Cloward and Frances Piven.[7] They found that the federal War on Poverty programs, particularly OEO's Community Action Program (CAP), had a direct effect on case loads through new agencies and organizations which provided information to potential recipients, brought litigation against local welfare bureaucracies, and nourished grassroots efforts by the poor themselves to ease welfare restrictions. While admitting that national political leaders did not intentionally expand relief rolls, Cloward and Piven maintain that:

The political circumstances of the 1960's made it crucial, however, that blacks get something in order to solidify their allegiance to the national Democratic Party, and in order to quiet them. As it turned out, welfare was the system that was made to do most of the giving — partly, perhaps, because black constituents needed money; more importantly, because it was easier to give welfare than to press for

Table 9-3

**The Relative Positions of Welfare Allowances and Wage Rates
in New York City, 1960–1970**

	1960	1961	1962	1963	1964
Weekly equivalent of welfare allowance for a specified family of four	$42.65	$43.72	$43.72	$43.72	$47.12
Wage rates as a percent of welfare allowance					
Weekly earnings at minimum wage	93.8	91.5	105.2	105.2	106.1
Weekly earnings in selected office jobs					
Office boy	NA	131.5	134.9	141.8	134.8
Office girl	NA	130.4	136.1	141.8	133.7
File clerk—class C	NA	NA	133.8	138.4	132.6
Average weekly earnings in selected industries					
Apparel manufacture	160.6	172.6	173.6	177.3	172.8
Leather manufacture	145.8	160.0	162.2	167.3	160.0
Retail trade	166.5	172.0	175.8	184.3	176.4
Hotels	152.1	156.2	160.9	163.4	156.2

NA—Not available.

SOURCE: Welfare allowance and minimum wage figures for 1960–1967 are from Elizabeth Durbin, *Welfare, Income and Employment,* tables 12 and 13; for 1968–1970 the figures are from data supplied by the New York City Department of Social Services and New York State

concessions that would challenge the interests of other groups in the cities. . . .

In other words, while the Great Society agencies often attempted to make gains for blacks in housing and health care and education and employment, resistance was stiff and sometimes virulent, for other groups in the cities had major stakes in these services and resources. But there were few other major groups in the cities with direct and immediate interests in welfare.[8]

Statistical evidence to support the political hypothesis is inconclusive. One study using data from 11 cities has found a significant correlation between CAP expenditures in a city and the percent of eligible poor on welfare (the ADC poor rate), but no significant correlation between Welfare Rights Organization (WRO)

1965	1966	1967	1968	1969	1970
$47.12	$61.86	$63.22	$72.98	$75.69	$81.00
106.1	80.8	94.9	82.2	84.6	91.4
139.0	111.5	113.9	105.5	110.3	113.0
137.9	107.5	110.7	101.4	104.4	106.8
135.8	106.7	110.7	101.4	105.0	107.4
176.4	142.1	150.4	137.2	141.0	139.2
166.9	128.7	136.5	121.7	118.6	121.9
178.3	142.5	142.7	131.3	135.4	133.0
169.4	131.4	135.7	124.8	136.8	129.6

Department of Labor. The selected office occupations data are from the annual Bureau of Labor Statistics, *Area Wage Survey*. Bulletins 1285-65, 1303-58, 1345-79, 1385-72, 1430-80, 1465-82, 1530-83, 1575-78, 1625-58 and 1660-89. The wage data for selected industries are as of December of the year indicated, as reported in monthly issues of *Employment Review*.

membership and the ADC poor rate.[9] A Rand Institute analysis of the impact of WRO membership and activities (demonstrations) upon welfare administration at selected New York City centers found that the major effect was to increase the grants of member clients. Political activity was found to have little effect on case closings or acceptances at welfare centers. However, the study suggested that WRO activities had an indirect effect on the level of applications by providing information and helping to reduce the stigma associated with public assistance.[10]

The changing attitude toward public assistance on the part of recipients, welfare administrators, and the general public undoubtedly has played a large part in the increasing number of applications and acceptances for public assistance. Throughout the decade more and more people, and especially the poor themselves, came to consider poverty an injustice rather than a misfortune. Accordingly, welfare was increasingly considered a right rather than a discretionary charitable function of government.

The effect of the changing attitudes held by clients and administrators was a sharp increase in the number of applications and the percent accepted. As Table 9-4 indicates, the average monthly rate of applications for ADC nearly doubled over the decade, from 4,326 to 8,210. The lack of reliable income data for New York City and the shifting eligibility standards make it difficult to ascertain the extent to which this increase reflects a greater propensity among the eligibles to apply, but we believe changing attitudes have significantly increased the willingness of poorer citizens to turn to public assistance. Changing attitudes on the part of administrators are apparent in their greater willingness to accept applicants. The acceptance rate rose from 54.1 percent in 1960 to a high of 80.1 percent in 1968 and since then has remained above 71 percent. One student of the welfare problem, Elizabeth Durbin, has calculated that the higher acceptance rate accounts for a much larger share of the increased case load than does the higher number of applicants.[11]

Table 9-4

Applications, Openings, and Acceptance Rates for ADC in
New York City, 1960-1970

	Applications	Openings	Acceptance rate
1960	4,326	2,342	54.1
1961	4,182	2,179	52.1
1962	4,156	2,172	52.3
1963	4,620	2,537	54.9
1964	4,632	2,768	59.8
1965	4,713	3,007	63.8
1966	5,412	3,801	70.2
1967	6,530	4,994	76.5
1968	7,504	6,011	80.1
1969	6,820	4,937	72.4
1970	8,210	5,835	71.1

NOTE: All figures are annual averages of monthly data.
SOURCE: Data for 1960 to 1968 are from Elizabeth Durbin, "Family Instability, Labor Supply and the Incidence of Aid to Families with Dependent Children" (Ph.D. dissertation, Columbia University, Department of Economics, 1970) Table 3-1. Data for 1969 and 1970 are from New York City Department of Social Services, *Monthly Statistical Report.*

In sum, the welfare crisis consists of a significant and rapid increase in the size of the population receiving public assistance, particularly ADC, ADC-U, and HR. The growth in the dependent population, though rooted in fundamental demographic and economic transformations taking place in the city (and in the nation), was given great stimulus by the more liberal income criteria, changed attitudes, and new political organizations which characterized the latter part of the 1960s.

EMPLOYABILITY, SELF-SUPPORT, AND WORKFARE

Efforts to reduce the size of the dependent population have focused upon their employment potential. Assessments of employability generally include the personal characteristics of clients, such as age, education, and previous work experience, and certain situational factors, such as the absence of child-care facilities, which may act as a barrier to employment for otherwise employable individuals. Yet even this multidimensional approach is often inadequate. Employability is a complex concept involving many variables, including subjective judgments on the part of individual clients, labor market intermediaries such as the employment service, and employers, about the suitability of a particular individual for a particular job. Each of these judgments is subject to change as labor market conditions improve or decline and is likely to vary along with the available opportunities. A mother who receives ADC might consider herself available for work as a salesgirl during the day while her children are at school, but not available for work as a nurse's aide during a hospital night shift. An older man with little education and a sporadic work history might actively seek employment, but the employment service may find none of its listings appropriate. When the economy is characterized by 6 percent unemployment, an employer might be unwilling to hire a mother on welfare who does not have a high school diploma, but when the unemployment rate is 3 percent, he might well be willing to hire her. Because employability is a function of many diverse and dynamic factors, any assessment of employment potential among welfare recipients is subject to change.

For obvious reasons, the aged, blind, and disabled are generally eliminated from discussions of employability. Traditionally, the employable welfare groups have been single adults in the HR category and male family heads in the HR and ADC-U categories. In New York City in 1970 this group totaled approximately 79,000 individuals, or 7 percent of the total welfare population and 19 percent of all cases (see Table 9-1). However, nearly one-fifth of this group, primarily underemployed HR fathers, are at work.[12]

Individuals falling into one of these two categories have always been the primary target population for employment efforts. Throughout the 1960s all recipients over 16 in the HR and ADC-U programs were required to register with the Department of Social Services' (DOSS) Division of Employment and Rehabilitation (DER), now known as the Employment Section. Employment interviewers then made a determination of whether or not the individual was available for work. According to an analysis of reports from the DER, about one-third of those required to report were employable and nearly half of this group were working and receiving only supplementary assistance. Of the remaining two-thirds a relatively small number were considered permanently unemployable. In the vast majority of cases either they were classified as temporarily not available for employment due to a variety of reasons including health conditions, family care, and attendance at school or training programs, or no determination was made for them.[13]

Efforts were made by the DER to place those considered available for employment in jobs. The department's workers conducted their own job-development efforts and also made referrals to the New York State Employment Service (NYSES). However, the DER was generally ineffective as a source of placements, and over time more reliance was placed on the NYSES. In an effort to improve employment services for employable clients, the New York State legislature mandated that effective January 1970 the DOSS must refer all clients it judges employable to the NYSES. Effective July 1971 it was further required that employable clients personally pick up their welfare checks at the Employment Service office. As of September 1971 there were 22,298 individuals reporting to the NYSES as a result of mandatory referrals from the DOSS.[14] Of this group, over 9,600 indicated that they were not available for employment primarily because of ill health. Subsequent interviews and medical examinations for these individuals have shown that over 90 percent are unemployable.[15] Another group of nearly 4,800 were in training. A total of 7,898 were immediately available for employment. Only 2,785 of these individuals were referred to a job by the Employment Service, and only 735 of these referrals resulted in a confirmed placement.

Also incorporated in the latest amendments to the state social welfare law was a provision that employables registered with the NYSES over thirty days and still unable to find a job must undertake obligatory unpaid work with municipal agencies. Congressional restrictions against work relief limit this program to unemployed persons in the nonfederal (HR) category, but because the WIN program (see below) is the preferred referral for ADC and ADC-U clients, these provisions apply effectively to most of those reporting to the Employment Service. While initial estimates were that 60,000 persons might be enrolled in the program, six months after it began only 3,805 recipients were at work as a result of the new law and the target for the end of fiscal 1972 was reduced to 7,000.[16]

Evaluation of the state-mandated actions ought to focus on its two explicit objectives—to facilitate the movement of employable clients into paid employment and to eliminate malingerers and ineligibles from the rolls. The placement record has been poor; the figures cited above indicate a placement rate of less than 3.3 percent for all those required to report and 9.3 percent for those reporting and judged available for work. With respect to the screening-out of ineligibles, initial claims by the Governor leading to publicized reports of potential ineligibility for 18 percent of the clients have subsequently been deflated to less than 4 percent of the employable population or about 1 percent of all cases.[17]

It should also be noted that no programmatic effort has been directed at the employed heads of households receiving supplementary assistance through the state's Home Relief program. A DOSS survey of this group in 1970 revealed they were predominantly married men between 30 and 50 years old with several children. Few had completed high school, and a majority had eight years of education or less. Most had histories of stable, full-time employment.[18] The demonstrated motivation and established work habits of this group would seem to make them a promising target for skill-development programs, yet no efforts have been initiated with this specific objective.

As noted earlier, ADC mothers have historically been considered unemployable because of the numbers who have young children who require care and because of the tradition against mothers working. This policy was reflected in DOSS operations throughout most of the 1960s, when mothers were referred to DER only on a voluntary basis and after consultation with a caseworker to ensure that proper child-care arrangements existed. This practice was dramatically reversed with the passage of the 1967 Social Security Act amendments which established the Work Incentive (WIN) Program for ADC and ADC-U adults. The shift in attitude toward ADC mothers is apparent in this passage from the New York City DOSS handbook describing the creation of WIN:

> Public assistance caseworkers today are confronted by what seems to be a challenge to one of our fundamental concepts. For years, we have emphasized the value of a mother's care for her own children. The very purpose of the ADC program, from its beginning, has been to enable mothers to remain in the home and care for their children. Now it appears, we have a Federal law that requires employable recipients of ADC to be referred for jobs or job training—and mothers are not excluded. Are we going to do an about-face and ignore risks to ADC children by referring all able-bodied mothers for employment or training? No, we are not—and the Federal legislation does not ask us to do so.
>
> We are, in effect, changing our *attitude* rather than our *policy*. We are not abandoning our belief in the value of a mother's care for her own children, nor our policy that children must be protected and family life strengthened. We are approaching each situation with an attitude of inquiry to see what course is best in that particular situation. Millions of mothers *are* in the labor force today work-

ing to provide better opportunities for their children, not only because living costs have risen, but because living standards have risen also. Many ADC mothers are likewise interested in opportunities to earn a better life for themselves and their families. And today there are millions of unfilled jobs, including work for the unskilled. Hence we can no longer take for granted that it is best, in every situation, that a mother stay in the home and ignore the world outside her home. We are becoming a bit more realistic, as many mothers are, in recognizing that there may be situations in which it is *better* for the mother to work.[19]

Although WIN was designed as a joint effort of the Department of Social Services (HEW on the federal level) and the Department of Labor, the participation of the DOSS is restricted to initial screening for employables, the provision of support services and income maintenance, and the supervision of child-care arrangements. The responsibility for training and placement is with the NYSES.

WIN is designed to use both carrot and stick methods to encourage employment and self-support. Financial incentives for participation include an allowance for work- or training-related expenses plus a $30 monthly stipend during training, a monthly unbudgeted allowance of $30 from wages earned ("income disregard"), and a reduction in the "welfare tax rate" (i.e., the proportion of earnings subtracted from the assistance allowance) from 100 to 66⅔ percent of earned income above $30 per month. Necessary child-care services are provided by the DOSS. By way of the stick, welfare recipients who refuse to undertake training or work can be dropped from the family budget.

WIN became operational in New York State in October of 1968. A review of the program's experience through June 1970 by the state legislature found that in New York City the DOSS had referred over 17,600 clients to the employment service for enrollment in WIN. Over one-third of this group were judged unemployable by the NYSES, further evidence of the variability inherent in the notion of employability.[20] Data on those who enrolled in the program in New York from its inception in late 1968 through the end of 1970 are presented in Table 9-5. The figures include

Table 9-5
WIN Enrollment in New York City,
November 1968 to December 1970

Total enrollment	*15,905*
Male	5,484
Female	10,421
Terminations	*5,669*
Completed program	545
Other reasons	5,124
Enrollment as of December 31, 1970	*10,236*
Orientation	741
Basic education	4,231
Job training or experience	1,587
Job follow-up	675
Holding and planned suspense	3,002

SOURCE: New York State Employment Service, *Operations*, January 1970 and January 1971 issues.

10,236 current enrollees and 5,669 former enrollees. Of those who are no longer enrolled, fewer than 1 in 10 had successfully completed the program by moving into paid employment; over 90 percent terminated because of ill health, child-care problems, or other circumstances. Those still enrolled at the end of 1970 were concentrated in basic education programs and, to a lesser extent, vocational training. About 3,000 current enrollees were in "holding," that is, awaiting an opening in a training program.

Experience with the WIN program demonstrates the many problems involved in assisting welfare clients, particularly ADC mothers, to move from dependency to self-support. Difficulties arise in selecting employable candidates, in coordinating the services they require, and in maintaining the sometimes tenuous child-care and other family arrangements which underlie employability. Finally, even those who overcome the numerous obstacles and secure employment are not likely to earn enough to remove themselves completely from the welfare rolls.

Leonard Hausman has used available national census data on the occupations and earnings of individuals with socioeconomic characteristics similar to those of welfare recipients to assess the potential for self-support among welfare clients. He concluded, "It appears that, given the conservative assumptions made in developing these figures, at least two thirds of the AFDC mothers and one third of the AFDC-U fathers could not, in the mid-1960's, have supported their families at the levels of income they could attain on welfare."[21] The inability of a working mother to support a family on her own income is not unique to welfare recipients. A review of the work experience of all female labor force participants pointed to this conclusion:

> Most working women were married and, although they were working to add to family income, most were supplementing the earnings of their husbands and were not fully responsible for family support. In fact, few of the working women could have supported an average family (four persons) from their earnings alone. Less than half of them worked full time the year round and half of those working full time had earnings sufficient to support a family of four at slightly above the poverty level, which in 1967 was considered to be about $3,500 a year. If, therefore, AFDC mothers do as well as all women in the population, about half of them would be working some time during the year, 20 percent would be working full time year round, and about two-thirds would have earnings below the poverty level for a family of four.[22]

The indefinite relationship between employment and self-support has important implications for expectations from the WIN program. In 1971 an ADC mother in New York must have had steady earnings of $3.08 per hour to remove herself from the welfare rolls when allowance was made for the work-incentive provisions.[23] Current data on wage rates of WIN graduates are not available for New York City, but a 1969 survey found that less than 10 percent of the completers (who, it must be recalled, are less than 10 percent of the enrollees) earned over $3.00 per hour.[24]

The experience to date with state and federally initiated work programs indicates that few people will be removed from the public assistance rolls as a result of these efforts. Employability is hard to define and harder to maintain. Placements are difficult to achieve, even at low wages. Most important, employment often does not mean self-support, particularly if the large number of low-level jobs in the economy is taken into account. One way of meeting this dilemma is via a wage policy that is geared to the elimination of poverty, a societal decision which has not yet been widely considered. In the future it is more likely that this problem will be met by a greater intermingling of earned income and public assistance allowances in the implementation of a national policy emphasizing work efforts and the elimination of a wholly dole-supported segment of the population. Welfare reform proposals presented to the 92nd Congress reflect this trend.

WELFARE REFORM: THE POTENTIAL FOR NEW YORK CITY

Encouraging employment among the dependent population is only one of the several objectives of various welfare-reform proposals recently under consideration by Congress. Other goals are the establishment of a national minimum-benefit level, extension of coverage to the working poor, and more dignified administrative arrangements. The Nixon Administration's welfare-reform proposal (HR 1), known as the Family Assistance Plan (FAP), was the most widely discussed proposal and can serve as a useful illustration of the potential gains for New York City. It proposed to achieve the desired ends by establishing a $2,400 minimum benefit in all states, eliminating the ADC and ADC-U categories, and extending eligibility to all families with children. HR 1 provided for federal administration of income-maintenance functions. Work incentives, in the form of an income disregard ($720 annually) and a reduced welfare tax rate (67 percent), similar to the WIN provisions were included, applicable to any family head and not limited to ADC mothers.

Enactment of such a program would constitute an improvement over the existing patchwork of state programs which comprise our national welfare system. It would also provide improved living standards for more than 3 million people in the 22 states which now pay less than $2,400 annually in welfare benefits to a family of four. But it can have little significant impact on the welfare problem in New York City. Most of the principal objectives of welfare reform have already been implemented in New York.

First, the proposed national minimum benefit level of $2,400 is irrelevant for New York. The current welfare allowance for a family of four in New York is now approximately $4,000 annually; the $2,400 standard was exceeded in 1964. After enactment of FAP, New York would undoubtedly continue to supplement the federal minimum. The possible benefits for the city are indirect. Increased allowances in states such as Mississippi, where the maximum allowance is now $720 annually, might slow the migration to urban centers. But how much is uncertain. Differential welfare benefits alone are rarely the factor motivating migration, and the young men and women who typically leave the rural South are unlikely to be deterred by somewhat higher grant levels which still do not exceed poverty standards.

FAF provisions for federal administration of assistance programs would also have a minimal impact on welfare procedures in New York City. Most of the administrative reforms which might be incorporated into federal practice are already operative at the DOSS. Eligibility is established by documented declaration, and the provision of social services is separated from income maintenance; the latter is handled by specially trained clerical personnel. Follow-up procedures include a face-to-face review of the case load and the issuance of photographic identification cards.

The extension of benefits to families with a working head also has little significance for New York's welfare system. The state's HR program has provided assistance to such families in need for many years, and it is not necessary that a father desert his family in order that they may qualify for welfare. The improvement represented by HR 1 is a federal financial participation in assistance to this group, a benefit for local taxpayers but not an innovation for the recipients.

In fact, the potential fiscal relief for the city government is one of the few significant improvements HR 1 provided for New York. Federal participation in programs for employed parents will save the city tax dollars, but, nevertheless, state and local programs would still be required for childless couples and single adults. Estimates by the New York City Bureau of the Budget indicate that total welfare expenditures will continue to rise through fiscal 1973. Had HR 1 been enacted effective in that year and assistance allowances maintained at 1971 standards, the city could have reduced its contribution to the total bill by up to $130 million because of offsetting increased federal participation. This amount constitutes over one-third of the city's projected contribution and about 10 percent of the total projected bill under the current system.

The employment provisions of HR 1 are essentially an extension of the existing WIN program to include newly covered recipients from the HR category as well as the ADC and ADC-U groups. As is presently the case, the Department of Labor would be required to provide employment services for those deemed employable. Registration would be mandatory for most able-bodied males and women without young children, but this is essentially the situation in New York under the present combination of WIN and state regulations. If experience with the existing programs is any indication, many of those required to register would be found unemployable. The significant employment-related proposal in HR 1 is the provision for 200,000 public service jobs nationwide and the extension of work-incentive provisions to two-parent families. However, the significance of the former is limited by the fact that the number of jobs proposed equals only a small proportion of the employable registered recipients. Most of those required to seek work would not be provided jobs. National estimates are that 77 percent of those required to register could *not* be offered training or a public service job under the provisions of HR 1.[25] While some of these individuals might be placed in private employment, the vast majority would remain untrained and unemployed.

From the vantage point of New York's poor the new work-incentive provisions constituted the most important innovation of HR 1. Its income disregard exceeded that of WIN ($720 versus $360 annually), and this provision, along with the reduced welfare tax rate, would be extended to the working poor in two-parent families. At present this group is eligible for assistance in New York, but they do not benefit from the work-incentive provisions of WIN. The working father in an HR family is still in theory subject to a reduction in his welfare allowance equal to 100 percent of his earned income. Elimination of this inequity is the single most important benefit which the FAP would bestow upon New York's poor.

However, liberalized work-incentive provisions bring about

new problems for states such as New York with relatively high benefit levels. If New York were to supplement the basic national grant to maintain the present welfare allowances, families earning over $6,000 would be eligible for supplementary assistance after work-incentive provisions are taken into account. Approximately half the city's population could theoretically qualify for welfare assistance. Since the incomes of many of those potentially eligible will never fall below the basic allowance, they would never actually enroll in the FAP. The effective result would be that, given two similar families with identical earned incomes and paying identical taxes, one would receive assistance and the other would not. The dilemma can be resolved only by reducing either benefits or work incentives, or by vastly extending eligibility to ensure equitable treatment for all similar families. Otherwise we will continue to treat welfare families more favorably than those who have continually been self-supporting, a situation with threatening political, economic, and social potential.

The work-incentive provisions also bring about new problems because of the fragmented nature of American social welfare programs and the regressive tax system. The multiple programs other than welfare which exist to aid the poor (Medicaid, public housing, food stamps) do not have sliding eligibility or fee scales equivalent to the work-incentive provisions. Consequently, what has been called a "notch" problem arises. For example, under HR 1 when an enrollee's earnings reach a certain point, he would become ineligible for Medicaid. The lost benefits from Medicaid, which average over $800 per family in New York, more than offset the gain possible under the reduced welfare tax rate, so that the individual's real net income actually declines and all work incentive disappears. The deduction of social security and income taxes also reduces work incentives, particularly in high-benefit states like New York. When these taxes are considered, the effective welfare tax rate would rise from the 67 percent specified in the legislation to over 90 percent at earnings above $4,000.[26]

Welfare reform along the lines of HR 1 will enhance our national welfare system by bringing the more backward areas into conformity with certain minimum standards. But for large metropolitan areas like New York it represents only limited improvements, specifically better work-incentive arrangements and some fiscal relief. These gains may be achieved only at the cost of new, and perhaps more complex, problems arising from the need to coordinate highly fragmented social welfare programs, tax measures, wage policy, and general economic planning.

10

AGING IN THE GHETTO

Dean Morse

SAMUEL JOHNSON REMARKED in one of his Rambler essays that "he who would pass the latter part of his life with honour and decency, must, when he is young, consider that he shall one day be old." Characteristically, Johnson added that he "must remember, when he is old, that he has once been young."[1] An extension of this remark might apply to a city or a nation. If a community does not understand the situation of the elderly, can it be considered honorable and decent? If a society which pretends to be concerned with youth and its problems forgets that those who are today aged were once young and that those who are young today will become aged, can it be called a civilized society? The question is poignant in the United States, which is becoming ever more youth-oriented. In this same society the numbers of the aging and the aged are, however, increasing rapidly

Our society has never faced up to the process of aging, to death itself. It has been a "young" country, a "growing" country where youthful qualities are at a premium—strength, daring, willingness and even eagerness to change. The United States is generally a healthy country, and one in which the unhealthy are too often shunned by the healthy. It has no unifying religion through which the aging and the aged can find material and spiritual support. The family itself has often tended to slough off its aged. The extended family once gave support to the elderly, but the urbanization of America has undermined this arrangement for the great majority of Americans.

179

In years past it was often possible for a farmer to grow older with at least the likely assurance of a home, relatives, and neighbors to provide a frame and support (even here we should not underestimate the hardships and the suffering of the aging farmer; often he simply worked himself to death). But the growth of the city in America (and throughout the world), which has always drawn the country's youth, offers little sense of community, and the old and the infirm tend to be lost in the general turmoil and anonymity of life.

Nevertheless, there have been efforts in the recent past to provide a shield for the aging and the elderly. Social security legislation provided an income floor, Medicare and other assistance programs helped the aged meet some of their pressing needs. Old-age homes, maintained by various religious denominations, provide asylum for some. Special housing projects for the elderly have been created with staffs who are expected to be sensitive to their needs. In 1971 a White House Conference on the Aging, characteristically referred to by such euphemisms as senior citizens or golden age citizens, was held. Intensive efforts have indeed been made to understand the situation of older Americans and to respond to their needs.

The situation of a particular group of aging and elderly Americans, black men and women in the central cores of our urban centers, however, is a matter which, even with the best will, is difficult for the rest of America, even other older Americans, to understand. A recent incident may indicate the differing frames of reference.

When the 1971 White House Conference on Aging was in the planning stages, a series of conferences, first on a community and then on a statewide basis, were held with the explicit goal of articulating the needs of the aged. In a large Eastern city, one of the sessions of such a conference dealt with the problem of income maintenance.

The panel of experts discussed the inadequacy of present social security payments, the erosion of private pension payments through inflation, the importance of supplementary income produced by part-time and consulting work, the disastrous effect of increasing property taxes upon elderly homeowners. The audience mentioned the effect of rising prices and taxes upon the value of pensions and fixed annuities. For many, discrimination against older jobseekers and rigid retirement ages were major grievances.

At one point, one of the half-dozen blacks in the room burst out, "This has nothing to do with us. What proportion of black men have a private pension, an annuity? Most of us don't even know what an annuity is. You talk about discrimination against older workers. But an older black worker in this city who becomes unemployed knows that no one is going to employ him. He's always been discriminated against. The jobs have left and he cannot move. You are talking about another world as far as he is concerned."

All the blacks in the room agreed with the speaker. They stated that public service employment is the only kind of paid work that can feasibly be developed for most of the older black men and women who are unemployed or have withdrawn from the labor force. These blacks felt that the need for the kind of services that public service employment would make available to the black community is obvious. In their view public service employment of older blacks, to minister primarily to other older blacks, is an essential part of a program to enable the community of older blacks to withstand destructive forces which, while disintegrating the community, wreak vast suffering and deprivation upon its individual older members.

Most Americans do not understand the condition of the older blacks of the central cities. The parts of the cities which are now called the Black Ghettos are strange, forbidding, remote from the day-to-day existence of much of the rest of the population. The current discussion of the ghetto focuses on youth; news reports center on the sensational event, the riots, the tensions and troubles in schools. The black athlete, the black entertainer, the black militant, the black prisoner—these are the faces and the voices that are seen and heard. They are overwhelmingly young. They are often harsh.

Since most Americans have little sympathy for the older Americans in general, the older black citizen is doubly rejected, first as a black and then as an old person. Black youth join in this rejection, and their rejection is the harshest. Moreover, this pattern involves an abrupt change in the traditional relations between the generations in the black community.

THE URBAN COMMUNITY OF OLDER BLACKS: AN OVERVIEW

In the great cities of the East Coast, particularly New York, one part of the black community consists of individuals who were born in the North, some of whom can trace their families to the Civil War. The majority of the black community, however, came in relatively large waves of immigration to the city over several decades.

One major period of immigration occurred during World War I and shortly thereafter. Shortages of workers, the enlistment and recruitment of blacks in the army, the effects of the exclusionary immigration laws at the end of the war, combined to bring a large number of Southern blacks into the large industrial cities. Many black immigrants from various parts of the Caribbean came to New York City. Those who came from the rural South tended to be physically vigorous, and they were inevitably drawn into industries and occupations in which a premium was placed on strength and a willingness to work in back-breaking and often dangerous occupations. They helped to replace the peasant immigrants of a previous generation who in their turn had provided the country with much of that kind of labor when machinery was still rudimentary and not widespread.

The community of older blacks in New York City, then, is made up of several fairly distinct subgroups: those whose roots are in various parts of the city, those who came from towns and cities of the South, those from rural areas of the South, and finally a relatively small but important group from the Caribbean. As a result, it has never been easy for older blacks to present a united front. Each group has vied for prestige and power within the black community. Those who can claim the longest residence in New York City tend to assert their preeminence, but at the same time they find themselves an ever-smaller minority of the black community of older persons.

Residential patterns, educational achievement, and occupational attachments have reflected these differences in origin. It is noteworthy, however, that the usual assumption that black migrants from the South are less educated and less skilled than those who were born in New York City is somewhat at variance with the facts. A significant proportion of black migrants from the South are in fact better educated and more skilled than many blacks brought up in Northern cities.[2]

Many black migrants, however, reflect the educational and occupational deprivations characteristic of rural Southern blacks. Moreover, as we have noted, some migrants were brought, as older blacks say, by "boxcar," to Northern cities to fill dangerous and exhausting jobs. At a recent discussion several older black residents of a large Northeastern industrial city recounted with wry humor an example, in some ways extreme, but familiar enough to older black workers, of recruiting tactics during and just after World War I.

A chemical company named Butterworth had developed a manufacturing process which had the unfortunate side effect of turning workers who were exposed to it a pronounced yellow color. The usual employees of the company were Italians, but confronting the prospect of their skin turning yellow, the Italian workers left the company en masse. The company then began to recruit blacks from the South to take their place. Many of the blacks who were brought up to work believed that they were to be employed in a butter works, and for many decades afterwards the fact that they had actually turned the color of butter when working in the "butterworks" would bring shouts of laughter to those who recalled the episode.

This incident emphasizes that black workers were exposed to more extreme occupational hazards than the usual lot of white workers. Examples of the occupational stresses and hazards to which they were exposed are legion. Black males, for example, were hired in large numbers by aluminum smelting plants because most white workers would not tolerate the heat and noxious fumes of the basic process of smelting aluminum. The most dangerous and debilitating occupations in the steel industry rapidly became largely the province of black males.

Several articles in the *Wall Street Journal* in 1971 called attention to the continued existence of dirty and dangerous jobs in particular industries. The authors seemed to assume that a disproportionate number of these jobs would be held by blacks and members of other minority groups. This characteristic of the labor market existed to a greater extent for earlier generations of black males. Interviews with black men who are now in their fifties or older repeatedly indicate that if they were large and powerful as young men, they tended to work many years at relatively well-paying but physically debilitating and dangerous jobs. Such experiences, of course, are not unique to twentieth-century America. Adam Smith called attention to the fact that men from disadvantaged backgrounds were induced by relatively high pay to work themselves literally to death in such occupations as sawyers.

The situation of many black older male workers today can be understood only by remembering the effects of their job environments. Historically, the black male worker has been exposed to a wide range of physical insults in his job environment—noxious fumes, excessive dust and dirt, physical shocks, excessively onerous tasks, a range of insults to body and soul which because of their diversity and pervasiveness in his life experience have been accepted as a natural state of affairs both by the society in which he finds himself and by himself.

The physical and psychic damage to the black worker brought about by his work environment has often been compounded by lack of access to or ignorance about medical services. Injuries which, if attended to, might have produced temporary disability become sources of chronic pain and physical deterioration. Life styles become affected by fatigue, pain, and boredom with routine tasks. Frequent change of jobs is one response, another is the palliative of alcohol. A greater willingness to withdraw from the labor force is another possible response, particularly for the black worker who has known nothing but hard physical labor, and who begins to sense that he can no longer stand the pace of work. Many older black male workers discuss the long and frequently agonizing period during which an awareness of decreasing physical vigor is pitted against a strong attachment to the world of work. Only when an individual "couldn't go another day" or "felt like dying on the job" did this attachment break. But once made, the rupture is usually considered complete; never again would they work at a "real man's job" but would engage in at most casual and "soft" work.

ATTACHMENT TO WORK

The Conservation of Human Resources project has begun a research effort to learn more about the interrelationships between the process of aging and the withdrawal from the labor force among black workers. Nearly 100 intensive interviews have been conducted with older men and women in Newark and New York City.

One of the striking characteristics of a good proportion of the men we talked with has been the strength of their attachment to work. As one man, still working every day as a substitute janitor for a large real estate firm, declared, "What would I do with myself if I do not work? I have no place to go and nothing to do and this keeps me alive." Since many black male workers have not had long attachments to a single firm, with foreknowledge of a pension and a mandatory retirement age, they are not apt to think of institutional arrangements which would effectively end their working lives at age 65. Moreover, most of them do not have resources—fixed assets, investments, or savings—which, along with social security payments and private pension income, would make retirement an attractive prospect. For black male workers who have prided themselves on their ability to provide for themselves and their families, who have avoided various forms of public assistance, one of the bitterest aspects of aging is the recognition that they may eventually have to "go on welfare."

Our conversations with older black male workers strongly impressed us, then, with the strength of their attachment to work and the importance of the meaning of work in their lives. In the face of often meager rewards, buffeted by the insecurity of their employment, the efforts of many of these older men to piece together work experiences of one kind or another to maintain a sense of independence and self-worth are often sagas of personal heroism. Of course attachment to work is not a unique characteristic of black men. The same extraordinary attachment is met in older black women. It is known that the labor force participation of black older women has for many years far exceeded that of white women of the same age group. And again, the black women with whom we talked stated that the rupture of this attachment to work is often made only with great difficulty. That many white middle-class Americans have working lives followed by nonworking lives, called retirement, is a situation which many blacks cannot emulate.

THE RUPTURE OF ATTACHMENT TO WORK

As we have pointed out, the circumstances of the black older workers have forced many to break their attachment to work. Labor force participation rates of older black men are somewhat lower than for comparable white age groups. And there is evidence that the differentials may be increasing. As we have seen, one factor which has contributed to withdrawal from the labor force of many aging black male workers is the steady erosion of the physical vigor and well-being which is necessary for the kind of jobs which they held. There are other factors.

In the past a relatively high proportion of older black workers in New York City found that one of the likely employment possibilities was blue-collar jobs, particularly those requiring little skill, in small and medium-sized manufacturing firms. In other urban centers which have larger manufacturing firms, such as Newark, black workers found similar opportunities during and after World War II. The migration of these firms out of the urban environment, either to entirely new regions, such as the South, occasionally out of the country entirely, or to suburban locations where better plant layout and better access to new transportation modes were attractive alternatives to the obsolete facilities and increasing traffic congestion of the older manufacturing areas of the city, has hit the older black community hard. Without the mobility which characterizes younger members of the labor force, often unable to relocate because of segregated housing patterns in the suburbs, older black workers are frequently in a tight bind. Since they tend to be employed relatively more frequently than white workers in plants with minimal or no unionization, collective bargaining agreements which provide job protection or severance pay have often been lacking altogether or of inadequate scope.

A number of the older black workers with whom we talked emphasized the hopelessness which faced them when the firm which had employed them, sometimes for many years, planned to move to a new location. Often the firm stated to a worker that he could keep his job if he were able to move to the new location. Long searches for housing, sometimes compounded by the fact that the worker owned his present home and was attached to his neighborhood, would result in his finding the cost of a new home near the new location of the firm far above his means. Mortgages were difficult to secure. The cost of moving itself and the disruption in living styles and routines frequently seemed more than the move was worth. Indeed, many interviewees declared that the only black who could afford to move out of the central core of the city was a professional or a white-collar employee. Even if the barriers to movement were exaggerated by those with whom we talked, the fact that they were perceived by them as insurmountable has effectively limited the number of older black workers who attempt to move out of the city with the firm.

After years of employment at demanding and minimally rewarding jobs, faithfully performed, perhaps with the hope and expectation of an eventual pension, older black workers perceive a decision taken by their firm in response to changing labor costs, increasing taxes, transportation problems, changes in technology and products, simply as a personal loss of employment. The result is their conviction that they are about to join other older black workers "on the ash heap."

When a firm relocates in a surrounding suburb and offers the older black worker a job at the new location, he faces another problem if he is unable to move to the suburb—namely, the almost insurmountable problem of transportation.

These remarks underscore the different perception of the world of work of the older black worker from that of the white middle-class white-collar or professional worker. What may represent for the latter a simple choice—to move to the new location of his firm or to commute by car—may for the other be not a choice at all, but two impossibilities.

Moreover, an important part of one's conception of a labor market is its spatial configuration. For every individual this configuration is more or less unique; space is perceived in part as a matter of the time required to move from one area to another. From that point of view the outer ring of the metropolitan area, which to the white man may be a familiar and accessible area, may seem to the older black worker to be *terra incognita* and psychologically impenetrable.

Indeed, those studying the operation of the urban labor market might well have a conception of the "maps" of the urban labor market which exist for important subgroups of the population. These maps would indicate the difference between physical and psychological space and pinpoint the different obstacles which truncate the field of labor market activity for the older black worker. It is certain that many older black workers operate as if parts of the urban labor market were inaccessible and dangerous. However, for many older workers the map (or image, in Boulding's sense of the term) of the urban labor market is in some important respects obsolete and inaccurate.

PROBLEMS OF GETTING LABOR MARKET INFORMATION

Difficulties of moving to the new location of firms which have been large employers of black workers but are now no longer in the central parts of the city, difficulties of finding transportation, public or private, to these new locations if the worker cannot find a home nearby, are compounded by lack of information about newly emerging jobs. When we talked with black workers about how a black older worker customarily learns about jobs, they emphasized, particularly when they had "good" jobs in mind, that friends and relatives were much the most important source of crucial leads to the job. Gate hiring is another important route of access and a way of acquiring information, but even here the information which leads to gate hiring frequently can be traced back to the comment of a friend or even casual acquaintance.

A number of older black male workers who were unemployed or had withdrawn from the labor force pointed out to us that many of their friends were in the same situation. They did not hear about employment possibilities and, as important, they knew from their friends the hopelessness of the situation of older black men out of work. Impressions and feelings that "it's just no use trying to find a job, no one wants me or a person like me," reinforced continually by the similar feelings of his friends, are a powerful force which restricts the range of job search and the willingness of the individual to accept information from other sources.

Other circumstances make it difficult for older black workers to gather information about employment possibilities. Many of them are not used to relying upon sources of information like *The New York Times* want ad section. Others cannot offer skills or work experience which might make them attractive to private employment agencies. All too often, older black workers who have tried to use the New York State Employment Service have been offered employment primarily at casual, relatively poorly paid work where, as some of them put it, the effort to get the job "costs more than the job is worth."

One group of black older male workers who live under specially handicapping circumstances are those individuals who are not attached to a family and who have lived in a succession of single rooms. In many respects these men are the older counterparts of the groups who are discussed in Elliott Liebow's *Tally's Corner.*[3] It is particularly difficult for these individuals to obtain information about stable employment opportunities. For many, their lifetime work experience has been at an immensely varied number of low-skilled short-term jobs. They have no records to produce. Many have difficulty in reading and writing. They are highly suspicious of people outside their immediate group and skeptical about the likelihood that their life chances can be changed or improved in any significant way.

SOME REMEDIES: THE CASE FOR COMPENSATORY ACTION

Gaining the confidence of older, unattached black workers, even to the point of obtaining their willingness to discuss their work experiences and their present labor force status, as we did, is often a delicate task. For many of them health problems are severe and chronic illness has reduced life to a day-to-day struggle to survive. Questions which ask them to look at the process by which they have arrived at their present situation or to examine their future prospects are painful. That there is a possibility that government action or changes in the operation of the labor market can alter their own lives favorably is rejected out of hand by most of this group. Who, they ask, is interested in them? Why should anyone care about what happens to them? And, unlike some subgroups in the black community, they cannot imagine that any kind of group action on their part can be effective.

Many of these unattached older black males feel strongly that they lack the education or skills which are required for employment today and that it is now hopeless to try to acquire these through training and educational programs. Many of them have never heard of the various programs that do exist and, when they have, feel that the programs are directed toward youth and that they have little possibility of entering them. To many, the idea of sitting in a classroom situation is ridiculous, even degrading.

If training and educational programs directed at this group are to have any chance of succeeding, they must be initiated, and carried out, in ways which are radically different from existing programs. To the maximum extent possible, they must be designed so that they seem as little as possible to smack of the classroom or the conventional teaching relationship. An obvious difficulty is that the kind of training and educational programs which might have some chance of success with this population should involve the attention of individual teachers to a wide range of individual problems. But even if a program of educational and skill rehabilitation were successful, the jobs which might be opened to this group would still be relatively poorly paid and of short duration. Consequently, in conventional cost-benefit formulation, such programs would rank quite low and would almost certainly have a negative rate of return. The only justification for such programs would involve considerations which go outside the usual cost-benefit framework.

Let us suggest one extended framework which could justify a program to provide education and training to older black workers. The failure of many black older workers to acquire education or training does not reflect a decision to forgo the investment, but because social and economic barriers prevented their having access to training at a time when it would have been economically justified by the resulting increase in productivity and the length of the individual's working life. The individual older black worker, therefore, has already paid a penalty for the failure of the society to offer him access to the education and training which was available to the average white man. Nothing can make up for the lost income and other benefits which would have been produced by adequate investments in education and training along with equal access to jobs. The amount of resources, however, which should now be made available to the black older worker, in the form of either income maintenance or training and educational programs designed to remedy the results of past deprivation, should not be based on a cost-benefit calculation which is appropriate to investment in roads and the like. Rather, they should provide some compensation for the losses which have accrued over a lifetime of work to the black older worker because of the failure of society to offer him access to education, training, and employment at an earlier stage of his life.

When the actions of government have imposed unequal sacrifices and burdens upon a particular segment of society, it is proper for government to undertake programs which will compensate that segment for those burdens. The GI Bill of Rights was based upon this proposition. To extend this principle to acts of omission on the part of government as well as the positive acts of government, such as the military draft, is not a large step. And this kind of action would amount to a recognition that a proper measure of the effects of discrimination, both in general social policy and specifically in the marketplace, should be not only the short-term effects of discrimination, such as differential wage rates that are discriminatory, but also (and more importantly) the effects which are developmental and often indirect and long term.

It is likely that even the most thoughtful and imaginative training programs directed at the unattached older black male worker will not involve more than a fraction of the group and will not materially change the life of even those it does attract, unless it is part of a program of providing employment opportunities which take into account the long-run effects of educational, training, and medical deprivation. For many, some kind of sheltered workshop seems the only framework in which gainful employment would be feasible. Here again the arguments which would justify training and educational investments, in spite of narrow cost-benefit calculations to the contrary, would also justify the institution of such workshops to make it possible for older black workers to maintain the sense of self-worth and dignity which, for a great proportion of them, is so strongly associated with gainful work.

For single older black workers sheltered workshops should be in propinquity to public housing designed specifically to take into account their life styles and particular needs. If such a combined workshop-housing complex is to be a success, it should be quite small scale. It should avoid an "institutional" appearance and permit maximum individual variation.

Since these complexes ideally should be small scale and personal in character, it should be possible to launch a number of them with varied format and programs so that over a period of time the successful programs would demonstrate how best to help this group, which is one of the most deprived of American demographic groups. The shame of this problem is that for a large proportion of older black men, the physical deprivation and sense of abandonment and hopelessness that characterizes their day-to-day existence are the result of years of hard work at the most dangerous, unhealthy, and physically exhausting tasks of modern industrial society.

PAST AND PRESENT: THE CHANGED POSITION OF THE OLDER BLACKS

We have pointed out how difficult it is for the outsider, particularly the white middle-class outsider, to understand the situation of the older members of the black urban community. One striking difference between the two groups deserves notice. It was first called to our attention by the former head of the Urban League of a large commercial and industrial Eastern city, one of the first black graduates of an Ivy League college. Now in his late eighties, he told of the transformation he himself had lived through in the situation of the older black worker in the large cities of the East Coast.

A generation and more ago, many of the older black workers in the cities were employed in providing various kinds of personal services—pullman porters, servants, waiters, porters, and so forth. For many of these individuals there was no such thing as retirement or formal pension. On the other hand, however, because they were involved in relationships with white employers who were strongly paternalistic, many of them found that they could continue to work as long as they were able to and when they could no longer work they were supported by their employer, perhaps in a minimal way, but at least they were provided with shelter and food. Thus their relationship with their white employers, personal and often of long standing, provided a shelter against the worst hardships of age.

Another feature of their situation deserves equal emphasis. Within the black community itself, the prestige of age was such that other groups deferred to the older black man and woman and at the same time protected them. Black churches and black social groups gave them status. In a fundamental sense old age had meaning and purpose. And since there were relatively few old members of the black community, this fragile and personal structure of support and status did provide, for at least an important proportion of the older community, a tolerable and relatively secure old age. Even then, for a significant minority of the older black population, circumstances were bitter. But others could anticipate that they would be able to keep body and soul together and that they would have close and satisfying relationships with their immediate community. The ingredients of a community, even if sparse, were sufficient to make old age an integral part of life. Although life was not generous, housing poor, medical services paltry, food often minimal in quality and quantity, there was, according to this old leader of a black community, a black community into which the older black man and woman fitted and in which they played an essential role.

The transformation that has taken place in the role and position of the older blacks in the great urban centers is typified by the change in the relationship between the very old and the very young in the past few decades.

When the head of the Urban League mentioned above was a child, a young man, even when he was middle aged, it was taken for granted that one of the primary disciplinary forces exerted over youth in the local neighborhood was that of the grandmothers and grandfathers of the neighborhood. A fight that threatened to get out of hand was ended by a word from one of the old people on the street. Today, in contrast, older black citizens, particularly in the heart of the poorer sections of the black community, sense that young people have rejected their authority almost completely and indeed often represent a threat to their physical safety.

THE PROBLEM OF PERSONAL SECURITY: THE LOSS OF MOBILITY

Indeed, if there is any one concern that seems to outweigh all others, a concern expressed equally by older black men and women, it is the problem of physical safety. So strong is their fear that it has partly immobilized many of the older blacks in the central parts of the ghetto. A number of the people with whom we talked indicated that they would be unwilling to accept a job that involved traveling any distance, particularly if it involved transfers at bus stops, or worse, if they had to walk any distance to a bus stop. The problem was considered most serious if it was necessary to wait or walk alone during the early morning hours or late afternoon, especially during the winter months. Most older blacks who are employed simply accept the risks of travel. But for those who are on the edge of participation in the labor force, considerations of personal safety may tip the balance against it.

The strength of attachment to work felt by some of the older black men is illustrated by a man, over 75, working full time as handyman for one of the major educational institutions of the city. For some twenty years he lived in an apartment near the institution, but far enough so that he had to walk through several blocks of a deteriorating neighborhood. For many of these years he enjoyed his morning and afternoon walks, but then, quite suddenly, he found himself the target of attacks by teen-agers. He finally decided that the only solution was to move to a more secure neighborhood where he could go almost directly from his apartment to the subway. After much time and effort, he eventually found an apartment in Brooklyn and took the subway to upper Manhattan. The cost in time and subway fare made him wonder whether he should simply have stopped working. But, he told us, "I would have been a prisoner in my apartment, like many of my friends, and what would I do if I do not work?"

The effect of the loss of mobility due to fear is, of course, not limited to labor market behavior. Another economic cost is the result of unwillingness to walk or travel any distance to take advantage of the lower prices in supermarkets and discount stores. One person after another told us that he could not go even a few blocks to buy food at a supermarket, although prices were considerably lower and his budget for food was pitiably low. When food budgets for older blacks who are receiving public assistance are calculated on the basis of average prices in supermarkets, they may amount to a considerable understatement of the actual prices they pay.

Some Conclusions and Their Policy Implications

At the beginning of this chapter we stated that the plight of the older black citizens of New York has been slighted, partly because of the attention devoted to the problems of black youth in the decaying areas of the city. The increasing numbers of black youth and the increasing severity of the problems they face have tended to dwarf the problems of older black people. The number of young blacks in the five boroughs of New York City has increased far more rapidly than that of any other age group. Blacks aged 15 to 24 increased by 110 percent between 1960 and 1970; in absolute numbers, from 150,887 to 336,144.[4] The group aged 5 to 14 increased at almost the same rate. Problems in the schools, problems of unemployment among teen-age and slightly older blacks have seemed to be so pressing and so corrosive that the problems of older blacks were shelved. It is not that nothing was done for them, but that a sense of the urgency of their needs and a resolution to divert major resources to meet them were generally absent.

Moreover, the problems of older blacks in the central city have been *silent* problems for the most part, because older blacks have lacked both the organization and style required to bring them sharply to the attention of the larger community. But they are not *small* problems. In New York City the rate of increase during the past ten years of older blacks outstrips that of all age groups in the city except for the groups of blacks aged 5 to 24. Blacks 65 or over increased 81 percent; blacks 45 to 64 increased 44 percent. In 1970 there were 307,382 blacks aged 45 to 64 and 98,425 blacks 65 or over in the city.

In contrast, whites aged 45 to 64 in the city actually decreased by 16 percent during the same time period, and those over 65 increased by only 11 percent. Nevertheless, whites still constitute the overwhelming majority of older New Yorkers—85 percent of the population 45 and over, although the proportion of the older population that is made up of blacks is increasing rapidly, rising from less than 1 in 10 in 1960 to almost 1 in 6 in 1970.

There is still a marked difference in the age profiles of blacks and whites in the inner city. In Manhattan itself, for example, almost 43 percent of the white population in 1970 was at least 45 years old and 30 percent fell into the age group 55 or over. Only 31 percent of the black population in Manhattan was 45 or older, and less than 19 percent were at least 55 years old.

The function of the inner city as a collecting point for the aging part of the population, white and black, particularly that part of the population that is poor and isolated, is a prominent feature of the demographic trends of the past decade. However, the rate of increase over the past decade of the population over 45, both white and black, in the suburbs has also been high. Whites in the 45-to-64 age group increased by 33 percent and in the age group 65 or over, by 37 percent. Blacks in these age groups increased by 44 and 80 percent respectively. Of course their absolute numbers remain quite small because few blacks in these age groups lived in the suburbs in 1960.

In light of the institutions and programs which do offer assistance to the aged within the inner city and their relative absence in much of the surrounding suburbs, the tendency of the inner city to collect the aging poor, white and black, particularly those 65 and over, is not surprising. Until it becomes possible to provide housing, employment, assistance, and supporting institutions within a metropolitan and regional framework to the aging poor (and most older blacks, according to their accumulated resources and employment opportunities, are among the poorest), their problems will have to be faced largely within, and with the resources of, the inner city. It is this prospect which makes the near future seem so bleak for the older blacks of the city. They feel trapped and abandoned, and their feelings are a reflection of the reality of their situation.

Let us attempt to sum up that situation. The older blacks live in those parts of the inner city which are physically deteriorated and are most subject to further deterioration. They live in areas of the city where some of the most important services provided by government and private organizations have deteriorated and will in all probability continue to deteriorate. They have the fewest resources. They are most apt to be the victims of illness, unemployment, and physical assault. They live in an inner city which finds its resources overly strained and the demands for additional services mounting steadily.

How high do the needs of the older blacks of the inner city rank in the scale of priorities which will determine the inner city's distribution of resources? We must return to our starting point. A community which is able to forget, or allowed to forget, that its older members once were young and that its young will be tomorrow's aged will not in all probability give high priority to the needs of the aged in general, or those of the aged blacks in particular. Unless the plight of the aging population of the inner city gets the attention of those who order national priorities, unless substantial resources are made available on a regional and metropolitan basis so that the larger urban community can tackle the problems of the aging members of the population, poor and rich, black and white, on a comprehensive basis, it is likely that the present situation will simply deteriorate further. Pressed on all sides by problems which increasingly seem almost beyond solution, the measures taken by the inner city to meet the needs of its older citizens will be at best holding operations and, at worst, simply a set of cosmetic devices which will permit the larger society to continue to dishonor its parents.

Part III

PLANNING

11

HIGHER EDUCATION

Ivar Berg

PLANNING IN AMERICA'S educational system calls to mind Boswell's remark about a dog walking on its hind legs: It is not done well, but one is surprised that it is done at all.

Whatever the measure, it is clear that the higher educational enterprise is as troubled as the primary and secondary educational systems. Alumni are restive; students, in large numbers, are restless; economic problems abound; the internal administration of many of even the finest, most reputable universities is typically a tangle of functions and a maze of "bureau-pathologies"; costs have skyrocketed; university faculties complain about the shrunken demand for their labor even as they thrash about for the best means for obtaining salary increases; the debates in Congressional committees concerned with the allocation of federal funds for education are mired in arguments that bypass many of the essential issues and gainsay many of the basic problems.

These sad circumstances are attributed to many different causes, depending upon the perspective of the diagnostician, but few deny that they are rooted in confusions about the roles of higher education. These confusions, in turn, are by-products of the fact that in higher education we have sought so many means to so many ends, that a day of reckoning, if not a collapse, is inevitable.

Consider that hardly a single public policy undertaking of any significance has been mounted in the post-World War II era that

201

did not have consequential impacts upon the educational apparatus, in general, and higher education in particular.

Whether the policy draftsman and his constituency were concerned about fighting domestic poverty, foreign communism, cancer, or crime, the academy has been an essential component in the order of battle. Whether for the nuclear race, the arms race, or the race to the moon, the runners and their coaches, it has been made clear, must be better educated. If health care is of grossly uneven quality and maldistributed, we focus upon medical education rather than upon the condition of management in the health services. If black youths find mostly dead-end jobs awaiting them in the labor market, we look askance at their educational achievements; meanwhile, we accept the higher incomes of white college graduates in the fashion of the chanticleer, as proof of the argument that, but for their educational deficiencies, blacks would be better off!

Were a foreign visitor to replicate the famous nineteenth-century study of *Democracy in America,* he would quickly remark that Americans have elevated education to a place equivalent to that reserved by de Tocqueville for committees, in that celebrated observer's assessment of American problem-solving techniques!

Now we shall perhaps always have to accept what may be termed fallout effects in education, and even to make the best of the fact that the society cannot guarantee that it will respect the parietal rules of the academy. The academy can seek to influence the effects of eternal demands through watchdog committees that review these demands in accordance with a set of policy guidelines, and thereby seek to protect important values. Thus, in the author's university, there is a "University Senate Committee on Externally Funded Research" that measures proposals influencing the utilization of its human and physical resources against an evolving set of standards. While such measures are typically of recent vintage, they do offer some limited promise of helping to shore up the useful walls that were all but dissolved during the long years when every national threat and opportunity was uncritically redefined into nuclear reactors, Russian studies centers, urban institutes, and myriad other programmatic attachments and appendages to the American university.

Even more serious than the educational fallout of political and related undertakings, however, are the direct impingements on the educational apparatus of public manpower and associated policies that seek, intentionally, to employ the education enterprise as a central means to specific ends. Any long-term plan regarding higher education in metropolitan centers must include assessment of the ways in which these impingements intensify and aggravate the fallout effects of the policies that have come to shape higher education. We may well argue that, in the absence of a coherent and well-reasoned overall policy regarding the role of higher education, we have encumbered ourselves with an apparatus that, like Boswell's dog, works in spite of itself.

It must be a matter of immediate and grave concern to educational planners and administrators at the state and local levels— particularly the big-city level—that we come to grips with questions regarding the appropriate role of higher education, lest we forsake what is a diminishing opportunity to straighten out, and thereby salvage, what is deteriorating through passivity, uncritical assessment, and well-intentioned but disastrously shortsighted patterns of utilization. New York State and New York City, regrettably, afford us with remarkable illustrations of many of the issues that need to be joined in an innovative assessment of future prospects regarding education at all levels.

First, and leaving aside for a moment the fallout effects, we can note that education was singled out to serve two national ends that were orthogonal, if not to an important degree incompatible. Thus we have long recognized—and in recent years could document—that education earns and produces significant economic returns to both individual beneficiaries and the nation.

After World War II, it was clearly perceived that a growing economy and a changing occupational structure require more citizens with the breadth of learning and disciplined intellects which are reasonably identified with a college education. An expanding public sector and the expansion in the ranks of the professions and management demonstrably require larger numbers of "better educated" manpower. Specific programs took sight of this need, and scholarships and grants soon joined program funds in a steadily increasing flow, the result of which was a building boom on existing campuses and a boom in college "starts," even as the fall-out effect manifested itself in the proliferation of special programs —from space medicine to oceanography.

At the same time that education experienced its economic takeoff stage, to borrow a phrase, it was singled out as the means for the solution of social problems as well. After all, went the argument, if education is necessary for national economic growth and for individual economic well-being, and if inequality and poverty are special kinds of problems which must be treated in economic terms, then we might expect education to be an instrument of social as well as economic policy. While manpower planners sought to identify the *specific needs* for scientists, engineers, teachers, and a host of other trained personnel categories, government poverty warriors and educationalists sought to facilitate educational opportunities for ever larger numbers of people on the grounds that education was the most direct avenue to higher income, and thereby to "upward mobility." The education enterprise thus expanded to serve the economy, in the narrow sense, by helping to qualify people needed in the economy and, in the broader sense, to serve the society as the mechanism by which its growing commitment to equality could be fulfilled.[1] Equality was regarded as a function of opportunity for mobility, and was defined in terms of labor supply.

In more recent years the very real possibility that the actual requirements for jobs were beginning to stabilize was noted by a few, but only a few, observers. A series of studies by economists who explored the personal and social returns on investments in higher education began to appear during the sixties, however, which concluded that the requirements for many of the nation's occupational classifications were legitimately rising! These economic studies, which assumed that the high positive correlation between education and income could be explained by the productivity of better-educated citizens, attributed a high rate of return on diplomas and degrees, and were based upon demographic data available at that time.

The methods utilized in these studies of "human capital" were indirect, as the previous paragraph suggests. The researchers looked not at *jobs* in relation to education, but at the different incomes of differentially educated groups. Incomes were thus taken as a measure of the demands for educated manpower, the rationality of employers was taken as a "given," and the assumption was that the market for such manpower would grow or at least remain firm in what was regarded as a competitive and growing economy. The effect of these studies, by some of the nation's most imaginative economists, was to underscore the economic importance of education.

At the same time, the education and income data were regarded by civil rights advocates as proof of the wisdom of expanding educational opportunities in order that more citizens might shift from the losing to the winning columns in the statistics on income distribution. The rest is by now an old story: "Universal higher education" and "open enrollment" were the new watchwords, and both educational plant and staff obviously needed to be geared up, in order that the colleges and universities could deliver the credentials that would simultaneously spell growth, opportunity, and equality.

The educational apparatus was thus chosen, as a major instrument of policy, to solve economic *and* social problems, knee-deep as it was in institutes, centers for research on almost everything, and special "crash programs" that kept its computers whirring with data on an endless list of matters from underground atom tests to outer-space travel, from personal to social disorders, and from the performance of rats in mazes to the performance of youngsters in inner-city schools.

No matter where one turned, higher education was the key ingredient in game plans of all kinds, while the basic statistics on education and earnings appeared on every subway car, every fifth matchbook cover, and in the preamble to literally thousands of bills offered to federal, state, and city legislators. "Dropout" became a dirty word while "stick-to-itiveness," and a host of other virtues, were credited to college graduates.

A number of facts and possibilities were overlooked in all this, however. The most important of these has already been mentioned, namely, that more direct measures of the economic requirements for education yielded a less optimistic picture of the demand for highly educated manpower in the absence of policies directed to the pursuit of aims that could be reached only by a large and continuously growing body of professional and managerial personnel. Studies by Folger and Nam,[2] by Ann Miller,[3] by Ruchlin,[4] by Folger and Astin and Bayer,[5] by the author,[6] by Folger[7], and by Ginzberg,[8] all of whom looked at jobs and job requirements rather than at income returns, strongly suggested a leveling off in the demand for highly educated manpower. Meanwhile, more recent versions of the earlier indirect approach, by Jorgensen and Griliches,[9] and by W. Lee Hansen,[10] suggest that the relationship between education and income, discussed in the "human capital" literature, is more complicated than had been contemplated. These later studies utilized more sophisticated methods and recognized changes in managerial perspectives regarding the marginal returns to the organization of purchasing additional increments of education.

Second, the labor force participation rates of women, particularly well-educated women, have gone up, for a variety of reasons, and thereby the competition among well-educated persons for jobs traditionally held by degree holders has increased.[11] At the same time, lesser-educated persons have faced increasing competition from college graduates for jobs hitherto occupied by those without college degrees.

Third, the early seventies have seen an economic recession in which the percent of unemployed workers in white-collar occupations is decidedly higher than that in blue-collar occupations.

Fourth, we have gradually overlooked the role of other means of work preparation, assigning colleges a virtual monopoly over credentials for work in almost every conceivable white-collar occupation.

Education, in fine, has been responsive to the urges and demiurges of those who pinpointed its crucial role in the economy and society. But opportunity has a demand side as well as a supply side to its manpower aspects, for which basically neo-orthodox policies were prescribed, even as the supply side was the object of the more numerous interventionist efforts involving education.[12]

The problems in New York are one set of the manifestations of the hodgepodge that has resulted. Where there was none after World War II, there is now a state university with multiple campuses. A number of the state's formerly small private colleges have been expanded and merged with a large number of the new state-built campuses to produce a geographically decentralized and growing system of higher education. The citizens and their political leaders saw a need for all this and got on with it. So far so good.

The City of New York, once the proud owner of City College, long famous as a point of departure for immigrants and first-generation city dwellers bound for significant roles in the community and the nation, now operates a citywide university *system*. Again, a number of formerly private colleges were expanded and merged with the city's higher educational plants to produce, for many more potentially mobile youths, the opportunities available only on a highly selective basis in other times.

The economy of the city, meantime, in common with that of the state and the nation, has been drifting sideways while, like other cities, it has been victimized by the drift—then massive shift—of middle-income families to the suburbs. And in the suburbs, community colleges have been springing up like crabgrass on middle-class lawns. And all—urban, suburban, and statewide systems—need money; all make their pleas before the state's legislators with the strong convictions that they have socially and politically certified mandates and missions, and that education is the young man's and woman's route to better jobs and higher incomes.

While the intrinsic or consumption benefits of education are never denied, it is the economic argument for education that is most strongly affirmed. While it once could be affirmed without cavil or reservation that a degree would, routinely, qualify a youth for a higher status and a better-paid job, this assumption now is based on an increasingly probabilistic argument regarding job opportunities.

It is still undoubtedly true, in the individual case, that a better job is a more likely reward for the better-educated than for the less-educated job applicant. But one commits the fallacy of composition when one now argues, from the statistical probability governing the single case, that the opportunities awaiting the aggregated members of the army of diploma-armed youths entering the labor force will be adequate to fulfill earlier promises. The fact is that educational achievements are outdistancing the changes in the occupational structure which previously elevated the demand for better-educated workers.[13]

The headlong race by nation, state, suburban county, and large city to provide increased educational opportunities for all their citizens has developed into a set of multilayered and competing educational arrangements, which has caused additional waste above and beyond the waste involved in the underutilization of educated manpower. At each level there is a rush to build, staff, and manage systemwide apparatuses while, simultaneously, private institutions are embarked upon development programs of all kinds.

The consequences of all this have not been happy in New York. Consider that in New York City there was, for many years, a leading private school of engineering, Brooklyn Polytechnic Institute, an institution of national reputation but with a local (New York City) student body. While its tuition was not much lower than that commanded by other private institutions, it was a "commuter college" whose students were spared the expenses of having to live on campus. The majority of these students had noncollege parents in modest, lower-middle income brackets.

When the New York City university system began to receive floods of applications, it explored the possibility of taking over Polytech to supplement its capacity to provide engineering educations. The state system, meantime, pursued the same course, while the Institute itself was beginning to experience the now well-known universal financial crunch. Over the past five years its status as an institution has suffered egregiously while city and state jostle each other to keep their options for offering engineering education open. A school that once was a vehicle which permitted mobility for low-income family sons may now actually go under for lack of support, even as the state and city seek to multiply precisely these opportunities on their existing campuses.

At the same time, engineering registrations have fallen off, and tuition rates at NYU and Columbia's engineering schools have shot up to $2,800 per annum. Both of these schools are a significant drain on the general incomes of their parent universities, and both of the parent universities (with enormous operating deficits), along with six other private institutions in New York, are in competition with the state and city systems for relatively scarce state and federal funds. The state legislature and the city council are understandably loath to bail out financially embarrassed private institutions, but they apparently feel no hesitation in building and operating low-tuition facilities in competition with the existing but faltering apparatuses on major private campuses. The eight largest private schools have organized into a lobby to force increases in tuition in public institutions, in addition to state capitation ("Bundy") money, which would be turned over to the private schools. But, it may be argued, the expenditure patterns of private schools reflect the tastes, preferences, prejudices, and aspirations of faculties and administrators in these private institutions without any eye to the public's interests.

The story is a sad one: duplicated facilities, underutilized personnel, unbalanced planning, unresponsive curricula, multi-layered expenditures, and expensive building programs all in competition, and all operated as though there were no such problems as recessions, unemployment, occupational credentialing despite manpower underutilization, and no alternative ways to ensure opportunity and equality other than by hodgepodge arrangements in higher education. The evidence is manifest in the fact that State University enrollments increased by 310 percent from 1961 to 1970, City University enrollments by 58 percent, and private institutions by 29 percent. But, whereas a majority of all college students in the state were enrolled in private institutions ten years ago, now only 41 percent attend private school.[14]

The operating deficits for 107 of the 140 private college and university budgets in the state for the current academic year (1971–1972) alone "may be in the neighborhood of $60 million," and half this deficit is in four major institutions, including Columbia and New York University, according to a report by New York's State Education Department. Only 27 private institutions among the 107 studied by the state "appear to have satisfactory prospects for the near-term future."[15] Juxtaposition of data about the shifting division of enrollments between public and private institutions with tabulations of the deficits in New York higher education affords some specific measure of the direct costs, and hints at the opportunity costs, of educational mal-planning in the state.

Thus, until a moratorium was recently placed by the New York State commissioner of education on new Ph.D. programs in the state, we witnessed an increase in public university doctoral programs at the same time that elite, private institutions, like Columbia, were in the early stages of cutting back on these programs. The long-term manpower implications of cutting back where quality is high and forging ahead where quality is, at best, aborning, must be deplored. The reassignment of experienced graduate faculty resources to other educational chores is among the implications that should cause serious concern.

The fact is that in 1963 New York State mandated master planning in public higher education, and statutes continuing in that direction, calling for quadrennial "updating," were duly passed by the state legislature. But the results have not been impressive. Until 1971 there was no requirement that this planning process take account of the plans (if any!) of the state's 140 private institutions, and when the education law *was* amended, it did not compel, but urged and encouraged "wider participation in the planning process by private institutions."[16] Since few private educational institutions do any real academic planning, as the author learned during his tenure as associate dean of Columbia's faculties, the good intentions will amount to precious little. And, so long after all the strategic building and location decisions have been made, it is hard to imagine that more than trivial consequences would result even if all the private institutions were to collaborate in the enterprise; the Stony Brook (SUNY) apparatus, for example, is not likely to be moved to another region in the state, although such a move would enhance Columbia's and NYU's positions.

There could, of course, be an increase in the orders of collaboration and cooperation among the schools in a given geographic area. But while one may devoutly wish for more coordination, one must realize that consolidation and reorganization even *within* one of the important schools will not take place without inducements generated by innovative budgeting techniques. Inventive budgeting techniques that would accomplish imaginative and reasonable "restructuring" in the institutions familiar to the writer are most uncommon. And the enduring patterns of institutional aid—such as "Bundy money" which, in New York, provides a fixed sum for each degree granted—fly in the face of both rational manpower *and* educational policy by rewarding the institutional status quo while they expand the supply of educated manpower without an eye to demand!

Among the needed reforms: a five-year moratorium on expansions in federal institutional aid to all institutions in favor of direct grants to students and post–high school trainees. If the planners do not in fact plan, then it would be far better to create a situation in which the consumer may spend his own tuition dollars, GI Bill fashion, and thus force changes in the structure of higher education. And, by providing *all* youths some funds for post-secondary education *or* training, we may well witness the emergence of alternatives to the conventional academy, as new agencies appear and apply for licenses which will enable them to vie for students' tuition grants.

Next, we simply cannot expect a better articulated process of educational and manpower planning as long as these needs are served separately, at local, state, and national levels, by totally differentiated education and labor apparatuses.

Consider that, in New York, the architects of the master plan for public higher education are supposed to build labor market estimates and forecasts into their calculations. But a spokesman for a commission made up of private college and university task forces, and assigned the task of facilitating the "wider participation" of private institutions in this planning, reports to the writer that he has been unable to uncover any significant manpower forecasts for the state.[17]

There is, of course, nothing very new in the statement that we could use more and better manpower forecasts but that we manage without them in both the private and public domains. The U.S. Department of Labor, in a 1970 Manpower Research Monograph on the subject, reported that few companies in a representative Minnesota sample ". . . were actively planning for manpower.

Almost none . . . were comprehensive in scope."[18] Interestingly, the firms that *did* undertake detailed forecasts experienced fewer errors in their judgments regarding manpower untilization. In general, ". . . manpower forecasting seemed to be almost completely isolated from other types of planning. Some 95 percent of the firms forecast needs for equipment, 90 percent for capital, 80 percent for plant, and 66 percent for raw materials." Only 36 percent of all responding firms forecast manpower supplies, 8 percent forecast only supplies, while only 43 percent forecast manpower requirements.[19]

Similarly, a couple of years after the 1959 steel strike, during which much was made of redundancy in the work force because of "work rules," the largest steel firms organized national raiding parties on other employers to locate skilled workers to man the mills during the Kennedy boom. And, after winning a "Mechanization and Modernization" agreement with the West Coast longshoremen, which permitted the introduction on the docks of capital equipment that would reduce manpower requirements, it was the stevedoring companies that neglected to introduce such devices as fork lift trucks.[20] Thus, there are many lessons about rationality, or rather irrationality, in manpower use that bear upon manpower planning, and we may conclude that the ineffectiveness of planning is rooted in the failures of employers as well as in the failures of educators and public servants in divided bureaucracies. One may accordingly sympathize with the young whose judgments are so badly shaped by the skewed realities which their elders repeatedly urge them to face.

The evidence, meantime, that young people will adjust their expectations, and thereafter their educational plans, to fit labor market realities is, paradoxically, greater[21] than the evidence that educational planners can adjust educational investments to take even modest account of short- and long-run changes in the manpower markets.

Evidence that educators, public bureau heads, and legislators can effectively use education as a means to achieving democratic ends, meanwhile, is virtually nonexistent. Thus, Hansen and Weisbrod, in a study of California's system of higher education, have shown that tax and educational policies in California exacerbate *in*equality: 40 percent of families with college-age children receive no subsidy for public higher education, while 10 percent receive subsidies in excess of $5,000. Students from families with incomes over $25,000 are *four times* as likely to be eligible for the state's higher educational benefits as those from families with incomes below $4,000. And California's system has long been held as a model for other states to emulate!

Nor is there evidence that typical present-day arrangements will encourage educators better to serve the population. Real reform on campuses, in educational terms, is as rare as chastity in a house of ill-repute; the well-educated reader is invited to flesh out the analogy according to his own lights.

That open-enrollment programs in the academy will help low achievers should also be doubted. Consider that an inventive and useful study of low achievers found that learning, training, and experience, *not* formal education, account for earning differentials among low achievers.[22]

The argument that higher education needs uncritical support, lest we deny ourselves the benefits of scientific discoveries and the rest, obtains only at the margins. Basic scientific and intellectual work is undertaken by a relatively small number of people at a very few institutions.

The fact is that we do not assess what we have, seek to assess what we need, or pursue policies that would give us flexibility in pursuing the implications of changing manpower requirements. The lessons for the nation, states, and cities need little explication, but it is perilously late to put off learning them.

The problems are particularly acute for cities like New York that have gone so far down the higher educational road in seeking solutions to economic and social problems, while doing almost nothing to make the first and more crucial twelve years of public education viable.

The evidence strongly suggests the need for a revamping of these policies so that we would have a balance between educational and other means to human and social ends. A useful equation will take account of statewide educational developments, the role of private institutions, both metropolitan and regional manpower requirements, alternative methods of job preparation, and the overall and specific demands for labor.

Large cities, close as they are to the front lines, must not continue to add credibility to the argument that the nation's larger problems can be solved by manipulating institutions that influence only the supply of labor.

12

LABOR MARKET INFORMATION

Dean Morse and Boris Yavitz

INTRODUCTION

In a number of the other chapters, the authors call attention to
linkages which presently exist or should be developed among
various institutions which play important, though sometimes
neglected, roles in the operation of New York City's labor markets. Through these linkages the decisions and effects of actions,
taken by one institution or by several in concert, are either transmitted to specific parts of specific labor markets or diffused
throughout the system of labor markets which underpin New
York's economic life.

    As is true elsewhere, in New York's labor markets a good
portion of the information used as the basis for decision making
by a particular participant is derived from others. Often decisions
are made jointly by several participants. There is, therefore, a
continual flow of information among participants in New York
City's labor markets—corporations, trade associations, trade
unions, and the city government's agencies such as the Human
Resources Administration, the Economic Development Administration, the Transportation Administration, to name only a few.
In addition, other levels of government, state and federal, are involved in the operation of the city's labor market, either as employers, as intermediaries, or as specialized sources of labor market information. The city government is by far the largest single

employer in the area. When the city's labor markets perform unsatisfactorily, city agencies, such as the Department of Social Services, bear the brunt of the burden of coping with the ensuing problems. If the health of segments of the city's labor supply is poor, the Health and Hospitals Corporation must attempt to patch up the pieces. If youth is floundering between school and work, the board of education and the police department often know the causes and consequences of the failure of the labor market to absorb new entrants.

Indeed, if jobs are moving to the suburbs and people are pinned in certain parts of the city, the mass transportation agencies and Transportation Administration ought to be among the first to know what and who is involved. If plans are underfoot to make heavy cutbacks in space programs and defense expenditures for specific weapons systems, the Defense Department is, of course, the first to know about what may become a serious unemployment problem in a formerly prosperous suburb.

It is not possible to describe in detail the intricate network of information channels that provides for the flow of information between participants in the labor market of New York City and its environs.[1] In this chapter, however, we will attempt to delineate in three sections the parameters of the network.

The first will be an analytical discussion of the basic features of New York City's economy and labor markets. An urban labor market information network is closely related to the character of a city's economic activity. A labor market information network appropriate to a one-industry town when that industry is in a period of rapid growth is at the opposite pole from the network appropriate to New York's mature and highly heterogeneous economy. In the first section, then, we will gather together a number of characteristics of New York City's economic life which, in our view, have important implications for its labor market information network.

The second presents a model of a labor market information network for New York City. This section concentrates on the linkages which exist between what we have termed those with "primary" roles in the labor market on the one hand—employers and job seekers—and, on the other, intermediaries in the labor market and agencies of the city and higher levels of government charged with developing manpower-training programs and education programs or with more general mandates to assist the region's economic development. This section concentrates on linkages which have significant policy implications.

The third and concluding section contains an outline of a proposal designed to provide a foundation for a strengthened labor market informational network for New York City, which draws upon what we feel have been hitherto neglected informational resources and is aimed at facilitating the achievement of several connected policy goals. We hope that it will provide an improved informational base for decision makers both in government and in the private profit and nonprofit sectors. In particular we would hope that our proposal provides strong incentives for those who occupy strategic positions in the labor market to pool their informational resources.

Decisions of major employers in the area to recruit, or dismiss, large numbers of workers have important repercussions on policy objectives of government. If, for example, major New York financial institutions decide to increase rapidly the employment of members of minority groups at relatively low occupational levels, those concerned with broad questions of social policy must ask whether such a step, desirable though it may be in itself, is tied to the opening up of higher occupational levels to the new employees and, if so, what training programs, public or private, are necessary for the successful implementation of this second step.

It is our conviction that the achievement of most of the labor market policy goals and, indeed, of most of the economic and social goals of the city depends to a great extent upon the willingness of strategic participants in the labor market to share information and with it the process of decision making.

The realization is growing that the decision-making process in any complex organization is becoming a shared one and that the effects of any important decision cannot be limited to one constituency. A sharing of information, therefore, is a first step in the process of shared decision making. We do not imply that it will be an easy step, but we suggest why and how it might be taken.

BASIC FEATURES OF NEW YORK CITY'S LABOR MARKETS

Since the urban labor market information network is related to underlying characteristics of the urban labor market, a preliminary sketch of some central characteristics of the New York labor market is in order.

Size. The first characteristic to note is size. Because of its scale, New York's labor markets equal or exceed in diversity those of the smaller nations of Western Europe. Compounding the effects of the diversity of New York's economic activities is the relatively small scale of the typical employer's operations. There are, of course, a number of establishments that employ thousands, but no single one of them, with the exception of the government itself, plays a dominant role. One out of every two employees in the city works in an establishment that employs less that 100 people.[2] Only one out of five works in an establishment that employs 1,000 or more, and the average size of these establishments is only about 2,500.

While the small firm is important in the city's labor markets, we also must call attention to the strategic importance, not of any single large corporate employer or institution, but of the totality of these employers. And to these large employers whose rolls contain hundreds or thousands of workers should be added those industries which, while consisting primarily of relatively small firms, have powerful trade associations and powerful trade unions; from many points of view, including an informational one, they amount to a combined set of employers facing a single group of employees. In this group of industries we can include several of the largest in the city—printing, apparel, transport. The combined employment of these highly structured industries—made up of small-scale employers united under a powerful trade association and confronting a powerful union, and of large corporate employers and institutions, governmental and nonprofit—includes a large proportion of the total employment in the "primary labor market" of the city.[3]

Diversity and specialization: New York City's comparative advantage. Several types of economic activity and several industries are concentrated in New York City to an extent unparalleled in any other location in the country. In the Central Business District of Manhattan is an array of central offices and other types of offices which is unique in the world, establishments whose major function is the processing of immense quantities of information with a primary aim of providing corporate executives with the basis for control and for decision making. Such establishments represent the epitome of bureaucratic organization of labor.

In addition to the immense amount of central office activity in the city, a vast range of wholesale and retail activities is concentrated in specific areas of the city. Connected to both central office and retail and wholesale activity are a host of industries and establishments which furnish specialized business and consumer services, from advertising to entertainment. Indeed, for much of the core of the city one of the most important features of economic activity is the dependence of individual establishments upon an immensely complex network of business and personal services.

This can be considered from another vantage. The division of labor has probably proceeded further in the few hundred square miles that make up Greater New York than it has in any other part of the world except for a few cities like London, Tokyo, and Paris. The information network that ties together the labor market of New York and its environs (and for some types of activity, the boundary of the relevant labor market is in Europe or the Middle or Far East) must therefore communicate a staggering amount of detail about a very large number of occupations to a vast number of establishments.

An important comparative advantage of New York City is its capacity to adjust to the shifting needs of employers and employees. Students of New York's economic life have long called attention to the "external economies" offered to employers by the existence of a large, highly variegated labor force.

Another factor is the change in the industrial and occupational mix that characterizes the urban economy. As we have noted, New York approaches a nation in the complexity and importance of "external" markets for a considerable portion of its output. To maintain a consistently high level of technological leadership and productivity, many of its industries must constantly be leaders in innovation. In New York, moreover, there are always a number of establishments, firms, and industries on the verge of a decision to move out of the central city, either into the inner or outer rings, or outside of the region altogether.

At the same time alterations in comparative advantage make it desirable for other economic activities, presently located outside of the region, to move to New York City itself or to other parts of the New York region.

In the past, one of the comparative advantages—perhaps the most important—which induced employers to locate in New York City was the quality, variety, and flexibility of its labor force. In the modern world in which many key resources are becoming more and more mobile, in which locational advantages turn less and less upon difficult-to-transport raw materials or differential access to capital, it is still probably true that man remains, as Adam Smith remarked, of "all baggage the most difficult to transport."

The presence of a large, highly trained, variegated, and flexible labor force will continue to provide, in our view, important comparative advantages to a few selected areas. New York City has had such an advantage in the past and can, if it is alert to its opportunity and its danger, increase this advantage in the future.

It has for this purpose a powerful tool: the existence of an immense educational and training establishment, at present beleaguered and uncertain about its role—an establishment which in the past has had many important linkages to New York City's labor markets, which has attempted to maintain such linkages, and which may be on the brink of discovering and utilizing new methods of connecting education and training with the needs of the city's labor markets. Let us put the case as sharply as we can.

As highly intricate technology becomes ever more widely diffused, as firms grow in size and complexity, the personnel practices of firms become ever more universalistic, impersonal, and rational. Manpower planning, over a long time horizon, becomes as essential as capital budgeting over a similar horizon. In fact the two become economically indistinguishable to all intents and purposes, and sophisticated firms have already begun to recognize this.

But another important change in the nature of manpower development emerges. In the past the importance of specific training has often outweighed the importance of general training, at least from the perspective of individual firms, if not from that of society itself. But the importance of specific training, in our view, will inevitably decline relative to the importance of general high-level training. In the past firms were willing to bear the cost of specific training because they could have a reasonable expectation that an employee in whom they had made heavy training investments would remain with them. After all, the very meaning of specific training is that it is valuable to an employee primarily within the firm which provided it.

If general training, particularly the most costly kind, is in the process of superseding specific training as the most important form of investment in human capital, then those regions (and from this point of view New York is a region) which have developed the capacity to deliver this kind of training most efficiently to employers who need trained manpower will offer crucial comparative advantages in the technologically advanced, and therefore the highest wage, industries and establishments.

It is from this point of view that the variety and depth of New York's educational and training establishment are most impressive. This establishment embraces a vast public school system which contains an array of publicly supported community and senior colleges along with the impressive beginning of a graduate school and a similarly vast array of private schools, colleges, universities, and professional schools. In addition, it has a wide range of private training establishments, ranging from the RCA Institute to highly specialized management-training institutes. It includes the training facilities of large firms themselves and the close links that such firms have developed with specialized schools.

The structure of the labor market. In recent years a number of students of labor markets have reached the conclusion that perhaps the outstanding characteristic of urban labor markets, including New York's, is the bifurcation into a "primary" and a "secondary" labor market. The boundary between the two is not always sharp and clear-cut, and there may be a large grey area in between. According to this view, employment in the primary sector tends to be relatively stable, wage rates and fringe benefits relatively high, and internal labor markets within firms well structured with recognized career ladders and ports of entry to the establishment.

The secondary labor market is different. Within it, firms are small-scale and numerous. Entry to and exit from industries, both by firms and employees, is easy and frequent (though not necessarily painless); little market power is exerted either by firms or by employees. Fringe benefits are usually small or nonexistent, working conditions are often minimal, and wage rates are relatively low. One consequence of these factors is that the employment experience of workers at any one job tends to be relatively short. It does not pay the firm to invest more than a minimum in the training of workers, and this is one reason that wage rates tend to be low.

The smallness of firms in the secondary labor market precludes the development of career ladders. There is little structure within the firm and little possibility that an employee will progress from a low-skilled entry job through a series of steps up the skill and wage ladder.

Demographic and other changes affecting New York City's labor markets. The continued migration of blacks to the inner cities, coupled with their relatively high rates of natural increase, and the rapid out-migration to the suburbs of white workers—a good proportion of whom are members of the "primary" labor market who found employment with firms located or locating in the suburbs—have combined to transform the character of the supply of labor in large cities, particularly New York itself.

Several other aspects of urban labor markets in general and of the New York labor market in particular should be noted. First of all, the changing spatial configuration of economic activity within the New York region (for example, the flight of industry to the suburbs) is one of the major determinants of the kind of labor market information that is needed, and one of the major causes of the emergence of gaps in the labor market information system. In the past all too little has been known about the movements of firms and establishments within the New York City region. The investigations of Stanback and Knight promise to throw much needed light upon the process of job creation and destruction that is involved.[4] In particular it is necessary to understand the relationship between the construction of new transportation facilities and the concomitant deterioration of older forms of transportation and the process of job creation and destruction. Similarly, the emergence of a new kind of suburb, in which the population is more working class than middle class, has transformed much of the region. Many working-class suburbs were based upon the economic fortunes of a handful of large concerns. Often, however, these firms have been among the technological leaders in the aerospace and defense industries. As such, they have been dependent upon a continued flow of government contracts and therefore particularly vulnerable to the radical cutbacks that many of the space and defense-related programs have undergone in the past few years.

IMPLICATIONS FOR NEW YORK CITY'S LABOR MARKET INFORMATION SYSTEM

The existence of a large pool of labor with diverse skills does not itself create comparative advantages unless the pool of labor is informed about and able to respond quickly to new employment opportunities. And such a pool of labor will stagnate and dry up if (in an environment of seasonality and rapidly shifting fortunes of establishments) workers cannot quickly find alternative employment opportunities when their jobs terminate.

What are the features of New York City's labor market information system, and how do they impinge on New York City's labor market?

First of all the city's labor market information network is highly decentralized and diversified. It ranges from the extremely informal transmission of information at street corners and in luncheonettes, which takes place in the garment district, to the services of specialized executive placement agencies, including among a host of other links the critically important role played by a single newspaper, *The New York Times,* in its daily want ads and Sunday section devoted to employment opportunities. In some industries and occupations, union hiring halls provide the central conduit along which information about employers and employees is transmitted, usually to a restricted audience. For prospective and present governmental employees, specialized publications provide information about employment and promotion opportunities along with assistance which helps the neophyte to negotiate the obstacle course of examinations and credentials. A number of governmental agencies provide selective labor market information for particular industries, occupations, and demographic groups. These range from the activities of the New York State Employment Service to the career guidance offered by public and private educational institutions. In the past few years, considerable attention has been given to the development of computerized job banks and even more sophisticated job-matching services.

The importance of the informal system. As we have noted, much of the information which makes possible the vast number of job transactions which occur in New York's many specialized labor markets is transmitted informally. But the term "informal" does not adequately characterize this transmitted information. Not only is it informal, it is highly personal. It is transmitted largely by friends and relatives and therefore has a restricted audience. Indeed, an integral feature of this kind of information transmission is its tendency to reinforce discriminatory barriers, often without conscious intention. Thomas Schelling has recently observed:

> If job vacancies are filled by word of mouth or apartments go to people who have acquaintances in the building, and if boys can marry only girls who speak their language, a biased communication system will preserve and enhance the prevailing homogeneities.[5]

Informational implications of a dual labor market. Although members of minority groups, particularly blacks and Puerto Ricans, are not the only workers who constitute the "secondary" labor market, an individual's chances of finding himself trapped within the secondary labor market are far higher if he is black or Puerto

Rican. Moreover, since the kind of information a person tends to accumulate about the labor market is influenced by the experiences of his friends and relatives and is peculiarly resistant to change, living in a neighborhood where a high proportion of the population is in the secondary labor market is apt to give a young person a sense that his own work experiences may also be episodic and unrewarding.

Asymmetry of information about the movement of firms and other changes. It seems easier for the city to be informed about potential losses of establishments, particularly if they are large (these movements are always rumored and given wide publicity by the press), than to know about potential gains, which often start in a small way. The planning process, particularly that part of it which involves an estimate of the demand for specific skills of the labor force, can therefore be distorted by this asymmetry of information about the near and long-term future prospects of the city's economy.

Similarly, it is not easy for the city to obtain reliable information about prospective immigration and emigration. Not only are predictions about gross movements notoriously unreliable (witness the inaccuracy of predictions about the inflow of blacks and Puerto Ricans and about the outflow of whites during the past decade), but it seems almost impossible to devise a means of projecting the supply of trained manpower in any fine detail because of unexpected immigration and emigration. A good deal of manpower planning in the past decade (and the projections upon which it has been based) is vitiated by a kind of neomercantilistic point of view which assumes that a particular region or state has more control over inflows and outflows than it has in fact.

A MODEL OF A POLICY-ORIENTED LABOR MARKET INFORMATION NETWORK FOR NEW YORK CITY

In this section, we will concentrate on the information links, either existing or desirable, among strategic institutions in the city's labor markets. In particular we want to emphasize those linkages

which are most closely related to pressing issues of public policy—
the equity of the city's labor markets, their efficiency, and ultimately, the character of the region's economic development insofar as it is affected by the operation of its labor markets.

First, however, we remind the reader of what we must omit.
The most important and pervasive of these omitted elements is
the network of informal links among individuals—friends, relatives, even casual acquaintances—through which a great deal of
the information which leads job seeker to employer and employer
to job seeker is actually transmitted. Every study of labor market
information emphasizes the essential role played by information
transmitted in this fashion.

We have left this flow of information out of our account, not
because we are unmindful of its importance, but because we do
not feel that it is the kind of information flow that can be affected,
certainly in the short run, possibly in the long run too, by policy decisions and objectives. Indeed we are not optimistic that attempts
spanning less than a decade to persuade New York City workers
to use formal information channels such as job banks will prove
successful, although recent decisions of the federal government
that require federal contractors to list their job vacancies with the
Employment Service may presage an enhanced capacity of the
Employment Service to penetrate that part of the labor market
in which good jobs are found.

Parenthetically, we should note that even if job banks and
other computerized job-matching facilities are not spectacular-
ly successful in terms of the number of job seekers who find good
jobs through them, they may still prove justified because of their
impact upon certain groups of workers, particularly minority
workers, whose access to such jobs through information links of
an informal nature has been impaired by patterns of discrimination. The informal transmittal of labor market information is clearly a repository of much of the legacy of discrimination that blights
urban labor markets.

A second set of links, in this case formal, has been omitted
from our model, again because we are skeptical that much can
be done through these links in the near future to help in the
achievement of policy goals concerned with equity or efficiency,
or economic development. The most important of these formal

links which we have omitted are those between the New York State Employment Service offices and the "secondary" labor market. Historically there have been compelling reasons for the Employment Service to have developed such links. If, however, it is to fulfill its present major policy objectives, it must strengthen its links to the primary labor market, and in the process, to assist its job seeker clients to make the transition to that part of the city's labor market. Incidentally, one of the effects of a decrease in the supply of workers offered by the Employment Service to the secondary labor market might well be an improvement in wages and working conditions for those who for one reason or another are forced to remain in it.

If, then, we concentrate our attention upon the remainder of the city's labor market information network, what does it consist of? We can distinguish a number of different levels, starting from those linkages which are closest to job transactions and moving to those linkages which are involved primarily in the process of job creation and manpower development, eventually reaching the level of policy decisions which are designed to improve the city's economic and social future.

At the first level there are the major employers—large corporations, major institutions such as hospitals, universities, museums, etc., and government itself, primarily the agencies of the city, facing a pool of existing and prospective employees upon which they now draw and expect to draw in the future. Closely associated with this level are the trade associations, which unite employers, and the employee associations, which represent workers.

While many workers, perhaps even the majority, have found employment with large-scale employers or membership in unions through informal channels, large employers are likely to use formal channels as well, and industries made up of small firms facing a powerful union are apt to have a trade association and to hire through union hiring halls. When large employers have to fill several thousand, or even tens of thousands of positions, during the course of a year, they cannot rely simply upon informal links to job seekers, even if they prefer to, but must develop more formal search procedures. These search procedures inevitably tend to become universalistic and impersonal in character.[6]

Although it appears that large corporate employers do not

rely upon the published information about labor markets that originates in various agencies of the federal government, they do use much of the information made available by trade associations or management consultants, much of which may have originated in the very governmental statistical programs and publications they ignore.[7]

At the level of labor market intermediaries in that portion of the city's labor markets that we have included in our model, we find a large number of specialized private employment agencies, the placement offices of schools and colleges, the hiring halls of unions, and the specialized offices of the New York State Employment Service. In addition, private training institutions direct a stream of trained workers toward the large employers. The employers themselves make extensive use of advertising to recruit specialized employees, particularly in *The New York Times,* but also in trade and professional journals and in business publications.

In the past few years a new kind of intermediary in the primary labor markets has emerged, born of efforts by various levels of government to provide more comprehensive manpower services, particularly training and upgrading, to the unemployed, the underemployed, and those workers whose wages are substandard. Of particular importance was the discovery that on-the-job training was vastly preferable to institutional (i.e., classroom) training for just those members of the labor force who are most subject to unemployment or underemployment. On-the-job training means the creation of links between administrators of manpower programs and those employers who are in a position to offer such training on a large scale.

From its inception in 1962, the manpower policy of the federal government has vacillated between programs designed to promote economic efficiency and development and a quite different set of programs which have been primarily equity-oriented, some of them as much eleemosynary as work-oriented. These programs have been designed to bring a major fraction of the population, particularly in the inner cities, into fuller participation in the benefits of employment in the primary labor markets.

The demographic changes in New York City's labor supply have made it more imperative than ever to discover ways by which programs designed to improve the relative position of inner-city minority groups in the labor market can be coupled with programs which would enable the number of good jobs available to these groups to expand sufficiently. In other words, equity objectives can be achieved only in tandem with the achievement of efficiency and economic development objectives.

It is at this point that a higher level of decision making and program development must be brought into our model of New York City's labor market information network. The basic equity objectives of the manpower programs of the past decade can be achieved, we repeat, only by a process of job creation within the inner city which will replace many of the jobs previously available to minority groups within the secondary labor market with jobs which must be created by firms which are located within the primary labor market.

But this kind of job creation depends to a large extent upon the willingness of large firms to remain in the city if they are already located there and upon the attractive force the city can exert upon other firms to induce them to locate facilities within the city. These firms must feel that it is worthwhile to make the heavy investments in facilities and manpower which job creation on a large scale entails. The decision to make these investments in turn will depend upon an improvement in the efficiency of New York City's labor markets and upon a process of economic development in which manpower development will play a critical role. It is essential, in short, to convince large employers—corporations, institutions, and government itself—that the city will continue to offer them significant comparative advantages through its supply of trained manpower.

If, to the various levels of the job-creation and manpower-development system we have already distinguished, we add the full potential of the educational and training establishment available in New York City, it becomes possible to visualize a process of interlinked job creation and manpower development which would promote the transition of workers from dead-end jobs, poorly paid, unstable, and degrading, to jobs which are securely based upon continuing technological leadership and high levels of investment in training and education.

Our proposal to strengthen New York City's labor market information network is aimed at fostering the linkages—first, informational and later, decision linkages—which would form the necessary underpinning to a dynamic labor market in the city. Such a labor market would be, we believe, responsive to changing technological opportunities on the one hand, and sensitive to the needs of its manpower resources on the other.

New York City has· already begun the process of creating a system of city agencies to play critical roles in the process of job creation and manpower development we envisage. The Economic Development Administration and the Human Resources Administration are, at least in concept, essential pieces in the network of institutions which must mesh if job creation and manpower development are to go forward in tandem. The City Planning Commission and a number of other institutions, private and public, are charged with the mission of developing both comprehensive information about the city's economic and demographic characteristics and a planning framework for action.

The proposed labor market information network (and the associated decision-making network) which would tie together these many different levels of action is at present embryonic in many of its important connective tissues. Many key elements in this proposed system of information and decision making, however, have already begun to accumulate critically important data which, if properly disseminated, could provide the basis for some first large steps on the path we have outlined.

For example, the technologically most advanced industries already located in the city—profit-making corporations and such institutions as hospitals, universities, and research institutions—already know a good deal about the kind of labor force they will need in the next decade and what kind of training it must have. They also have some idea of likely areas of shortages of trained personnel as well as those of oversupply. Educational and training institutions have developed in the past few years a much greater sophistication about learning processes. They have a much clearer idea than they had a few years ago about the resources required to carry out successfully their projected training programs. Those agencies of government which have been charged with the development of manpower resources now have more knowledge than a decade ago about how to involve minority groups in training, guidance, and career programs.

Many of the pieces that New York City needs to solve the puzzle of how to provide a more equitable labor market and simultaneously to stimulate the city's economy to provide a large increase in stable, relatively well-paid jobs are already known or becoming known.

If the strategic institutions of New York City's labor market can be brought into an informed relationship with each other, the future of the city, at least from the point of view of its continuing to offer a comparative advantage to those industries which would provide the best employment opportunities, seems propitious. And a favorable economic climate, particularly one in which the process of creating a large number of good jobs is matched by a process of education and training which would enable a large proportion of those who are unemployed and consequently discontent to find and hold jobs, is essential if the city is to attack successfully the other problems of the city which are associated with poverty, despair, and a sense of removal from the mainstream.

IMPROVED INTEGRATION OF NEW YORK'S LABOR MARKETS THROUGH SYSTEMATIC INFORMATION EXCHANGE: A PROPOSAL FOR A CONSORTIUM OF LABOR MARKET INFORMATION USERS

The lack of integration among the various levels of New York City's labor markets—direct participants, intermediaries, government policy framers and implementers—is exemplified by the fact that there is no clearing house through which major participants can exchange information on an ongoing and systematic basis. The result of the situation, however, is clear. Large bodies of information about New York City's manpower, employment, and related issues, scattered in literally thousands of sources and repositories, is not available to many of the major participants in the city's labor markets, although a considerable portion of this scattered information would be extremely useful if it could be disseminated to them in a coherent and digestible form.

Let us be specific. Many large corporations—for example,

the New York Telephone Company—and many agencies of government—like the City Planning Commission—spend considerable amounts of money and effort in collecting and analyzing data which bear upon the operation of the city's labor markets. Trade associations and trade unions are repositories of large amounts of information about their members. Schools and colleges have files that are bursting with information about students (and their parents too).

Yet despite the enormous efforts involved in the collection of all these data, each of the major participants in the city's labor markets often finds gaping holes in essential labor market information, needed in some cases simply to enable the participant to comply with the law. A large corporation, for example, may find that a federal government directive requires that it hire a labor force which approximates the racial balance of the area from which the establishment draws its labor force. However, there may be no data which indicate what that racial balance actually is. Or administrators of manpower programs may not be able to follow up the graduates of their training programs over a sufficient period of time, although most graduates who do not obtain employment show up on the rolls of the Department of Social Services.

In some cases, of course, the desired information may simply not be available, or at least not economically available. In other instances, however, the needed data (or a reasonably close surrogate) may lie in the files of another participant. Some data circulation is quite naturally restricted by political considerations and in other cases compelling reasons involving the rights of privacy of individuals or institutions justify the retention of information within narrowly guarded boundaries.

But in many instances purely technical factors make it difficult for strategic participants to take advantage of information which is in the hands of other users. These factors include the following:

1. There is no formal mechanism through which much of the data now being generated can be located, inventoried, and categorized.

2. Even for known data sources, there is no systematic procedure for distribution.
3. There has been no careful consideration or estimate of the costs and benefits which participants in a cooperative labor market information sharing system might reasonably expect, either in the immediate future or in the long run.
4. In the maze of participants, agencies, and firms, governmental policy framers and implementers, statistical bureaus and so forth that should be brought together, there is no single institution which stands out as the most logical candidate to take on the role of coordinator and administrator of a labor market information clearinghouse.

In light of these technical factors and the potential gains which accrue to New York, we recommend that a consortium of strategic institutions and firms be formed to explore the setting up of a "clearinghouse" system. Such a system would integrate to the maximum extent possible both private and public sources of information relevant to the city's labor markets. It would transcend conventional categories of labor market information to bring into the system information dealing with, among other matters, social transformations, transportation and housing developments, and technological change.

A working assumption, at least at the outset, is that it would be more efficient for the consortium to explore the potentialities of existing but underutilized sources of information than to attempt to create new sources and types of information. In our view, the city's labor market information network suffers primarily from the lack of coordination, analysis, and adequate dissemination of the immense body of information which now is in existence. We recognize that the statistical purist may have considerable doubts about the quality of much of this information. One benefit of the consortium approach, indeed, would be that the quality of presently collected data would be upgraded by the suggestions of others about limitations and deficiencies in present methods of collecting and analyzing these data.

A consortium, of course, cannot function unless one of its members is given a clear mandate, along with the necessary resources, to coordinate its initial efforts. It is not enough to have several conferences of interested parties. Moreover, the resources available to the executive leadership of the consortium must make it possible to indicate to the members of the consortium specific promises of mutual benefits from the interchange of information. Without the promise of reasonably quick results, it is certain that the consortium would soon fall apart. The leadership of the consortium, on the other hand, must also be in a position to look at the labor market information network of the city from a general perspective.

Fortunately, several recent administrative developments indicate that we are on the verge of a consortium approach to the coordination of labor market information for the New York City region. The proliferation of manpower programs during the 1960s overstrained the control and planning capacities of the various levels of government which took part in these programs. In an effort to bring some order into what threatened to degenerate into administrative chaos, it was hoped that the establishment of CAMPS (Cooperative Area Manpower Planning System) and the development of computerized information systems like MARS and ESARS (Manpower Automated Reporting System and Employment Service Automated Reporting System respectively) would provide coordination and control.

Although the establishment of CAMPS did not bring about a nice and neat integration of manpower programs, it was a step in the right direction. It has been followed by the inauguration of the New York Manpower Area Planning Council. It is our impression that the Manpower Planning Council could well prove to be the agency whose mission and point of view is most congruent with the leadership role in the labor market information consortium we envisage.

There are other possible agencies which might carry out this function, particularly the Employment Service itself. Indeed, it might be possible that the consortium would prefer to set up a new agency, perhaps one on the order of the National Bureau of Economic Research but specifically focused upon the city's manpower and employment challenges. But we believe that the leadership of the consortium must not allow it to become purely a research or information center. Rather it should hold out the prospect that the consortium might eventually fulfill an "indicative planning" function insofar as the supply of and demand for trained manpower must be related to the general economic development of New York City. The consortium would then be in a position to make an invaluable contribution to the solution of the region's economic and social problems.

13

INSTITUTIONS AND LINKAGES

Beatrice Reubens

THE EXISTENCE OF A COMPREHENSIVE, sharply defined, and clearly organized governmental manpower agency does not in and of itself give assurance that manpower programs will be well conceived and executed. Nor does the mere establishment of liaison between the manpower agency and all other involved institutions and groups eliminate conflict, overlapping, duplication, and waste. But it is virtually certain that an agency with poor organization and inadequate interagency relationships will not produce satisfactory programs. Therefore, there is a high premium on discovering the elements of effective internal and external organizational structures.

A listing of some of the tasks of the manpower authorities may suggest the preferred lines of internal organization and external linkages:

—Anticipating the manpower effects of general economic, fiscal, and monetary policies and preparation of programs which can make both short-term and long-term adjustments. The separation of the short-term from the long-term effects and the reconciliation and balancing of programs intended for each situation.

—Forecasting long-run trends and planning for adjustment to them both in the size and quality of the labor force and in the economy of New York City (e.g., the growth of white-collar jobs and decline of manufacturing).

236

—Providing advisory services for employers in connection with manpower planning at the enterprise level, which includes personnel policies (especially with regard to educational qualifications and racial or other discrimination), labor utilization, increasing of labor productivity, location of facilities, recruitment, dismissals, labor shortages, on-the-job training.

—Obtaining advance notice of large-scale dismissals, whether due to adverse business conditions or a decision to move out of the city. Special assistance to firms and individuals in such cases.

—Providing information, guidance, testing, placement, training, job-creation services to job seekers and jobholders.

—Undertaking efforts to locate jobs in the suburbs, to relocate workers, and to provide inexpensive transportation to the suburbs.

—Conducting studies regarding work attitudes and satisfactions; attempting to enhance job status and pay in low-level jobs.

To carry out the functions described above, manpower officials require information, defined general policies, specific programs, coordination among the concerned agencies, and machinery for executing and enforcing programs. How well does New York City measure up to this standard?

In New York City there are three main contenders for the role of chief manpower agency, a situation which hints at less than perfect administrative arrangements. The three agencies are: the New York State Employment Service, the Human Resources Administration of New York City, and the Manpower and Career Development Agency, a subdivision of the Human Resources Administration. None does the job completely. Indeed, all three combined do not perform all the reqired tasks.

In an ideal world, New York City would not have established a manpower agency independent of the State Employment Service. Preferably, the city manpower agency would be part of a national manpower organization which would have branches at the state, area (inter- or intrastate), and local levels. This form of organization need not negate the city's initiative, influence, or administrative power. In several European countries, the manpower agency is comprised of both a strong national organization and local units which operate with their own staffs under supervised autonomy. Such countries generally have more successful programs than those which use central government employees at all levels, including the local.

In a complicated economy which does not respect political boundaries, an independent city manpower agency operates at a disadvantage. But in the United States, there has been inadequate manpower organization at higher levels of government, and the cities have had no choice but to create independent bodies.

The Employment Service has not become the manpower agency in New York City because it did not adjust rapidly or completely enough to the new directions and imperatives. In particular, the demand for more services for the disadvantaged was not met in a fashion which satisfied the antipoverty movement. For example, it has not established suboffices in the poverty neighborhoods and has declined to send its employees to storefront offices which lack amenities. It has made special efforts to aid the disadvantaged within its traditional modes of operation, but these have been insufficient because of the prevailing social mood.

Only a few countries have been able to bring about major transformations in their manpower programs without creating new organizations. Two types of countries can be distinguished: those where new programs can be implemented through existing administrative structures and personnel, and those where the interests and programs of entrenched agencies defy attempts to introduce new ways and thus the only remedy is to establish a new and sometimes competing agency. The United States and its political subdivisions usually fall in the latter class. This is unfortunate, because the countries which have adapted without duplicating agencies seem to have superior performance records.

The city's alternative to the State Employment Service has been the Human Resources Administration (HRA), a superagency consisting of five agencies and one department with seven major subdivisions. In addition to the Manpower and Career Development Agency (MCDA), the HRA encompasses the Addiction Services Agency, the Agency for Child Development, the Community Development Agency, and the Youth Services Agency. To these is added the Department of Social Services, which supervises programs for income maintenance, employment, food stamps, medical services, special services for adults, special services for children, and community social services. While many of these programs are not unrelated to manpower issues, they primarily serve people who temporarily or permanently are out of the labor market. To the extent that there is an overlap of interests between MCDA and HRA's other programs, coordination could as easily be achieved by interagency relationships as by a superagency. HRA seems less suitable than its subsidiary MCDA to be the city's manpower authority.

The failure to establish a broad scope and independent role for the Manpower and Career Development Agency may be attributed to several factors: a genuine conviction on the part of the officialdom that the disadvantaged are the proper and only clientele; community pressures which lean in the same direction; the influence of federal and state fundings and programs; and the prior claims of the State Employment Service to serve the larger public.

Concentrating on aiding the disadvantaged, particularly those from minority groups, the Manpower and Career Development Agency has not created the image of a strong manpower authority with comprehensive coverage and interests. All 4.5 million people who work or seek work in New York City should be the concern of a manpower agency, although special interest and programmatic emphasis still might be directed toward the disadvantaged.

It has been a European criticism of American manpower programs that they have not moved from their initial concern for the disadvantaged to a broad, integrated approach, and New York City is no exception in this regard. Effective, sustained programs for the disadvantaged cannot be developed in New York City without the reinforcement of a general manpower policy which encompasses the entire labor force and the whole economy of the city and its environs.

Looking ahead, it appears doubtful that New York City will

soon scrap its own manpower agencies. Nor has the State Employment Service given evidence that it could fill this gap and also
carry out the other responsibilities that a proper city manpower
authority should exercise. Since the possibility of establishing
one manpower agency in New York City seems remote at this
time, the challenge is to divide the tasks among the existing agencies and to establish responsive and responsible cooperation
among the various federal, state, and city agencies which operate
in the manpower field. At the same time, the Manpower and
Career Development Agency should be strengthened and broadened so that it has the primary role in manpower planning and
programming in the New York City administration.

Perhaps all placement functions eventually should be trans-
ferred to the State Employment Service's city offices, suitably
enlarged and restructured. The most favorable arrangement
would detach the State Employment Service offices located in
New York City and make a separate unit of them; they would
have an organizational connection with both the State Employment Service and the city manpower agency. To reconcile differences of policy and operations, a representative of the State
Employment Service would be in the top councils of the city manpower agency and a representative from the city Employment
Service would have a similar position on the state body. This is
the model followed in Sweden, and as it functions in the largest
city, Stockholm, it seems a viable arrangement.

Surely all the many public vocational training activities in the
city should be centralized and coordinated through the city manpower agency, but the reality today is far from this model. Any
research and forecasting service that a broadened city manpower
agency might establish should take full advantage of the excellent
regional office of the Bureau of Labor Statistics and its research,
as well as the research capacity of relevant state agencies. With
some care, the wastes of duplicated agencies can be held to a
minimum.

In addition to a reallocation of tasks and better cooperation
among the manpower agencies, improvement in internal operations should be sought. One of the key questions is the role of
management, labor, and community organizations in the man-

power agency. Abroad, in countries where the manpower agency is not located in a government department but has a quasi-independent status, it has been found useful to include representatives of labor and management in the active executive; the direct participation of these groups has been a distinct asset to operations in Sweden, Norway, and West Germany.

In other countries the manpower agency, organized under a government department, uses these interest groups in an advisory capacity at all levels. Community organization is not well developed in Europe, and these groups have not yet achieved adequate representation. Another approach is to recruit persons with industry and union experience to work for the manpower agency, especially in those aspects of its operations which involve direct dealing with employers and workers.

To recruit effective personnel for the manpower agency, it is desirable that the jobs have social acceptance and status, that salary levels be attractive relative to other available jobs, that the leadership of the agency be strong, and that the educational standards for recruitment be related to the actual requirements of the job. In-service training courses and institutes can remedy deficiencies of formal education and add specific job skills. Personnel assignments should be characterized by flexibility and mobility, including ready transfers of staff among the various local offices, so that special short-term personnel requirements can be met without an increase in total staff.

The relationships of a city manpower agency with other bodies determine to a large extent whether it can carry out its mission. It is evident that the city manpower agency must maintain close and satisfactory connections with the state and federal agencies from which the funds flow. Other links may be required with these levels of government as well as with the political subdivisions surrounding New York City. These are the suburbs from which many jobholders come into the city and in which some city residents, especially minority workers, look for blue-collar jobs. As Westchester, Nassau, Suffolk, and Rockland Counties, as well as northern New Jersey and southern Connecticut, develop and expand their agencies, the job of achieving coordination can be simplified.

In any event, some means of communication should be maintained with responsible officials in these peripheral labor markets. The political boundaries of New York City are too large to incorporate a single labor market, but the multiple labor markets do not necessarily end at the city's boundary lines. Therefore, the political view of New York City's jurisdictional lines must be replaced in the manpower field by a regional approach. Of course, the vast majority of New York City's labor force will continue to consist of residents, and only a fraction of the city's working population will seek jobs outside the five boroughs.

The most significant linkages to be forged are those with other departments of the city government. Many of these departments are involved in activities affecting the quantity and quality of the labor supply, such as the board of education and the board of higher education. In addition, municipal government agencies are a most important source of jobs. In 1969, local government showed the fastest job growth in New York City, followed by the securities and banking industries, business services, medical services, and educational services.[1] Therefore, the manpower agency must maintain close relations with other municipal authorities from the viewpoint of both supply and demand.

There are several different institutional situations in which persons under the primary jurisdiction of a department of the city government may prepare for entry or reentry into the labor market and thus need the services of the manpower authorities. The most common institutions are schools, prisons or probation, hospitals and nursing homes, rehabilitation institutes, sheltered workshops, special schools, programs for addicts or alcoholics, welfare rolls. Even when the institutions or programs are run by private or nonprofit organizations, some city department may have administrative relationships with the organization which would permit the manpower agency to make its contribution. Direct negotiations with private and nonprofit groups should be initiated by the manpower agency if they cannot be reached through the established governmental channel.

Two main kinds of influence can be exerted by the manpower authorities. They can help institutions under the supervision of other city government departments to use work orientation and exposure to work situations as a part of their regular procedures. And the manpower agency can give specific assistance to individuals who are about to leave the institutions and wish to enter or reenter the work world. Whether the individual is a recent school leaver, a prisoner about to be released, or a person on welfare deemed employable, the manpower agency can provide occupational guidance and information, specific local labor market information, aptitude and work tests, placement in jobs and follow-up, and, where appropriate, referrals to specifically created jobs. Of course, the manpower agency should play a key role in the planning and administration of such jobs.

It is apparent that a program such as this calls for substantial change and cooperation on the part of other city government departments so that they will seek and accept the manpower agency's advice or intervention. For example, it may be a very slow process to enable the high schools to recognize and assist the large number of students who cannot or should not undertake higher education and who therefore need vocational preparation, information, and guidance while still in the high school. It should be borne in mind that many graduates of even junior and senior colleges, having had only a general education, are at a disadvantage when they arrive in the job market and that many of them would benefit from training courses which are shorter and less arduous than professional or postgraduate work, but which provide specific skills.

As long as any of New York City's youth obtain a high school education or less, the schools must be concerned with relating them to the labor market. Fortunately, the projections of the labor market for the 1970s for New York City show that 75 percent of the jobs will require no more than a high school education; this is due to the importance of replacements for workers in existing jobs. Those who focus only on the fields where the total number of jobs is expanding place undue stress on the need for higher educational attainment. But this is misleading because the actual job vacancies still call for large numbers of male blue-collar and service workers and female office workers and sales persons.[2]

The youth work situation in New York City is difficult and unlike that in Western Europe in two important respects: Vacancies for young people in New York do not usually exceed the number of unemployed; and alternatives to work exist in the New York poverty areas to a degree unknown in, say, the London slums, where illegal activities are generally undertaken after working hours, except by the very small group which rejects work entirely.[3]

Among the needs of New York City high schools are: work/study programs for those who lack academic interests; business, technical, and vocational education which is respected and relevant and which draws employers into every aspect of the curriculum; free post–high school technical courses for those not enrolled in a junior college, competing with the fraudulent or expensive private courses; counselors dedicated to helping high school students go on to work; relating the basic literacy skills to the clerical jobs that many girls, black girls in particular, will hold in New York City.

The schools should draw in as visitors to classrooms and assemblies those employers who say that they are contemplating leaving New York City in part because of the inadequate quality of the city's high school graduates as office and clerical workers. The success reported by industry programs to improve literacy should be studied, and their methods should provide a model for the high schools. Those who think that it is difficult to prepare high school girls for New York City's demanding office jobs should reflect on the fact that in Belgium it is considered a virtual necessity that girls seeking office jobs be fluent in two, preferably three, languages!

It should be possible to bring to New York City's schools some of the basic attitudes which prevail in Western Europe. The head of an English school whose 15- to 16-year-old boys generally leave school for jobs said recently:

> A school is very much part of society, and as such has a responsibility to prepare its pupils for the world of work. If it neglects this responsibility it fails not only society but also its pupils. Boys may then be unemployed, employed below capacity, become irresponsible or be completely baffled by the pattern of work relationships and values.[4]

The specific measures taken to prepare "pupils for the world of work" need not conflict with the demand, so prominent in the United States, for constantly higher levels of educational achievement. To aid those with the desire and ability to undertake higher education is not inconsistent with giving a different kind of assistance and direction to those who dislike or fail at academic education and prefer to begin to work.

This extended discussion of the New York City schools is prompted by the large number of potential labor market entrants and the excessively academic orientation of the schools. However, other New York City institutions also prepare their clients inadequately for the labor market. Some, limited by lack of funds and staff, would be happy to institute the preparation-for-work programs found in the most advanced institutions in the country. However, other municipal institutions which may accept and implement suggestions by the manpower agency to increase and improve internal manpower-related programs still may be unreceptive to efforts of the manpower agency to use outreach methods within these institutions on behalf of individuals soon to depart. The manpower agency must prove itself before it can insist on the privilege of working within the institutions; it must have a great deal to offer which is not to be obtained elsewhere.

A useful method of conducting this type of outreach is through the "contact man," as the Swedish manpower authorities call their officials who devote their time to work within institutions among individuals soon to be released. An intimate knowledge of individual institutions is also useful for the manpower agency in its efforts to help members of the labor force who need referrals to remedial treatment of some kind. Of course, the community-based outreach efforts which have been directed toward individuals, apart from their institutional connections, should be continued by the New York City manpower agency.

Much of the good which a manpower agency can do along these lines rests on the willingness of employers to work directly with the institutions concerned. The manpower agency is the broker in the relationship, and its success depends on the extent to which employers accept the fact that they have a role to play in the development of the quality of the labor supply. This has not been a strong point with American employers as a whole, and much less with New York City employers, who are characteristically engaged in small-scale and marginal operations.

Among the additional tasks of a manpower agency are negotiations with other municipal departments which deal with such matters as the amount and location of low-income housing or the allocation of industrial space. These policies have indirect connections with the employment and well-being of the labor force and should not be regarded as extraneous. It is the duty of the manpower agency to intervene in all municipal decision making which has any bearing on the labor force.

If what has been reported above seems too expensive to implement or too visionary to accept, let it be noted that manpower agencies in a number of countries have done this much and more.

14

HUMAN RESOURCES PLANNING

Alfred Eichner

IF THIS ESSAY WERE NOT a chapter in a larger work, it would be best entitled "What to Do about a Market That Is Not a Market." This title is appropriate because the analysis of what has come to be known as the urban "labor market" is complicated by two factors. The first is that the process by which individuals obtain long-term employment corresponds to the theoretical construct of a market only superficially. The second is that the urban milieu is one in which the immobility of land further distorts the pattern of resource use. An understanding of both these complications is essential if the functioning of what is termed the urban labor market is to be improved through public policy.

The essay which follows falls into three main parts. The first indicates the critical characteristics of an equilibrating market mechanism which are missing from the process by which individuals obtain long-term employment. The second part explains how certain trends in urban development have made the absorption of recent migrants into the permanent labor force more difficult. This part itself is divided into two sections, one describing how modernization and economic development lead to the growth of a peripheral labor force in urban communities, the other pointing out how recent changes in urban land settlement and transportation patterns have made it more difficult for members of the peripheral labor force to be absorbed into the permanent labor force. The third part of the essay suggests what limited steps an urban governing body can take to facilitate the work attachment process. It, too, is divided into two sections, one pointing out what can be done to improve the quality of the labor force, the other pointing out what can be done to assure better linkages between institutions preparing individuals for work and those which offer employment opportunities.

WHY THE "LABOR MARKET" IS A MISNOMER

Economists have found the notion of a market extremely useful in explaining how, within an economic system, goods of a certain kind and quantity come to be purchased by families. The separate influences of supply and demand can be isolated, and the process by which a balance is struck between them described in such a way that a picture of a self-regulating cybernetic mechanism emerges. For example, if too much of a particular good is produced, market demand will be insufficient to clear the market, and this will signal the firms which supply the good to reduce their prices and/or curtail output. Alternatively, if too little of a particular good is produced, shortages will develop, and this will signal firms to expand output and/or raise prices. In either case, it can be assumed that supply will adjust to the level of demand which reflects the preferences of buyers. Thus the process not only is self-regulating, it also imposes the consumer's will on the economic system insofar as quantity, if not quality, is concerned.

The temptation to treat labor services as simply another "good" which is distributed through the market process has been too great for most economists to resist—especially in the absence of a better explanation. The fact is, however, that services are not just another economic good. They represent the utilization of human competences or, more familiarly, human skills, and these competences and skills are the output of an entirely different societal system—the anthropogenic, or human development, system. This system involves different processes from those entailed in the economic system and requires a different mode of analysis.

In the most general terms, the anthropogenic system is that set of institutions, including the family and the schools, through which human competences are developed. The competences themselves encompass more than just the skills used by business firms to produce the physical goods which are the output of the economic system. They include also the skills necessary to make the political system function effectively—from the ability to distinguish between the positions of two opposing candidates for public office to the ability to build a winning electoral coalition. They include the skills essential to the anthropogenic system itself— from the ability to create a wholesome family life to the ability to provide inspirational teaching to the young. Finally, they include the skills necessary to evaluate critically the norms, or values, of the society.

These various types of competences are acquired in varying degrees by the individual as he moves along a unique developmental path, beginning with his birth into a particular family group, either nuclear, extended, or some variant thereof. The initial orientation (inculcation of values) and training (acquisition of skills) come from his family. But in any relatively developed society, the family is not likely to prove sufficient for training youngsters beyond a certain age. At some time following early childhood the individual must, either through his own efforts or those of his family, become affiliated with a more specialized developmental organization, one that can provide him with the training and experience (even the orientation) which his own family is unable to offer. Indeed, in more advanced societies, he must achieve a sequence of such affiliations. The most common type of developmental organization with which an individual is likely to become affiliated is a local, publicly supported school system. In the United States, this type of affiliation generally covers most of the early years, usually beginning at the age of 5 and continuing through the teens. It may be supplemented by private instruction —from music teachers, vocational institutes, and the like—and it may be followed by more years of college and graduate training.

The acquiring of competences does not cease, however, with the individual's departure from the formal educational system. It continues even after he is affiliated with an employing organization, whether it be a business firm or not. Indeed, most of what is commonly recognized as a skill is acquired on the job, when the generalized types of competences developed during formal schooling are adapted for particular purposes to enable the individual to carry out specific tasks. For this reason, the employing organization is as much a part of the anthropogenic system as the family and the schools.

The point is that the same organization may function as part of more than just one societal system. The business firm, when it produces goods for other groups in society, is operating as part of the economic system. By providing the various individuals affiliated with it, either as workers, creditors, or suppliers, with money which can be used to command a part of the total output of goods and services, it is also operating as part of the economic system. But when the same business firm offers employment opportunities to individuals, especially employment opportunities that will enable those individuals to enhance their previously acquired skills, it is operating as part of the anthropogenic system. What is commonly referred to as "the labor market" represents, therefore, the point at which the economic and anthropogenic systems impinge upon one another.

Of course, when the individual, in proceeding along his developmental path, first enters the labor market in a serious way—that is, seeks a job or long-term affiliation with an employing organization—the rate of money payment is likely to be one of the relevant considerations. And while this may not be the first time that affiliation with a developmental institution hinges on a pecuniary arrangement—for example, the individual or his family may previously have had to pay tuition to a private school or college—it does mark the point along the developmental path at which, as matters now stand, the payment flows are reversed. Nevertheless, in attempting to understand why affiliation with an employing organization takes place, it is a mistake to place the entire emphasis on the amount of compensation which will be paid. The reason is that both parties, the individual seeking affiliation and the organization seeking labor, are likely to attach greater importance to other factors.

For the employing organization, the more important consideration is whether the individual has the requisite competences for the job. These competences may include qualities only marginally related to the immediate demands of the position—for example, the ability of the individual to get along with fellow workers or his potential for advancing to a more responsible position. Nevertheless, they are qualities which may be critical to the effective functioning of the organization over the long run. Once satisfied that the individual has these qualities, the employing organization is likely to be willing to pay the prevailing wage in either its industry or community, depending on the relevant reference group.

For the individual seeking affiliation, the important considerations are more variable. To one whose only concern is the immediate present, the conditions of work are likely to be the critical factor—whether the job is onerous, how easily he can reach the place of employment from home, if there is opportunity for social intercourse, etc. For one with a longer time perspective, security of employment is likely to be at least as important as, if not more than, these other aspects of the job. Finally, to one with professional or career ambitions, it is the additional opportunities to which the job may lead—the higher or more responsible positions for which it enables the individual to qualify—that are likely to prove decisive.

The rate of compensation is, of course, important. But if there is a proper articulation between the anthropogenic and other major societal systems so that the impact of the former is balanced with the demand for competences throughout the society and equivalent wages are earned in comparable types of positions, the affiliation decision is likely to depend on factors other than money.

If there is not proper articulation between the anthropogenic and other major societal systems, what is now often referred to as a manpower problem will arise. A sudden expansion of demand in a particular sector of the economy requiring labor of a highly specialized and/or sophisticated sort is one way in which an imbalance between the supply from the anthropogenic system and the manpower demands of the other systems can occur. A technological innovation, such as the development of the computer, or a shift in governmental priorities, such as the establishment of Medicare and the space programs, may be the cause of a sudden shortage of trained personnel. In either case, one can expect that the rates of compensation for the required types of labor will rise in a manner that suggests the impersonal working of the theoretical labor market. And this rise in relative rates of compensation will serve an important purpose; it will signal the anthropogenic system to increase its outflow of persons with the required competences. With the highly developed anthropogenic system that exists in the United States, the response will in fact be prompt, as the recent increase in computer programmers and space technicians attests. Only the gestation period required to produce the skills—or the artificial restraints imposed on new entrants by those already in the field—will cause any time lag, as the recent experience with health personnel indicates.

The other way in which the outflow from the anthropogenic system and the manpower demands of the other societal systems become unbalanced, thereby creating a manpower problem, is when the other systems cannot absorb the entire output of the anthropogenic system. Unfortunately, this is the more typical condition. Cyclical downturns in economic activity dramatically compound the problem, but the situation is actually chronic in the United States, and probably in other developed countries. Moreover, in this case, lowering the rates of compensation which employing organizations are prepared to offer is unlikely to correct the problem.

MODERNIZATION AND THE PERIPHERAL LABOR FORCE

The situation is chronic not because of any inherent defect in "capitalism," or whatever other word is used to describe a modern, technologically advanced economic system, but rather because of the system's superiority, and particularly because of its ability to provide a higher standard of living. This success has the effect of attracting persons from traditional, preindustrial societies—and even from the more backward parts of the advanced society—and consequently the economic system must absorb not only the outflow from its own anthropogenic system but also the migrants from less-developed regions.

In most cases, deficiencies in orientation and in training bar these recent migrants from the jobs which offer both security and the prospects for advancement—and when these barriers are insufficient to reserve the better jobs for the progeny of the indigenous population, artificial barriers are likely to be erected. The discriminatory practices of the craft unions in the construction industry, therefore, should come as no surprise. However, apprenticeship rules are only one of the ways in which those safely ensconced within the developed society seek to protect themselves and their children from the competition of those on the outside seeking a place within.

Because of the barriers to preferred employment, both natural and otherwise, which must be overcome, the movement of persons out of traditional, preindustrial societies is likely to take place in at least two stages. The first is the actual, physical relocation of the migrants from the countryside to the city, where they then become part of what is termed the peripheral labor force. The peripheral labor force consists of workers whose background and training are so deficient that they can qualify only for the marginal jobs in society—those which offer a minimum wage, which hold out little or no hope of promotion, and which may terminate at any time. Gradually, as the migrants acquire more skills and, more important, become better oriented to the world of work and the urban milieu in general, they begin to qualify for the second stage—absorption into the permanent labor force. This consists of workers who hold full-time jobs, jobs which offer security, which follow a well-defined career ladder, however humble the career may be, and for which the pay is likely to rise with the general standard of living. Usually, because of the gap in the two cultures, a shift to the permanent labor force can be accomplished only intergenerationally.

It is to the members of the peripheral labor force that the theoretical construct of a labor market has its greatest applicability. In the first place, unskilled labor is more of a homogeneous input than the various competences found among the members of the permanent labor force. There is, therefore, greater interchangeability of personnel and, as a result, greater competition among the members of the peripheral labor force for the jobs available to them. In the second place, there are not the institutions, such as trade unions, which insulate the members of the permanent labor force from market pressures. Finally, the existence of many workers in rural areas who need only slight encouragement to move from the countryside to the city assures that the supply of labor—at least within the peripheral labor force—will be responsive to any increased demand for manpower. Since the peripheral labor force includes, besides migrants from rural areas, youths who have somehow fallen between the cracks of the anthropogenic system and mothers who are no longer fully occupied by their child-rearing duties, it can in fact respond quite rapidly to an increase in the demand for manpower.

Unfortunately, when the demand for manpower falls off, the peripheral labor force is less capable of adjusting. The migrant from the countryside will not immediately return home from the city. Indeed, between the excitement which the city has to offer and the dearth of opportunity in the region from which he has fled, the migrant may not return home at all. Similarly, the youth and the mother, once attracted into the labor force, will be reluctant to leave it. The result is that when the economic system fails to expand and the demand for manpower is curtailed, the unemployed portion of the peripheral labor force will swell. The peripheral labor force, then, serves as a buffer, protecting the anthropogenic system from the main shock of reduced economic activity. Still, the anthropogenic system is not likely to escape entirely unbuffeted. A certain proportion of its graduates, instead of obtaining the employment opportunities they had anticipated, will probably have to settle for less-attractive positions or even go without a job.

Now if there were something similar to the equilibrating mechanism of a market at this interface between the anthropogenic and economic systems, this swelling of the numbers of unemployed members of the peripheral labor force during a recession would lead to a self-correcting response—as it does when, alternatively, the demand for manpower increases. But in fact, since the outflow from the anthropogenic system is geared to the life cycle of the individual, and not the business cycle of the economic system, the adjustment can hardly be expected to come from the economic side. Indeed, as noted above, withdrawal from the peripheral labor force is always slow and halting. The notion of a labor market, however, implies a feedback into the economic system itself which will produce the necessary corrective action. It is here, then, that a need for an equilibrating mechanism is most felt.

Theoretically, an increase in the number of unemployed and unskilled workers would lead to a reduction in the rates of compensation which the members of the peripheral labor force are willing to accept, which would then enable employing organizations to hire additional workers. In practice, it may well be that a swelling of the unemployed ranks will force the members of the peripheral labor force to accept a lower rate of compensation— although with wages already close to the minimum level, there is not much room for downward adjustment. But it simply is not true that a reduction in the rates of compensation will increase the number of employment opportunities. The number of employment opportunities can be increased only through aggregate economic policies. This is the basic point which Keynes sought to demonstrate more than thirty years ago. The essential feedback mechanism from the peripheral labor force to the economic system does not exist.

Of course, from the perspective of the economic system, no problem exists. Business firms will be rid of the burden of having to pay for unneeded labor. To this extent, something resembling a labor market appears to be working. But from the perspective of the anthropogenic system, it will be clear that the problem has been exacerbated. The number of persons placed in the limbo of the peripheral labor force and, even more significantly, in the hades of its unemployed core, will be increased. Even if some of these persons eventually escape back into the protected environs of the anthropogenic system, by returning home or to school, this means that the problem is being covered over. The essential fact is that, after a certain point in the development path of an individual, further competence can be acquired only through actual work experience. When that work experience is not available, the individual's skills stagnate and eventually atrophy.

The problem is especially acute for the recent migrant from the countryside. With little formal schooling, a job is the only means through which he can acquire competence, and even more important, a better orientation to the urban milieu. Without a job, there is little chance of his being integrated into the alien society to which he has migrated, while the inability to provide for the material needs of his family may create unmanageable tensions within the connubial circle. Thus what begins in one generation as a manpower problem on the demand side may well become, in another generation, a manpower problem on the supply side as the breakdown of family structure deprives the offspring of a better chance in life. The recent migrant, like the other members of the peripheral labor force, has little control over his employment prospects. Because of the rush of others to enjoy the putative benefits of the urban life, his prospects will be marginal at best. But when this more chronic manpower problem is compounded by a cyclical downturn in economic activity, the employment prospects of unskilled migrants may well become nil.

The only way to solve the manpower problem created when the outflow from the anthropogenic system is too large to be absorbed by the other major societal systems is to step up the rate of expansion of those other systems, the economic system in particular. It is only in this way, and not through a reduction in the rates of compensation which employing organizations are required to pay, that migrants recently arrived from the countryside can be more quickly absorbed into the permanent labor force and the size of the peripheral labor force kept from swelling. Indeed, it is the question of how to integrate these rural migrants into the permanent labor force of an industrial society, with the degree of orientation and the level of skill thereby implied, that constitutes the "urban problem" in its broadest sense. Much of human history for the past 400 years has revolved around this question, and the final outcome, as the present travails of the less-developed countries indicate, remains to be recorded.

The Changing Urban Milieu

Still, when someone speaks of the "urban crisis" in the United States today, he probably has something else in mind. He likely is referring to the plight of the American cities, including New York. This plight is, of course, not unconnected to the migration from the countryside. But it goes beyond that phenomenon to encompass the decay of the inner city, the breakdown of municipal services, and the growing estrangement between those trapped in ghetto enclaves within the city and those who have escaped to the surrounding ring of suburban communities. These various elements in the contemporary urban pathology serve to impair the process by which individuals obtain long-term employment, and each can be traced in one way or another to the peculiar characteristics of the resource that makes the city a separate and distinctive unit of study.

That resource is, of course, land. Each city is likely to have come into being because the land upon which it is located was deemed at one time to offer unique locational advantages. If it is to remain viable, the city must continue to offer those or other locational advantages. As an economic resource, however, urban land has certain peculiar characteristics. For one thing, it cannot reproduce itself. Humans may beget other humans, and machines other machines, but the amount of surface area is immutably fixed. Underwater areas may be filled in and buildings increased in height to exploit the vertical dimension, but these expedients face an asymptotic limit—the amount of land area falling within the urban boundary. That boundary can be expanded outward through the appropriate investment in transportation, but in this direction another asymptotic limit is likely to be encountered— that imposed by the traveling times possible with the existing state of transportation technology.

The effect of all this is that, to conserve the scarce land resource, large numbers of people must be concentrated within a relatively small area. It is concentration of people, in fact, which sets the urban community apart from the rural landscape. And it leads to a second peculiar characteristic of urban land, its tendency to produce external, or neighborhood, effects. Because people in the urban community live in such close proximity to one another, they are likely to be significantly affected by their neighbors' actions, particularly by the use those neighbors make of the land which they control. If one house on a block is allowed to deteriorate, the block will be a less pleasant street on which to live. In the vast expanse of the rural landscape, however, one deteriorated structure is not likely to be noticed.

A third peculiar characteristic of urban land pertains to the structures likely to be erected upon it. To avoid danger to neighbors, urban buildings must be substantial ones, with strong skeletons and virtually indestructible outer skins. Consequently, once a building is placed on a plot of urban land, it is likely to remain there for many years. The relative permanence of structures, together with the neighborhood effect, make it difficult to alter the pattern of urban land use. All three of these peculiar characteristics, it should be noted, distinguish urban land, like labor services, from other types of economic resources. When to these peculiar characteristics of urban land are added the two historical factors which have complicated the recent vast migration from the countryside, the present urban crisis in the United States is not hard to understand. Those two complicating historical factors are, one, rapid technological change, and two, the confrontation with America's legacy of slavery and discrimination.

The effect of the technological change has been to make the nineteenth-century city, both the types of living quarters which it provided and the types of manufacturing establishments it boasted, obsolete. The children of the city's older inhabitants, fortified by the higher incomes which economic progress has made possible, have in general sought more spacious dwellings on the periphery, dwellings that more readily lend themselves to the evolving household appliance technology. With the spread of the highway network, supplementing the earlier railroad spokes, it has been possible for large numbers of exurbanites to live in large homes in the uncluttered countryside even while retaining their jobs in the city's Central Business District. Manufacturing firms, meanwhile, requiring more land on which to enclose their horizontal, flow-through processes, have followed a path of their own to the suburbs with the highway network making it possible to secure a labor force.

The housing stock deserted by the children of the city's older inhabitants, instead of being torn down to make way for better utilization of the land, has been taken over by the recent migrants from the countryside. The process has been a slow one, but no less insidious for that reason. To compete in the marketplace for the available housing, the migrants have been forced to double up and triple up, and thus pay rents at a level which, under private ownership, still warrants continued use of the land for residential purposes. The higher densities have, in turn, accelerated the physical deterioration of the housing stock, but this added cost has been reflected not so much in the rents paid as in the squalid surroundings which the migrants must bear.

Because of the neighborhood effects, community decline, once it passes beyond a certain point, is all but impossible to arrest. A slippage in the maintenance of one or two buildings on a block makes the street a less desirable one on which to live. This adds a push to the pull of the open spaces and newer structures which attract middle-class families to the suburbs. If the homes which they leave behind can be filled only by recent migrants from the countryside—an economic arrangement made possible both by the willingness of the recent migrants to accept less living space and by the depreciated property values—the process of community decline is set on its irreversible path. Racial animosities and unwarranted fears, to the extent they exist, further expedite the flight from the inner city, leaving the older housing stock in the hands of the recent migrants from the countryside. The only exceptions are likely to be in areas contiguous to the Central Business District which, if the business district should expand, will be taken over for commercial purposes.

By itself, this capture of the older housing stock by recent migrants from the countryside would not be serious. The same process has, after all, occurred continuously throughout the history of the city. What makes the current situation different is that the type of economic activity which in the past offered recent migrants their main source of expanding employment opportunities is no longer located primarily in the city. Moreover, the transportation system, built to serve the needs of an earlier era, cannot be used to take the migrants to where many of those expanding employment opportunities are found—in the suburbs.

It is there, on the periphery of the city, that new manufacturing plants are being built. The manufacturing activity which remains in the city is likely to be marginal—offering lower wages and little hope of advancement to something better. It is the counterpart of the deteriorated housing stock which the recent migrants have inherited. To the extent that the city continues to have a viable economic base, it consists primarily of tertiary activities— for example, central office management, insurance, finance, and government—which require, not the unskilled labor of the recent migrants, but the high-level competences of the educational system's graduates.

To reach the suburbs where the better jobs in manufacturing are found is usually not possible with the existing modes of public transportation, and when it is possible, it is too expensive, in both time and money, to make it worthwhile. The present public transportation system is largely a leftover from another age. Many of the bus lines follow routes originally laid out for horse-drawn cars and later electric trolleys. This system provides reasonable access to various points within the city, but little or no access to the suburbs. Of course, commuter trains, supplemented by bus lines, bring many of the persons who live in the suburbs to work each morning and take them home at night. This commuting network is, however, ill-suited to the needs of the inner-city resident who tries to reach a place of work in one of the surrounding communities. For one thing, the scheduling of service is geared to the needs of the reverse flow, and any inner-city resident who tries to travel in the opposite direction during the twice daily rush hour may find himself forced to wait long intervals for the right bus or train—especially since express service is often lacking in that direction. Furthermore, the fares are based on the higher incomes earned by those with jobs in the Central Business District, and not on the incomes of those who hope to find semiskilled jobs in the suburbs. Finally, the inner-city resident usually does not have one of the critical links in the commuting network—the private automobile.

The suburban commuter, even if he takes public transportation into the city each day, may still have to drive his own automobile to the train station or bus stop, since there is very little public transportation to cover the first leg of the journey—from home to commuter line. For the inner-city resident trying to reach a place of work in the suburbs, this is, of course, the final leg of the journey. Frequently, when he steps off the commuter train or bus, he is still quite a distance from the factory or plant.

Underlying the urban crisis in the United States today, then, is the fact that recent migrants from the countryside have flocked to the inner cities, there to take over the low-paying jobs and housing stock abandoned by the children of another generation's immigrants, only to find themselves handicapped in the quest for better jobs by educational and transportation barriers. The discriminatory housing practices which make it all but impossible for ethnic minorities and low-income inner-city residents to relocate in the suburbs where the employment opportunities are greater complete this broad-brush picture. Thus, to the skill and orientation deficiencies which have always acted to impede the transition of recent migrants from the peripheral to the permanent labor force must now be added a new factor, the inner-city–suburban dichotomy.

IMPROVING THE ANTHROPOGENIC SYSTEM

What room for maneuvering does this leave the government of an inner city, genuinely concerned with improving the welfare of the migrants trapped within its ghetto communities? A partial answer, pertaining to the economic policies which are best pursued, has been suggested in an essay in a previous Conservation of Human Resources volume, *Manpower Strategy for the Metropolis*.[1] There it was argued that what the inner city, acting alone, can do is secondary to what national and state governments must do. The primary need, within the economic sphere, is for housing and transportation programs that will enable large numbers of the recent migrants to relocate on the periphery of the city. The optimum strategy involves the coordinated construction of new towns in the surrounding outer belt and of rapid transit links to and from the urban core. In accomplishing these goals, the inner-city government, because of its limited jurisdiction, can be expected to play only an advocate's role. Its role is critical, however, in ensuring that land usage within the city's boundaries is continuously upgraded, through condemnation and foreclosure if necessary (supplemented by satisfactory relocation programs), to assure that the city remains economically viable and thus able to offer the range of services which, among other things, will facilitate the adaptation of the recent migrants and their children to the urban milieu. In the remaining part of this essay, the emphasis will be on the role which the inner-city government should play with respect to the purely manpower aspects of the problem, that is, with respect to the process by which the outflow from the anthropogenic system is absorbed by the economic system. It is the outcome of this process which is often termed, not completely accurately, the urban labor market.

To understand how a local government can play a constructive role in this process, intervening to increase the chances of an individual to obtain the type of affiliation with an employing organization that will remove him from the peripheral labor force, it is necessary to return to the analysis of the developmental path which is unique to each individual. The purpose of this exercise is to indicate which factors determine whether an individual takes one or another fork along that path, and particularly which of those factors a local government can influence. Here, too, it will turn out that what the inner city, acting alone, can do is supplementary to what the national government must do—but no less important. What the local government can do is to ensure that those who graduate from its educational institutions have the minimum amount of competence necessary for affiliation with an organization at the next higher level of development. As a further step, it can even assist those graduates in making the transition from a developmental to a manpower-utilizing institution, thereby placing them firmly on a career ladder. Only the national government, however, can ensure that the economic system expands at a rate sufficient to provide employment opportunities for all who emerge from the anthropogenic system.

The individual's progress along a developmental path depends on the types of organization, both anthropogenic and manpower-utilizing, with which he is able to achieve affiliation at each successive fork along that path. For example, entering a vocational high school will reduce his chances of going to college; successfully completing an Ivy League law school, on the other hand, will increase his chances of eventually becoming a partner in a Wall Street law firm. And becoming a partner in a Wall Street law firm will increase his chances of becoming either a director of a corporation or a Cabinet officer.

During his early years the individual has little control over the particular anthropogenic organization with which he will be affiliated. This is especially true of the child with low-income parents. For him the public educational system, with assignment to a school based on residence, is the only real possibility. But income is not the only factor that influences movement along the development path. Since the young child is incapable of making an intelligent choice it is incumbent upon those who make the affiliation decisions for him to act in such a way as to foreclose as few of his later options in life as possible.

On the face of it, the public education system seems to place no limits on how far an individual can go. Free schooling has long been provided from kindergarten through high school and now, with Head Start programs and open college admissions, the period of subsidized learning is being extended at both ends. Enabling an individual to attend school is not the same thing, however, as bringing his skills up to a certain level. A child may sit in class, yet learn nothing. This is an important point, because affiliation with an anthropogenic or manpower-utilizing organization at the next fork along the developmental path may well depend on whether a certain level of competence has been acquired. Even if promotion within the public school system itself is automatic, the youngster, unable to benefit from the classroom, may decide at some point to drop out. Should he decide to stay in school and eventually receive a high school diploma, he may find that, because of his reading or mathematical deficiencies, no college or employing organization will open its doors to him. The educational system may fail in ways that are not immediately obvious and for reasons that are not easily separated out from the past train of events.

Such failure should come as no surprise. It is inherent in any type of human activity. But it is essential to recognize this probability and then to determine how the anthropogenic system, or that portion of it which is susceptible to government intervention, can be redesigned to minimize the incidence of failure.

The educational segment of the anthropogenic system is intricate, involving as it does the sequential movement of individuals from one grade level to the next, with the ability to perform at any given level dependent on success at all the previous levels. Each of these grade levels can be considered a separate component of a single, complex system. So far, efforts to improve the success rate of the educational system as a whole have focused either on reducing the probability of failure at each grade level—for example, through the more intensive commitment of resources as in the More Effective Schools program in New York City—or on lengthening the entire chain—as in the Head Start program. In other words, all the efforts have been directed toward improving the reliability of the individual components and augmenting their number.

As cybernetic theory indicates, this is a faulty strategy. In any complex system, the greater the number of components, each with its own probability of failure, the greater is the probability of failure of the system as a whole. Improving the reliability of any one component scarcely affects the success of the overall system. The better strategy is to provide back-up services for the components which have the greatest probability of failure and which play the most critical role in eventual success. It is only in this way that the reliability of the system qua system can be significantly improved.

The back-up services within the New York City educational system, as in most educational systems throughout the United States, are an uncertain thing. There is little assurance, for example, that a child with a reading problem will, if it is detected, receive the remedial help he needs. Yet failure to maintain a certain rate of reading growth will certainly hinder the child throughout the rest of his life. The lack of resources committed to these back-up services is only part of the problem. Even more to be criticized is the way in which these services are organized and coordinated. No one within the educational system is directly responsible for seeing that the lagging child receives special assistance, and thus no one can be held fully accountable when the child eventually drops out of school.

Educational back-up services are only one type of back-up service that is needed, however, to improve the reliability of the overall anthropogenic system. Even with the best of educational back-up services the child may fail to develop a minimal level of competence; the reason most often is that the family, as the primary developmental institution, has in some way failed him—by not providing sufficiently for his material or emotional needs. As numerous studies of education have pointed out, including the noted Coleman Report,[2] family background is the single most important variable affecting the child's likely success in school. What are required, then, even more than educational back-up services, are family back-up services. The present systems of welfare, child placement, and mental health are most inadequate. Indeed, it is an exaggeration to view them as part of an integral family back-up system. Services, when available, are not necessarily directed toward improving the functioning of the family; they are likely, in any case, to be splintered among different agencies and poorly coordinated.

Thus the first and most important task for city government, sincerely concerned with enhancing the life chances of those entering the labor force, is to see that the educational system's rate of failure is reduced. And the key to accomplishing this is the better provision of educational and family back-up services. Not only must the amount and variety of such services be augmented, but, even more important, they must be reorganized into overall systems capable of responding quickly and automatically when the need arises. It is much easier to correct a reading deficiency or a family problem when a youngster is 8 years old than when he is 16. If the deficiency or problem is not adequately dealt with soon after it manifests itself, the individual is likely to emerge from school without the competence necessary to qualify for satisfying career employment.

BETTER LINKAGES TO THE WORLD OF WORK

As a further step toward enhancing the life chances of those entering the labor force, city government can also attempt to create a more structured linkage between the anthropogenic and economic systems, especially for those who, without family connections, are at a disadvantage in establishing an affiliation for themselves. The city government can do this in two ways—by providing those coming out of school with employment opportunities and by assuring that those already at work for the city receive the education and training, on the job and off, necessary to qualify for careers outside the civil service. In other words, municipal employment can be used more imaginatively than at present to assure better articulation between the anthropogenic and economic systems. Given the decline in manufacturing jobs within the city's borders and the manpower needs of the businesses that have remained behind, this better articulation may well be a necessity.

The high school dropout is unattractive to a prospective employer, less because he lacks some skill critical to the job than because he does not have what the employer considers a proper work attitude or orientation. Staying in school long enough to acquire a diploma is largely testimony to the ability of the individual to get along in a system that makes unnatural demands upon him—precisely the quality required for most jobs reserved for high school graduates. This can also be said about the college dropout or the person who does not go to college at all—though here the quality sought by the prospective employer is likely to be some capacity for independent judgment. Once an individual has acquired a record of steady employment, however, fears about his orientation to work are likely to be allayed. It is for this reason that municipal employment can serve to ease the transition from school to work, especially when the school record is not a flattering one.

The City of New York hires a substantial number of new workers each year, many of them in jobs which require only minimal skills. Various public agencies which receive their funds from the municipal budget add to this figure. The annual turnover of low-level municipal and quasi-municipal employees provides a pool of employment opportunities which, if intelligently managed, can be used to place young people on career ladders that would not otherwise be open to them. To this end, however, the city's personnel policies must be altered to take into deliberate account their anthropogenic impact. Just as the government's fiscal policies can be used to stabilize the economic system, so governments' personnel policies can be used to shore up and reinforce the anthropogenic system, especially at the critical interface between it and the economic system.

In broad outline, to improve the interface between the anthropogenic and economic systems, the city must reserve a certain portion of its job openings for individuals selected by the high schools as well as through manpower-retraining programs. The positions to be created and subsidized through the Emergency Employment Act of 1971 represent an important first step in this direction. The individuals chosen would be youngsters who are unlikely to finish high school or, if they have finished high school, are unlikely to qualify for a job on their own. When these individuals are hired, they would be told that their employment is for a limited time—time enough to enable them to overcome their educational deficiencies and to qualify for employment outside the civil service. These individuals would be assigned to counselors who would advise them both of the training they need and the types of jobs for which, after employment with the city, they could expect to qualify. In this way, individuals who might otherwise be forced to join the peripheral labor force could acquire both the work experience and some of the skills which would make them attractive to employers in the private sector. At the same time, since this group of employees would continuously turn over, the program could proceed at a steady pace without swelling the city government's payroll. Indeed, since the employment would be for a limited time, there would be savings in both rates of compensation and deferred payments which could offset the costs of counseling and administration. An imaginative use of New York City and Emergency Employment Act funds would make it easier to initiate such a program.

The city government's objective in setting up such a program should be in part to set an example for other employing organizations—to show how personnel policies can be used to place individuals at the start of a career ladder rather than to allow them to languish at low-level, low-skill jobs. At the heart of the plan is the limitation placed on the time an individual can hold a particular entry job, together with the simultaneous grooming of that individual for a better position. This is a strategy which sophisticated large organizations, such as the military and large corporations, have often followed to develop new leadership from within their own ranks. The suggestion here is that the same strategy be adopted to create career patterns across organizational, and even sectoral, boundaries for individuals not normally thought of as leadership material. If such a program could be successfully implemented by city government, it might lead to imitation by other employing organizations. Indeed, there is probably no better way to assure success for the manpower-training programs now in operation by almost every large city. Manpower-training programs work best when they are directly tied in with employment.

This last point brings to mind, however, the major limitation of this as well as other efforts by city government to improve the life chances of those entering the labor force. As noted earlier, the outflow of the anthropogenic system can be absorbed only at the rate dictated by the expansion of the economic system. Because of the interrelationship between work and training, even the rate at which the anthropogenic system develops human competence is likely to depend on trends in the economy. Unfortunately, city government has virtually no control over the rate of economic expansion. This is a matter entirely in the hands of the federal government.

Still, while city government is not the master of its own economy, it should not ignore the problem; it can, in fact, be an important advocate for more vigorous expansionary policies by the federal government. Indeed, this should be its accepted and normal role. Moreover, city government can put the lie to the argument most frequently advanced against vigorous expansionary policies —that because of tight "labor markets," inflation would be accelerated. City government cannot, of course, guarantee that inflation will not follow in the wake of the expansion. But it can guarantee that the cause of the inflation will not be shortages of personnel. Moreover, it can demonstrate the validity of this position by keeping an accurate tally, preferably as an outgrowth of its efforts to improve the articulation between the anthropogenic and economic systems, of all the persons who would like a better job—or even just a job—but cannot find one. In other words, city government can serve as a gadfly, reminding the federal government that the economic system is falling short of providing jobs to all who want them.

City government can also commit itself to overcoming, through its various anthropogenic programs, whatever shortages of personnel the national government can demonstrate exist. Cooperation among governments toward achieving this end, if such a system could be developed and routinized, would improve the responsiveness of the anthropogenic system, necessarily locally centered as it is, to the national needs of the other major societal systems. If the national government can be thus prodded into adopting more vigorous expansionary policies, city government will have taken the single most important step to assure that the process by which individuals obtain long-term career employment functions adequately. Only then will what is termed the urban "labor market" function adequately.

Part IV

POLICY

15

PRECIPITATIONS

Eli Ginzberg

ALTHOUGH INITIAL ATTEMPTS have been made by Doxiades, Forrester, and others to develop dynamic models for understanding the growth, stability, and decline of urban centers, the gap between the structural and functional complexities that characterize a large city and the ability of the scholar to construct a useful model is substantial. The present effort, restricted to the labor market of a single metropolis, provides reinforcement for the proposition that the dynamics of urban development represent an order of complexity that far exceeds the ability of investigators to encompass, describe, and evaluate the multiple forces whose interaction determines whether the metropolis will grow and prosper or whether it will stagnate or decline.

Yet the only prospect of narrowing the gap between the present limited capability of the new discipline of urbanology and the horrendous complications of urban realities is to distill the principal findings from successive studies in the hope that they will provide some useful building blocks for an improved analytical model of urban development. This is the task of this penultimate chapter. We will seek to extract from each of the preceding chapters its core contribution in the hope and expectation that they will provide leads and insights for future investigators. Moreover, such a precipitation has an important secondary use. It will provide the foundation for the following and final chapter, which is addressed to policy issues—that is, the preferred actions that

different decision-making groups should undertake, on their own
or in collaboration with each other, to strengthen the manpower
resources of New York City and, in the process, to contribute to
the continuing viability of the metropolis and to the increasing
welfare of its citizens.

The first group of precipitations is drawn from the chapters
that are concerned with delineating and evaluating the parameters of New York City's economy. In the summary below we
will follow the order of the chapters and will present one central
proposition for each chapter. While this will necessarily ignore
much of interest and relevance and may occasionally extend the
analysis, it will have the virtue of calling attention to the high-
lights.

1. The economy of New York City is vital; so far, at least, it
has been able to meet the repeated challenges from ongoing
changes in the size, nature, location of domestic and international
activities with which its fortunes are linked. While the city has
not been able to maintain its relative position with respect to each
sector in which it had earlier established a leadership role, it has
repeatedly demonstrated a capacity to generate or expand in new
directions, i.e., air transportation and financial activities, while it
has retrogressed in others, i.e., manufacturing and water transportation. From the vantage of long-term perspective, the more serious challenges that New York faces are to find the capital resources with which to renew its aging infrastructure, particularly
its critically important intraurban public transportation system,
and to control the growth of illicit and illegal operations that extract a heavy toll both in economic and human terms. A metropolis
in which people are afraid to venture forth in the evening is in
jeopardy.

2. There are two major threats to the viability of a large city
such as New York. On the one hand, people and plants can move
to another city where the environment is more favorable, or they
can leave the city and relocate in the inner or outer ring within the
metropolitan area. A detailed analysis of the nation's 30 largest
cities revealed that while, with respect to certain pathologies such
as crime and per capita welfare costs, New York ranks close to the
top, it is in a preferred position with respect to many crucial in-

dices such as its unemployment rate, its ratio of nonwhite to white unemployment, and its rate of job loss to the outlying areas.

The conclusion from this comparative analysis was that much that is dysfunctional in New York City has its counterpart in the other large cities of the nation. From a competitive point of view, then, it is unlikely that New York will suffer serious losses as a result of employers' opting to locate or expand elsewhere. Moreover, some of the indices which show New York in a relatively vulnerable position, such as high welfare costs, do not foreshadow only threats. The more income the poor have to spend, the better the prospect of their rearing their children free of physical and emotional disabilities. While Phoenix and Houston, among others, have shown more rapid rates of growth, the major metropolises, Los Angeles, Chicago, Philadelphia, Detroit, do not appear to be displacing New York as the vital center of the country.

3. The conclusion that New York City is holding its own vis-a-vis its major competitors is important but not conclusive with regard to its future. Since World War II, there has been an accelerated redistribution of population and economic activity from the central cities to the suburbs, a relocation that does not appear to have exhausted its momentum. An analysis in depth reveals that the suburbs around New York City have experienced rapid growth in population (white middle class), retailing, manufacturing, and, more recently, the expansion of business and governmental services. This growth has been at least in part at the expense of the central city.

But this is only part of the story. The other part points to the fact that the inner suburbs, Westchester and Nassau, are no longer growing; that they are increasingly plagued by what were formerly thought to be exclusively city pathologies, such as crime, racial conflict, high welfare costs, and traffic jams; and that the low densities of suburban use, if continued, will slow the rate of growth in and/or increase commuting costs among home, job, and shopping centers. And if land use is altered to resemble more closely that prevailing in the city, the dysfunctional urban elements are likely to be reproduced, as is already happening, in suburbia and even exurbia. The suburbs are encountering major difficulties which redound to the advantage of the city, especially if the city acts

while it still has time to remove some of the hurdles that are inter-
fering with its renewal.

4. One of the many difficulties with urban studies is the
choice of an appropriate time perspective. If the period under
study is foreshortened, exaggerated weight may be given to transi-
tory phenomena; if focus is placed on long-term trends, important
new factors may be ignored or minimized. The preferred approach is one that will take account of long-term trends while it is
sensitive to new forces that are impinging on the city and that
will shape its future.

Hence the importance of the critical review of the manpower
record of the last two decades. This review revealed that none of
the generalizations about the city such as the erosion of its employ-
ment-generating capacity, the absence of occupational opportunities for minorities, the excessive burden of welfare, and the malfunctioning of its educational system obtain in fact. While the city
was experiencing difficulties on each of these fronts, the difficulties have been exaggerated. A reading of the manpower record for
the 1960s does not justify a pessimistic projection, although it
identified weak spots that should be attacked and remedied.

5. A key measure of the performance of a city's economy,
particularly its labor market, is whether or not it can provide jobs
for all who are able and willing to work as well as whether a
worker who conscientiously performs his duties is able to earn a
living and support his family. New York City provides the largest
number of high-paying jobs of any city in the nation, in fact, in the
world. But it also has a large number of jobs which pay so little
that a fully employed worker is not able to earn enough to support
a wife and even two children. Moreover, New York City, because
of its high rents and high service costs, is an expensive community,
except for those with the lowest incomes, which adds to the difficulties that many families face in trying to make ends meet. Most
of those who succeed have two wage earners. If a wife can supplement her husband's earnings, a family is likely to enjoy a reasonable standard of living. But families with only one wage earner,
especially if he or she is not skilled, are likely to be hard pressed.

This then is what a review of the critical parameters reveals:
New York City is very much alive although other cities and the

suburbs have been able to snip off some of its valuable assets, such as some middle- and high-income earners and blocks of attractive jobs. However, these losses have not stopped the city's growth, which has been sufficient to provide jobs and incomes for its recent in-migrants and their children. For the minority who succeed in rising to the top, New York provides high incomes; families with two wage earners are able to enjoy a reasonable standard of living. But the family with one unskilled worker is under pressure.

But the future of New York City cannot be deduced simply from a study of the foregoing parameters. Also important is an identification of central problem areas and an assessment of whether solutions are in the making. For problems that are ignored can multiply to a point where they may become intractable. A city with a large number of intractable problems will lose its capacity to grow and adjust. Its decline is foreshadowed in its failure to respond. We will therefore review the principal findings emerging from our analyses of five problems in the manpower arena.

6. The simplistic assumption is that New York and most other large American cities are doomed as desirable locales for residence and work because of the large inflows in the post–World War II period of minority group members and the flight of corresponding or larger number of white middle-class families. The tacit postulate is that blacks and Spanish-speaking minorities are undesirable, uneducated, unskilled, given to crime and violence, allergic to work, looking for welfare grants, bad workers, and bad neighbors. In light of the deeply entrenched racism that has been the curse of American experience and the confusion between caste and class, these gross judgments are not surprising even though they have little basis in fact.

A careful look at the changing role of minority groups in New York City reveals that the English-speaking white majority still outnumbers the minority groups in the ratio of 2:1. However, a look at the age distributions indicates that minority group members below the age of 24 account for 45 percent of the total. By the end of the 1970s, members of the minority groups will account for almost one out of two new entrants into the labor force.

Therefore, the faster the city moves to integrate fully its minority groups and the more it can speed the development of their potentialities, the better will be its prospects for survival and growth. The real challenge it faces is to blur the distinctions between majority and minority and to recognize that its strength and well-being depends on how well it succeeds in developing the skills and competences of *all* its citizens, irrespective of the color of their skin. New York City has moved a fair distance in opening opportunities for minorities. But it must force the pace.

7. The American dream places great importance on the ability of a man who extends himself at work to improve his circumstances and to increase the opportunities available to his children. We noted above that New York City has a large number of low-paying jobs. A critical question, therefore, is the range of opportunities available for workers in such jobs to improve their position through upgrading. An analysis in depth revealed that the potentialities for climbing up the occupational and income ladders, particularly for blue-collar and service workers, are fairly restricted. In several large industries, including apparel and food services, the number of better jobs is seriously limited. In the health services, educational requirements interfere with the promotion of workers on the basis of their experience. In construction, union control tends to block the opportunities available to minority groups.

More determining than these specific impediments is the logistical consideration that there are a great many more competitors for good jobs than there are good jobs available. The incontestable fact is that many will be doomed to a working experience that constricts and restrains them to low-level work at modest pay. This is a fact of life of New York City's economy. Improving the conditions of this segment of the working force must start from this reality: Upgrading holds limited promise.

8. One of New York City's vaunted strengths has long been its system for public higher education for qualified students. A second source of strength has been its specialized high schools. A third, its large and recently expanded system of private and public occupational training institutions. In addition, the scale and variety of employment opportunities in New York City pro-

vide many work and career opportunities for those who know how to negotiate the complex world of work.

However, it is difficult for newcomers to the city or those whose families are poorly connected to become knowledgeable about the many educational, training, and career opportunities that exist, and even more difficult for them to know how to avail themselves of these opportunies. Career guidance in and out of the educational system should be able to help those who need help most, particularly members of minority groups, women, men seeking a job where they can improve their prospects. But a critical review of the operations of the guidance system demonstrates wide-ranging weaknesses resulting from poor staff preparation through too many clients per counselor, to the absence of effective liaison among critical institutions, such as schools and employers, and nonexistent or inadequate supporting services. The path of the poor could be eased if career guidance were strengthened.

9. If there is one belief that has led to the conviction that the city is in its death throes, it is that so many of its members are unable or unwilling to work and look to welfare for their sustenance. In New York City the welfare case load approximates 1.2 million, or almost one out of six persons in the population. But these figures hide as much as they disclose. They obscure the fact that half of all welfare clients are minors, preschoolers and children of school age. They also obscure the fact that about one-third of the adults on relief are old or disabled. This still leaves a considerable number of potential employables, estimated by the Human Resources Administration at about 200,000. But again the figures fail to indicate that many among this latter group move from work to welfare and back again to work depending on the changes in their personal condition and in the economy. There are many difficulties in this arena which even the passage of the President's welfare reform would not solve. The principal challenge is to provide many on welfare with an opportunity to become self-supporting. But this requires a great many changes on a great many fronts—from an expansion of federal job-creation efforts to a more effective administration of welfare at the local level.

10. American society is child-oriented, although it has not succeeded in providing a supportive environment for the growth

and development of children from disadvantaged families. Our actions have not been congruent with our words.

But as we have neglected many of the nation's children, we have met even less well the needs of our older citizens, especially those belonging to minority groups. In years past, New York and other large cities have harbored only a few older minority group members, but the passage of time since their in-migration and some improvement in their longevity is resulting in a rapid increase in their number. There are currently 100,000 blacks in New York City over 65 years of age. Many have few or no social security benefits; many are in poor health; many live without family ties; many are locked into a constricted ghetto neighborhood where they live in fear for their person and possessions. No civilized society, surely no city that pretends to be a center of culture and sophistication, can continue to turn its back on the needs of this deprived population. A man or woman whose life has been beset by trouble and turmoil should receive a helping hand in his old age.

There is no question that New York City faces many problems that warrant attention and solution. Since its minority population will soon account for half of the entrants into the labor force, the city must do more to ensure that the potentials of this population are developed and utilized. Although the opportunities for upgrading blue-collar and service workers are limited, more can be done to avoid discrimination in allocating such opportunities. If guidance services were strengthened, the less-advantaged members of the community would be in a better position to take advantage of the many developmental and career opportunities that exist in New York. The welfare population is large and still growing. Significant improvements by federal, state, and local governments in programming, financing, and administration of welfare are required. More attention, more sympathy, more resources must be directed to easing the declining years of older persons in the ghetto. Their continuing neglect is scandalous.

If New York City's problems are to be solved and its potentialities realized, planning mechanisms must be strengthened. Manpower is a unique resource in that it takes between eighteen and twenty-five years to develop, educate, and train a human being to a point where he can assume a productive role in the economy. But manpower planning is complicated because of the number of institutions that have a role in the process, the tensions that exist between private and public institutions, and the difficulties of aligning public institutions funded and operated by different levels of government.

11. New York City did take the lead in developing a publicly supported system of higher education which contributed significantly to increasing the output of trained personnel required to staff the professional and technical sectors of the local economy at the same time that the tuition-free system contributed to expanding career opportunities for young people from low-income families. However, a closer look at the present interface between higher education and the demand for trained manpower indicates that much is left to be desired.

First, educational planning has been conspicuous by its absence. The City University expanded rapidly without consideration being given to how such an expansion would impinge on the State University or on the many privately supported institutions in the city and in the suburbs. Furthermore, no part of the higher educational structure considered the long-run as well as short-run effects on the labor market. As a result, in the early 1970s many institutions are in a greatly weakened position and the essential planning and control mechanisms are not yet in place. Here is one arena where improved planning is urgently required and where effective planning should result in marked gains in the utilization of human and financial resources.

12. The scale and variety of New York City's labor market and of its related institutions, such as the education, health, and welfare systems, point to the potential role of information in improving the decision making of diverse groups: individuals preparing for or actively in the labor force; employers looking for more or better qualified workers; corporate, nonprofit, and government agencies faced with formulating long-range plans in which information about the city's manpower resources is a critical input. While the current output of labor market information is considerable, an assessment reveals serious lacunae that hobble the decision making of all major participants. Moreover, much of the

information that is currently collated and disseminated is not directly apposite to the priority requirements of the major participants. The finding is unequivocal: Major opportunities exist for improving the effectiveness of New York City's labor market through the mundane task of facilitating a better match between available workers and available jobs and the important long-run challenge of assuring that the city will have a properly qualified labor force to meet the requirements of a vital and changing economy.

13. An urban labor market can be affected, for good or bad, by the performance of its key manpower institutions. A close look at New York City reveals that at least three agencies perform some, but by no means all, of the services of a manpower agency and that none of the three is doing more than a part of the job and even that part leaves a great deal to be desired. But the shaping of a central manpower agency and its effective staffing would be only a step in the right direction. It is inevitable that a great many diverse institutions in the public and private sectors will continue to be heavily involved in one or another facet of manpower development and utilization. Consequently, a major challenge to the manpower agency would be to establish and maintain effective cooperative relations with these organizations. Here is an arena where much remains to be done.

14. While the concept of a labor market is taken for granted in legislation, administration, and analysis—including the present work—a critical consideration reveals that human beings cannot be treated in the same manner as commodities and that at best the market for labor operates quite differently from that for other resources. Family, society, and the individual are involved in the development of human skill, and as was pointed out above, the process extends over two decades. Moreover, no individual is in a position to assure that he will be able to put the competences which he has acquired to productive use. That depends on the demand for workers in total, in his locale, and in his area of specialization. In fact, no individual by his own actions can assure that he will acquire the general and specific competences that will enable him to earn enough to support himself and his dependents. He is dependent initially on his family and later on the developmental institutions provided by society, above all the school. If either or both fail to perform effectively, the neglected and deprived child will turn into an ineffective and dependent adult. Since the scope for slippage is great within the family, within the school, within the world of work as well as in the passage from one to the other, there is much room in New York City as in every other city for support and reinforcements that would lead to a strengthening of manpower resources. This is a major challenge to government and to the principal nongovernmental agencies concerned with improving the quality of life of the urban population.

Clearly, manpower planning is a major function that invites more attention, resources, competence. It is difficult to believe that New York or any other large city will make much progress to improve the development and utilization of its manpower resources unless the many agencies and organizations with responsibility in this arena strengthen their manpower-planning capabilities and cooperate with one another to improve the career opportunities of individuals as an essential step in strengthening the economic foundations of the urban economy.

These then are the principal precipitations from this collaborative research investigation:

—New York City continues to have a vital economy.

—New York City continues to be in a strong competitive position relative to the other large cities at home and abroad.

—While the economic development of its suburban regions has been and will probably continue to be rapid, New York City's future is not in jeopardy from this trend.

—If the manpower record of the last decade or two is a reliable index of performance, New York City is surmounting many of the challenges it confronts as a result of the recent shifts in its population.

—While New York City offers high rewards to the few who rise to the top, most families that enjoy a reasonable standard of living do so because they have two wage earners.

—Blacks and Puerto Ricans are no longer a small minority in New York City. In the age group below 25 they account for close to half the population. If New York is to flourish in the future, the potentialities of all its residents must be fully developed and utilized.

—The number of blue-collar and service workers seeking better jobs vastly exceeds the number of available opportunities, but access to the opportunities that exist should be on a nondiscriminatory basis.

—The improvement of career guidance services in and out of the school system could contribute to expanding the options available to disadvantaged groups.

—Despite the large numbers of persons on welfare, there are hurdles to transferring the employable group into productive employment because of their child-rearing responsibilities, the low wages available, and the shortfall in job opportunities.

—There are 100,000 blacks over the age of 65 living in the ghetto, most of whom are deprived and who need more income and services if their last years are not to be an oppressive period spent waiting for death.

—The proliferated system of higher education is grossly deficient when it comes to manpower planning, and there are consequent huge wastes in human and monetary resources.

—The operation of the New York labor market could be strengthened through a selective expansion of the quantity and quality of information and its improved dissemination and use.

—Improving the linkages among the principal institutions involved in the development and utilization of the city's manpower resources could contribute significantly to the wellbeing of the citizenry and the strengthening of the economy.

—Because many families fail to rear their children effectively and because many schools fail in their tasks of socialization and instruction, public and private agencies must seek to establish a network of supportive and second-chance institutions to compensate for these malfunctions.

16

PRIORITIES

Eli Ginzberg

BEFORE SETTING FORTH the priority recommendations that flow from these analyses, we will review the framework of the study and thus recall its boundaries. This work does not attempt to provide a comprehensive picture of the manpower dimensions of New York City. Nor does it explore except incidentally the interfaces between manpower and the other critically important policy and programmatic areas such as the economic, the political, the social.

Even within the arena of manpower, there are a host of issues which affect the well-being of the population and the city that were not analyzed; some were not even identified. Among the important issues that were not considered here are the role of trade unions, particularly the bargaining relations between the city and its employees; the extent to which the city's expenditures and capital budgets reflect efforts to improve the development and utilization of human resources; the political and administrative machinery and decision-making processes involved in distributing over $5 billion of city funds annually for such human resources programs as welfare, education, and health.

Moreover, this analysis did not explore in any depth such important determinants of the city's economy as the alternative uses of land, the deterrents to new residential construction, racial conflicts, the malperformance of the public educational system, the impact of tolls and taxes on nonresident jobholders, and a great many other important forces that help shape the city's labor market.

This book has sought to provide a selective rather than a comprehensive approach to that complex organism called the New York City labor market. The recommendations that are set forth below must, in turn, be selective rather than comprehensive.

Since the authors of the individual chapters have pointed out certain policy and programmatic recommendations that flow from their analysis, this concluding chapter will follow a higher order of generalization. It will concentrate on relatively few issues where changes hold promise of significant improvements in outcome, rather than detail a large number of specific recommendations. The priorities listed below will cover policies and programs, institutional arrangements and alignments, and the need for new knowledge and understanding of the structure and functioning of the New York City labor market. These selective recommendations are informed by the fact that in most areas improved outcomes depend on cooperation and coordination among different levels of government—local, state, and federal—and joint action by the public and private sectors. Although the need for cooperation and joint action adds to the difficulty of improving the effectiveness of current policy and programming, to ignore this necessity would result in paper rather than real solutions to the urgent problems facing the city.

1. With an expenditure budget of about $8.5 billion, the majority of which funds are spent for welfare, education, and health, the city is in a preferred position to exercise leverage on the size and quality of the manpower pool. At present the city government does not have nearly as much leeway as it would like with respect to specific programs and the allocation of funds among them. Its freedom of action to initiate, change, and terminate programs is limited by both the state and federal governments. But the federal government, which has substantially increased its contribution in recent years to the city's budget, is moving toward revenue sharing, which implies more funds for the city and more discretion over the use of such funds by the city's government. There is a reasonable prospect that one or another revenue-sharing proposal will be passed, and there is a likelihood

that the state and federal governments may free part of the city's budget by assuming responsibility for welfare, education, and possibly other high-cost programs. Even if neither eventuality is realized in the proximate future, it would still be highly desirable for the mayor to instruct the Bureau of the Budget to begin a systematic study in depth of *how the present pattern of government spending for human resources development might be altered so that the employability and earnings of the beneficiaries of these expenditures might be enhanced in the short and long run.*

At present, most of the welfare funds are directed to helping the poor meet their minimum needs. If there are numerous employables on the welfare rolls, as senior officials believe, there is clearly scope for imaginative reprogramming of some part of these expenditures to facilitate the transfer of some of this large group into productive employment if only in public service jobs. Specifically, it might be desirable for the city to explore, at least on an experimental basis, converting disability grants into wages for training and jobs for youthful drug addicts.

To take another example: It is generally acknowledged by most investigators who have studied the high schools in New York City that the present program is failing to educate or train a significant minority of students in the classroom and that many are becoming hostile and alienated young people because they are forced to remain there, regardless of their inability to learn in that situation. Since the per capita annual cost for each student is about $1,500, the city would be well advised to explore whether a reallocation of a considerable proportion of this sum for the development, supervision, and work allowances of a work/study program might yield a greater net benefit.

Each of the major program areas concerned with human resources should be reappraised to determine the potentialities of increasing the productivity of public expenditures through a process of reallocation. The experience of the 1960s demonstrated unequivocally that simply putting more money into established channels is not likely to prove constructive. The special grants to improve ghetto schools, the large sums devoted to Medicaid, and the expanded expenditures for manpower training all underscore the need for critical reappraisals aimed at making the efforts of government more responsive to the needs of the people it seeks to serve.

2. While a government as large as New York City's must rely on departments and agencies to carry out discrete missions, many citizens who need services are dependent on more than one governmental unit. For instance, when prisoners are paroled or patients discharged, their ability to succeed in their community depends in large measure on whether they receive supportive services and special assistance. Unless they do, they are likely to break down again. These returnees to society may require clinic services, a training program, help in locating a job. A major challenge to every government is to analyze its present and potential clientele for special services in sufficient depth to recognize the strategic types of assistance that may make the difference between continued dependency and independence and to strive to coordinate its resources to provide the critical assistance. *The city's public agencies must be better coordinated if they are to serve its population more effectively.*

The reorganization of several departments into superagencies such as the Health Services Administration and the Human Resources Administration represents a serious effort to facilitate better planning and coordination within city government. But this reorganization remains incomplete and its results to date are inconclusive. Equally important is the fact that the superagency concept is limited to agencies with similar missions. New efforts are required to ensure the coordinated delivery of diverse services which may be required by an individual. Although this is a formidable task, unless major efforts are directed to the end of improved coordination, a high proportion of all governmental expenditures will run to waste.

3. Although government is an important factor, the past, present, and future economic well-being of the city depends in the first instance on the continuing vitality of the private sector. Unless large corporations, small employers, and the self-employed are willing to invest, expand, and work in New York City, the economy has no future. The very size and diversity of the private sector inhibit the emergence of a business leadership with clearly defined goals and needs. Partly because of the difficulty of identifying a recognized business leadership, the governmental leader-

ship has been slow to establish mechanisms for joint planning and programming. The politicians have tended to be responsive to special interest groups which have real or putative power at the polls, while the different business groups have found it difficult to identify the centers of governmental decision making which might have a sympathetic understanding of their problems and might be able and willing to lend a helping hand.

Although the economy is becoming more and more pluralistic, that is, although urban dynamism depends on the intermingling of private, nonprofit, and governmental efforts, New York City still lacks effective coordinating mechanisms. In their absence, any small, well-organized minority can interfere with, even prevent, essential expansion or renewal. The ability of a small, but vocal, group of citizens to prevent the construction of a large department store on Manhattan's West Side is an outstanding example of this process at work.

It is essential that *the several leadership groups in the city attempt to fashion mechanisms that will facilitate decision making involving the three sectors in which the gains from growth can be balanced against the losses from upheaval.* The city's 62 Community Planning Boards have provided a framework for the participation of diverse interests. If given continued support and additional resources for staff and technical assistance, the community boards could become a spokesman for broader segments of the population. In the absence of effective mechanisms there is a real danger that the dynamism of New York's economy—the foundation for employment and income—will be undermined by the vetoes of small minorities.

4. There is a widespread belief that a major drag on the economy of the city is the inadequate preparation of young people, particularly minority youth, for white-collar activities. A gap between the educational achievement of young people and the requirements of employers, especially a wide gap, can be a deterrent to the attraction and expansion of business, especially if competing locations do not suffer from a similar liability. The fact that New York City has even more nonmanufacturing employment than most large cities makes this particular handicap of new entrants into the labor force more serious.

Although intensified efforts have been made during the past

few years to improve the performance of the public educational system, the results have not been conspicuous. A great many young people drop out of or graduate from high school poorly prepared to enter white-collar employment. Others are so negative, hostile, or alienated from society that they balk at searching for employment for which they might be qualified. One measure of their negativism is the high truancy rate characteristic of so many junior and senior high schools.

Beginning efforts are being made to expand the relations among schools, business, trade unions, and municipal government with an aim of improving guidance, work/study programming, and job placement, to help many young people to relate their school work and plans more effectively to their career objectives. About 7,000 students are enrolled in cooperative education programs, satellite schools have been created, and an innovative work/study plan is being developed at Franklin K. Lane High School. *These school-work linkages should be strengthened and expanded, and the chancellor of the public school system and his associates should redouble their efforts to elicit the support of private and public employers and trade unions to this end.* Their goal for 1975 should be to provide at least 10 percent of all high school juniors and seniors with paying jobs related to their course work. Young people who learn that an improvement in their performance in school may lead to better jobs and higher wages are more likely to extend themselves. But they need concrete evidence of this relationship, not just words, and this points to the importance of structured transitional devices.

5. Even if the efforts outlined above at improving linkages between school and work are greatly strengthened—as they should be—large numbers of young people will still come through the educational system poorly prepared to find a place in the world of work. Many will need a second chance, a second opportunity to acquire the knowledge or skills which they failed to master while at school.

During the past decade considerable manpower-training funds have become available to the city, funds provided primarily by the federal government and to a lesser degree the state. Additional sums have been added by the city out of its own resources.

Federal funds have also been channeled into the private Coalition JOBS program. While some of the manpower-training programs underwritten by these governmental funds have helped youngsters to acquire skills and secure a job, many have accomplished relatively little. Because of the requirements of employers for better-qualified new workers, an attempt use governmental manpower-training monies to finance preemployment and work/training programs that are geared to definite job offers should be pursued. The efforts to date have been too small. *The city's Manpower and Career Development Agency should encourage key trade associations, among others, to take the leadership in organizing and conducting job-related training programs, which should be financed partly with public manpower-training funds.*

Many young people who drop out of school in the tenth or eleventh grade, even if they are behind in their reading and calculating skills, could probably be brought up to the job-entrance level in six to eight months or less in an effective work/training program. It is important that large employers and strategic industries, such as banking and finance, recognize that they cannot wait for the reform of the educational system. They must help themselves and seek help from the city to qualify many of the new members of the labor force whom they will have to employ.

6. The foregoing recommendation looks to an improved employability of the youthful entrants into the labor force through joint planning of business and the city for job-related training efforts under employer direction and supervision. There are related opportunities within the governmental sphere where the city should take the lead. With multi-billion dollars of welfare funds passing through its hands, with access to about 400,000 municipal jobs, with a small but potentially increasing number of federally financed emergency jobs at its command, the Human Resources Administration in cooperation with selected voluntary and business groups, should seek *to increase the number of welfare recipients who can be placed in public service jobs, if only for a transitional period while they acquire training, skill, and orientation to the world of work.* There are many people on the periphery

of the labor market who would welcome a helping hand. On their own they are unable to break into employment, surely not into steady employment. But with a little skill and an assist in job placement they might be able to make the grade.

7. An expansion and improvement of the jobs available in New York City depend in considerable measure on how successful the city is in attacking the principal forces in the environment that are acting as brakes on the willingness of people to invest, work, live in the core city. While it is easy to draw up a long list of environmental factors which would stimulate the economy and pari-passu strengthen the job market, a highly selective approach would focus on the following: improvements in the use of land, an efficient transportation system, and enabling people to enjoy the special advantages of metropolitan life. The city has been moving, albeit slowly, to rationalize the use of land by consolidating parcels for manufacturing and other business uses while at the same time expanding opportunities for new residential construction. It has also been attempting, with the Metropolitan Transportation Authority, to expand and modernize its subway system, and it is striving to increase safety in the streets, a precondition for enabling residents and visitors to make greater use of public and private recreational, cultural, sport facilities. *More efforts are required to enlist private and nonprofit agencies to prevent neighborhood deterioration and to facilitate housing rehabilitation; to encourage such nongovernmental groups to participate more actively in local security efforts, street cleaning, and beautification efforts; and to encourage publicly supported work programs utilizing employable welfare recipients to enhance the special attractions of the city—including parks, museums, and other unique urban attractions.*

The thrust of these recommendations is twofold: to single out a few critical areas where further deterioration spells danger, and to emphasize that the municipal government, acting on its own, does not have the resources to turn the situation around. More and more New Yorkers must become engaged in stemming the forces of decline and in the process expand the urban amenities which have long been the dynamic of metropolitan growth and prosperity.

8. A related challenge stems from the pervasive nature of illicit and illegal activity in New York City which, it will be recalled, was estimated to provide employment and income for about ¼ million persons. The repeated efforts to control, reduce, and eliminate crime and crime-related activities have clearly not succeeded, among other reasons because of the stakes of so many individuals and institutions in these activities. Buyers, middlemen, and sellers are willing to pay the extra premiums and run special risks because of the potential gains from crime. The drug addict will stop at nothing to get the money he needs for his next shot; the head of a numbers syndicate can afford to pay off a large number of law enforcement officials, so large is his take.

Although the city cannot eliminate crime, it can take a series of constructive actions: *It can expand the more successful of its present efforts aimed at rehabilitating drug addicts and explore new approaches; it can press the state legislature to legalize certain types of gambling and solicitation for sexual purposes; and, with the assistance of the state, it can aim to improve its law enforcement machinery.* Even if these approaches were followed energetically, crime would remain a major industry, but assaults against people would probably decline.

9. A major result of this research investigation has been to highlight the rapidity with which the new minorities—blacks and Puerto Ricans—are beginning to play a dominant role in the city's labor market. Consequently the economic, social, and political hegemony of the city depends on how quickly and how effectively the established white groups make accommodations and adjustments for the rapidly increasing numbers of newcomers. The evidence we reviewed suggests that New York has done more than most other large cities to initiate necessary and desirable changes. But much remains to be done. *The city's Office of Contract Compliance and Commission on Human Rights should be given the legal, financial, and human resources to expand their efforts to remove all arbitrary barriers which still confront blacks and Puerto Ricans.* Since enforcement of antidiscrimination laws is an intergovernmental responsibility, *these city agencies should seek to establish a regional law enforcement program involving the cooperation of state and federal offices of contract* *compliance and the U.S. Commission on Civil Rights and its New York State Advisory Committee, as well as interested private groups, in order to coordinate the efforts of these bodies and to assign priorities in the selection of cases.*

10. One of the critical findings of the present investigation is the gap between what is known about the major trends and tendencies in the city's labor market and what people in government, business, and nonprofit organizations need to know to improve their decision making. *There is urgent need for expanded and improved labor market data collection and data analysis which will involve cooperative action by governmental and nongovernmental organizations. The New York Manpower Area Planning Council should seek the cooperation of its member agencies, as well as private firms and other interested parties, in creating a consortium for the collection and distribution of labor market information.* In the absence of a strengthened data base a great many planning and operating decisions will be faulty. In an environment such as that of New York City and its environs, which is characterized by rapid change, especially population changes, various decision-making groups must be able to assess and monitor these changes to shape sound policies and programs.

11. The final recommendation arising out of this study of the New York City labor market is the urgent need for a strong planning and operating manpower organization concerned with the development and utilization of human resources which will take the lead in improving coordination among the several levels of government and the private sector. To this end, the *city needs to fashion a broadly based, well-staffed manpower agency with broad responsibilities over the gamut of governmentally supported labor market services.* Given the present fragmented structure of manpower programs, the Manpower and Career Development Agency seems most capable of serving as the primary municipal manpower organization. In addition, key governmental and nongovernmental groups must organize themselves to participate effectively in joint manpower planning and programming. Such strengthened organizational efforts are essential for improved outcomes.

For quick summary, the foregoing principal recommendations are recapitulated below:

—Municipal government should study in depth how its present pattern of expenditures for the development of human resources might be altered to enhance the employability and earnings of the clients of these public programs.

—Effective municipal services to people entail improved coordination among the several municipal agencies.

—Improved decision-making mechanisms must be fashioned in the governmental, nonprofit, and profit sectors, including coordination among them, to assure that potential gains from change are not sacrificed because of the opposition of special interest groups.

—The support of business, trade unions, and governmental and nonprofit employers should be elicited to strengthen the linkages between the schools and the world of work.

—The municipal government should encourage, through financial assistance, key trade associations and other employer representatives to play a larger role in organizing and conducting job-related training programs.

—Municipal government should seek to increase the number of welfare clients on publicly supported work projects with an aim of enhancing their employability and eventual economic independence.

—The mayor should seek to elicit the more active cooperation of business and nonprofit organizations in neighborhood-improvement efforts.

—With the assistance of the state government, municipal government should redouble its efforts at rehabilitating drug addicts and seek to reduce nonviolent crime by legalizing various types of gambling.

—In cooperation with state and federal agencies and the leadership of nongovernmental groups, municipal government should press ahead with its efforts to remove all forms of racial and ethnic discrimination.

—In cooperation with other governmental and nongovernmental organizations, municipal government should seek to expand and improve the available data and analyses relating to the changing structure and functioning of the New York City labor market.

—Municipal government should fashion and staff a broadly based manpower agency and seek to improve its liaison with key governmental and nongovernmental groups to improve the quality of manpower planning and programming.

NOTES

CHAPTER 1

1. Data in this and succeeding paragraphs in this section are drawn primarily from Tri-State Transportation Commission, *Measure of a Region*, May 1967.

2. Richard Knight, "Metropolitan Trade and Employment Expansion," unpublished Ph.D. dissertation, London School of Economics, 1972.

3. See *Fortune*, May 1971, pp. 170-201.

4. Data in this and succeeding paragraphs dealing with business and related services are drawn primarily from Planning and Development Department, Port of New York Authority, *Industries Servicing the Corporate Headquarters Function in the New York-Northeastern New Jersey Metropolitan Area*, June 1971.

CHAPTER 2

1. U.S. Bureau of the Census, *Statistical Abstract of the United States, 1971*, 1971, pp. 830-899.

2. U.S. Department of Labor, Bureau of Labor Statistics, *Work Stoppage Trends in the New York-Northeastern New Jersey Area*, Regional Report no. 25, November 1971, table 10, p. 25.

3. U.S. Department of Labor, Bureau of Labor Statistics, *Some Facts Relating to the New York Scene*, Middle Atlantic Regional Office, April 1971, p. 18.

4. Stanley Friedlander assisted by Robert Shick, *Unemployment in the Urban Core: An Analysis of Thirty Cities with Policy Recommendations*, New York: Praeger, 1972.

5. Growth rates for all sectors except government are based upon figures reported in the 1959 and 1970 issues of Bureau of the Census, *County*

Business Patterns (see Tables 2-1 and 2-2). Government employment figures are based on annual averages reported in the Bureau of Labor Statistics publication, *Employment and Earnings.*

6. U.S. Department of Labor, Bureau of Labor Statistics, *Understanding the Social and Economic Challenges for New York in the Seventies,* Middle Atlantic Regional Office, May 1971, p. 4.

7. U.S. Department of Labor, *Manpower Report of the President,* April 1971, table D-13, p. 288.

8. U.S. Department of Labor, Bureau of Labor Statistics, *Poverty Area Profiles,* "The Working Age Population: Initial Findings," table 1.

9. U.S. Department of Labor, *Manpower Report of the President,* April 1971, loc. cit.

CHAPTER 3

1. No rigorous definition of the suburbs has yet been put forth. In general, it includes that area outside the geographical and political boundaries of the city but within its commutershed. In the analysis of larger cities (e.g., New York, Chicago, Boston) it is often useful to conceive of a metropolitan region which is considerably larger than the SMSA and includes all counties which may be regarded as part of an overall metropolitan system. The region is divided into a core and two or more outlying rings. These rings are classified primarily on the basis of intensity of land use: see Edgar M. Hoover and R. Vernon, *Anatomy of a Metropolis.* New York: Anchor Books, Doubleday & Company, Inc., 1962, pp. 14–19.

2. Except where otherwise noted, the definitions of inner and outer rings used here are those of Hoover and Vernon, ibid.

3. The process described so briefly here is an example of the Keynesian income multiplier at work. For a more complete discussion see Thomas Stanback and Richard Knight, *The Metropolitan Economy.* New York: Columbia University Press, 1970, pp. 62–64.

4. The ring counties of the New York SMSA are Nassau, Suffolk, Westchester, Rockland. The core counties are the five boroughs. This definition is more restricted than that of Hoover and Vernon.

5. *Stores.* August 1970, p. 8.

6. Data are from U.S. Department of Commerce, *Census of Manufacturers,* 1967.

7. The data and classification scheme presented in this section are based on the work of Regina Armstrong, *The Office Industry.* Cambridge: MIT Press, 1972.

8. Westchester County Department of Planning, *Westchester's Economy,* White Plains: August 1970, p. 35.

9. New York City Planning Commission, *Planning for Jobs,* March 1971 supplement to *Plan for New York City.*

10. Ernest W. Williams Jr., "The Urban-Intercity Interface," in *The Future of American Transportation.* New York: The American Assembly, 1971, p. 158.

CHAPTER 4

1. New York City Planning Commission *Planning for Jobs,* March 1971 supplement to *Plan for New York City,* p. 2.

2. U.S. Department of Labor, Bureau of Labor Statistics, *Strengths and Weaknesses of the New York Area as an Employment Center,* November 1971, p. 33.

3. U.S. Department of Labor, Bureau of Labor Statistics, *Some Facts Relating to Earnings and Wages in New York City,* March 1970, pp. 4–5.

4. New York City Council on Economic Education, *Fact Book: 1972.* New York: the Council, 1972, p. 11.

5. Ibid., p. 46.

6. U.S. Department of Labor, Bureau of Labor Statistics, *Changing Patterns of Prices, Pay, Workers and Work on the New York Scene,* Regional Report no. 20, May 1971, p. 11.

7. Regional Plan Association, *Summary Report: Growth and Location of Office Jobs in the United States and the New York Region.*

8. Ibid., pp. 10–11.

9. Ibid., p. 22.

10. *Fact Book: 1972,* p. 129.

11. *Changing Patterns of Prices, Pay, Workers and Work on the New York Scene,* p. 17.

12. Ibid., p. 16.

13. *Fact Book: 1972,* p. 86.

14. Ibid., p. 87.

15. *Changing Patterns of Prices, Pay, Workers and Work on the New York Scene,* p. 35.

16. Ibid., p. 37.

17. *Fact Book: 1972,* p. 140.

18. Ibid., p. 137.

19. Ibid., p. 141.

20. *Changing Patterns of Prices, Pay, Workers and Work on the New York Scene,* p. 17.

21. *Fact Book: 1972*, p. 32.

22. Ibid., p. 113 ff.

23. *Planning for Jobs*, p. 6.

24. *Strengths and Weaknesses of the New York Area as an Employment Center*, p. 5.

25. U.S. Department of Labor, Bureau of Labor Statistics, *The Statistical Background to Manpower Directions in New York City in the Seventies*, January 1971, p. 33.

CHAPTER 5

1. Union Bank of Switzerland, *Prices and Earnings Around the Globe*, Zurich, 1971. The reader should keep in mind that data cited throughout this chapter come from a variety of sources and pertain to different years. They are, however, valid for their major purpose here, which is to illustrate relative magnitudes.

2. U.S. Department of Labor, Bureau of Labor Statistics, *Changing Patterns of Prices, Pay, Workers, and Work on the New York Scene*, Regional Report no. 20, New York, Middle Atlantic Regional Office, May 1971, p. 29.

3. Ibid., p. 31.

4. Peter B. Doeringer and Michael J. Piore, *Internal Labor Markets and Manpower Analysis*. Lexington, Mass.: D. C. Heath, 1971.

5. Melvin W. Reder, "A Partial Survey of the Theory of Income Size and Distribution," in Lee Soltow (ed.), *Six Papers on the Size Distribution of Wealth and Income*. New York: National Bureau of Economic Research, 1969, pp. 205–250.

6. Dean Morse, *The Peripheral Worker*, New York: Columbia University Press, 1969.

7. U.S. Bureau of the Census, *U.S. Census of Population: 1960, Subject Reports, Characteristics of Professional Workers*, Final Report PC(2)-7E, 1964, pp. 1–2; New York State Department of Labor, Division of Research and Statistics, *Manpower Directions in New York State 1965–1975, Job Requirements and Labor Force*, vol. 2 (March 1968), pp. 39–40.

8. U.S. Department of Labor, Bureau of Labor Statistics, *Professional, Administrative and Technical Pay in New York, 1970*, Regional Report no. 18, New York, Middle Atlantic Regional Office, February 1971.

9. Ibid., p. 18.

10. New York State Department of Labor, Division of Research and Statistics, *The Structure of Earnings and Hours in New York State*, vol. 1 (May 1968), table 3B.

11. Ibid., table 2B.

12. Internal Revenue Service, *Statistics of Income—1967, Business Income Tax Returns*, 1970, p. 22.

13. Irving F. Leveson, "Nonfarm Self-employment in the U.S.," Ph.D. dissertation, Columbia University, 1968.

14. William A. Johnson, *Changing Patterns of Employment in the New York Metropolitan Area.* New York: Rand Institute, 1971, p. 31.

15. Martin Segal, "The Relation between Union Wage Impact and Market Structure," *Quarterly Journal of Economics,* vol. 78, February 1964, pp. 97–114.

16. *The Structure of Earnings,* vol. 1, pp. 84, 89, 114, 119.

17. U.S. Department of Labor, Bureau of Labor Statistics, *Employment and Earnings,* Bulletin 1312-7, 1970, p. 354.

18. New York State Department of Labor, Division of Research and Statistics, *The Structure of Earnings and Hours in New York State,* vol. 4, November 1968, p. 43.

19. New York State Department of Labor, Division of Employment, Research and Statistics, *Employment Review,* vol. 24, nos. 2 (February 1971), 4 (April 1971), 5 (May 1971), 7 (July 1971).

20. *The Structure of Earnings,* vol. 1, pp. 98–99.

21. New York State Department of Labor, *Employment Review,* vol. 24, nos. 2, 4, 5, 7.

22. U.S. Department of Labor, Bureau of Labor Statistics, *Year-end Report on Jobs, Prices, and Earnings in the New York Area,* Regional Bulletin no. 25, December 1970, pp. 34–35.

23. *The Structure of Earnings,* vol. 1, p. 132.

24. Ibid., p. 116.

25. Marcia Freedman, *The Process of Work Establishment.* New York: Columbia University Press, 1969, pp. 100–101.

26. David Lewin, "An Analysis of Wage Parity for Protection Services in Local Government Employment" (unpublished paper), p. 12.

27. U.S. Department of Labor, Bureau of Labor Statistics Summary Report, *Work Stoppages in 1970,* August 1971.

28. U.S. Department of Labor, Bureau of Labor Statistics, Regional Report, no. 20, op. cit. chart 9.

29. U.S. Department of Labor, Bureau of Labor Statistics, *Job Tenure of Workers, January 1968,* Special Labor Force Report 112, 1969, table 1.

30. Elizabeth Waldman, "Changes in the Labor Force Activity of Women," *Monthly Labor Review,* vol. 93, June 1970, chart 1.

31. Cited in U.S. Department of Labor, Wage and Labor Standards Administration, *Facts About Women's Absenteeism and Labor Turnover,* August 1969.

32. Wade Greene, "Can Ma Bell Really Be Sexist?" *The New York Times,* Dec. 5, 1971.

33. Anne Fribourg, *Clerical Jobs in the Financial Industry in New York City.* New York: New York Department of City Planning, July 1972.

34. I am indebted to Thomas Stanback for this observation.

35. New York State Department of Labor, "Private Household Workers, New York State, 1970," Special Labor News Memorandum 141, June 1, 1971.

36. Stanley Lebergott, "Labor Force and Employment Trends," in Eleanor Bernert Sheldon and Wilbert E. Moore (eds.), *Indicators of Social Change.* New York: Russell Sage Foundation, 1968, p. 99.

37. U.S. Bureau of the Census, *Income in 1970 of Families and Persons in the U.S.*, Current Population Reports, P-60, no. 80 (October 4, 1971), table 4.

38. H. V. Hayghe and K. Michelotti, "Multiple Job-holding in 1970 and 1971," *Monthly Labor Review*, vol. 94, October 1971, p. 38.

39. Estimates prepared from census data by Raymond A. Glazier, Community Council of Greater New York, 1970 Census Bulletin no. 10, Aug. 26, 1971.

CHAPTER 6

1. Population figures in this section are estimates based on U.S. Department of Commerce, Bureau of the Census, *1970 Census of Population and Housing,* Final Report PHC(2)-34, "General Demographic Trends for Metropolitan Areas, 1960 to 1970," August, 1971; New York State Department of Labor, Division of Employment, *Minority Manpower Statistics,* July, 1971; and estimates prepared by the New York City Human Resources Administration and the Community Council of Greater New York discussed in Edward Burks, "Blacks and Puerto Ricans Up Million Here in Decade," *The New York Times,* Mar. 6, 1972.

2. See William Johnson, *Changing Patterns of Employment in the New York Metropolitan Area.* New York: Rand Institute, December 1971.

3. New York State Department of Labor, "Minority Group Membership in Selected Unions, New York State and Metropolitan Areas, 1969," Special Labor News Memorandum no. 139, February 1971.

4. U.S. Department of Labor, *Manpower Report of the President,* April 1971, table D-13.

5. See New York City Cooperative Area Manpower Planning System, *CAMPS Plan for Fiscal Year 1970–71,* September 1970.

CHAPTER 7

1. U.S. Bureau of the Census, *Current Population Reports,* ser. P-60, no. 81, "Characteristics of the Low Income Population, 1970." 1971, table 20.

2. New York Urban Coalition, *The Working Poor,* September 1970, p. 1.

3. See Howard Hayghe, *Work Experience of the Population in 1969,* U.S.

Department of Labor Special Labor Force Report no. 127, 1971; and Dean Morse, *The Peripheral Worker.* New York: Columbia University Press, 1969.

4. U.S. Bureau of Labor Statistics, *Recent Trends in Wages and Related Benefits of Hospital Workers in New York City,* Regional Labor Statistics Bulletin 20, May 1970; and Bureau of Labor Statistics, *Earnings of Hospital Workers in New York City, April, 1970,* Industry Wage Survey Report 71-1, February 1971.

5. New York Urban Coalition, *The Working Poor,* p. 7.

6. Recent discussion of the subject is found in Industrial Relations Research Association, *Proceedings of the Twenty-third Annual Winter Meeting, Dec. 28-29, 1970,* IRRA, May 1971, pp. 106-146.

7. For details on this data source see William Johnson, *Changing Patterns of Employment in the New York Metropolitan Area.* New York: Rand Institute, December 1971.

8. See William Grinker et al., *Climbing the Job Ladder: A Study of Employee Advancement in Eleven Industries.* New York: E. F. Shelley & Company, 1970; and Charles Brecher, *Upgrading Blue Collar and Service Workers.* Baltimore: The Johns Hopkins Press, 1972.

9. U.S. Department of Labor, *Formal Occupational Training of Adult Workers,* Manpower Automation Research Monograph no. 2, December 1964.

10. Florence Stern, *Upgrading Nurse's Aides to LPN's through a Work Study Program,* Final Progress Report, Education Department, District Council 37, 1970.

11. Institute of Public Administration, *Training Incentive Payments Program, First Year's Operations,* June 1971.

12. City University of New York, *Enrollment Report, Fall 1970.*

13. Quoted in *Monthly Labor Review,* June 1971, pp. 79-80.

14. Quoted in Arnold Lubasch, "City's School-Job Tests Barred as Biased," *The New York Times,* July 15, 1971, p. 1.

CHAPTER 8

1. Eli Ginzberg, *Career Guidance: Who Needs It, Who Provides It, Who Can Improve It.* New York: McGraw-Hill Book Company, 1971, p. 41.

2. Robert Birnbaum and Joseph Goldman, *The Graduates: A Follow-up Study of New York City High School Graduates of 1970,* The City University of New York, May 1971, p. 37.

3. *Annual Census of School Population October 30, 1970, Summary Tables,* Board of Education of the City of New York, Office of Business Administration, publ. no. 340, P.N.S. 411, April 1971, table 1.

4. Birnbaum and Goldman, op. cit., p. 41.

5. Citizen's Committee for Children of New York, *A Report on New York City High Schools,* January 1970, p. 2.

6. Birnbaum and Goldman, op cit., p. 5.

7. "Open Admissions at the City University of New York," Testimony of J. Joseph Meng before Joint Legislative Committee on Higher Education, Nov. 17, 1971, p. 20.

8. "Open Admissions at the City University of New York," Testimony of Dr. Robert J. Kibbee, p. 3.

9. Birnbaum and Goldman, op. cit., p. 74.

10. "Open Admissions at the City University of New York," Testimony of Dr. David E. Lavin, p. 32.

11. New York State Department of Labor, Division of Research and Statistics, *Jobs of Young Workers, 1952–1968,* Special Labor News Memorandum no. 133, February 1970, p. 3.

12. Ibid., p. 5.

13. U.S. Department of Labor, Bureau of Labor Statistics, *Some Facts Relating to the New York Scene,* Middle Atlantic Regional Office, April 1971, p. 10.

14. Birnbaum and Goldman, op. cit., p. 88.

15. *Some Facts Relating to the New York Scene,* p. 5.

16. Ginzberg, op. cit., p. 278.

17. J. G. Bachman, S. Green, and I. D. Wirtanen, *Youth in Transition: Dropping Out—Problem or Sympton?* Ann Arbor: Survey Research Center, Institute for Social Research, 1971, vol. 3, chap. 8..

18. Birnbaum and Goldman, op. cit., p. 127.

19. "9% of 38,555 City University Freshman Are Getting Aid from Welfare," *The New York Times,* Jan. 18, 1972, p. 28.

20. "Open Admissions at the City University of New York," Testimony of James J. McGrath, p. 28.

21. Ibid.

22. Ginzberg, op. cit., p. 82.

CHAPTER 9

1. Estimates are from Stanley Lebergott, *Manpower in Economic Growth: The American Record Since 1800.* New York: McGraw-Hill Book Company, 1964, table 2-4, p. 65; and *Manpower Report of the President,* April 1971, table B-2, p. 235.

2. See New York State Department of Social Services, *Characteristics of AFDC Families in New York State, May 1969,* Program Analysis Report no. 44, December 1970; and U.S. Department of Health, Education and Welfare—New York State Department of Social Services, *Report of Findings*

of Special Review of Aid to Families with Dependent Children in New York City, 1969, p. 39. The latter report found no statistical evidence to support a "calculative hypothesis" explaining increased AFDC rolls as a function of deliberate migration to receive welfare in high grant cities.

3. David Gordon, "Income and Welfare in New York City," *The Public Interest,* Summer, 1969, p. 83.

4. See Elizabeth Durbin, "Family Instability, Labor Supply and the Incidence of Aid to Families with Dependent Children," Ph.D. dissertation, Columbia University, Department of Economics, 1970. pp. 198–199; and Blanche Bernstein, "Welfare in New York City," *City Almanac,* February 1970.

5. Blanche Bernstein, *Welfare and Income in New York City.* New York: New School for Social Research, 1971.

6. Edward Banfield, "Welfare: A Crisis Without 'Solutions,'" *The Public Interest,* Summer, 1969, p. 93.

7. Richard Cloward and Frances Fox Piven, *Regulating the Poor: The Functions of Public Welfare.* New York: Pantheon Books, Inc., 1971.

8. Ibid., p. 286.

9. U.S. Department of Health, Education and Welfare—New York State Department of Social Services, op. cit., pp. 48–50.

10. William Johnson, *The Welfare Crisis: The Growth of Dependency in New York City.* New York: Rand Institute, in press.

11. Elizabeth Durbin, *Welfare, Income and Employment.* New York: Frederick A. Praeger, Inc., 1969.

12. Estimates based on figures provided in the New York City Department of Social Services, *Monthly Statistical Report,* May 1970.

13. Durbin, *Welfare, Income and Employment,* pp. 120–131.

14. Except as noted below, all data in this paragraph are from New York State Department of Labor, Division of Employment, *Operations,* October 1971, table 6-A.

15. See "Job Test Speeded for Relief People," *The New York Times,* Jan. 24, 1972, p. 36.

16. Peter Kihss, "3,805 on Relief at Work under New Law," *The New York Times,* Jan. 20, 1972.

17. Governor Rockefeller made the initial statement in August 1971. A detailed memorandum prepared for New York City Human Resources Administrator Jule Sugarman supporting the 4 percent figure was released by the Human Resources Administration on October 4, 1971.

18. Lucinda White, *A Profile of the Working Poor,* New York City Department of Social Services, November 1970.

19. New York City Department of Social Services, Procedure 68-67, Dec. 18, 1968, p. 10.

20. New York State Legislative Commission on Expenditure Review, *Manpower Training in New York State,* Feb. 16, 1971, pp. 27–38.

21. Leonard Hausman, *The Potential for Work among Welfare Parents,* U.S. Department of Labor, Manpower Administration, Manpower Research Monograph no. 21, 1969, p. 15.

22. Irene Cox, "The Employment of Mothers as a Means of Family Support," *Welfare in Review,* vol. 8, no. 6, p. 11.

23. See U.S. Department of Labor, *The Work Incentive Program,* Second Annual Report of the Department of Labor to the Congress on Training and Employment Under Title IV of the Social Security Act, June 1971, table 9.

24. New York State Legislative Commission on Expenditure Review, loc. cit.

25. U.S. Congress, Senate, Committee on Finance, *Hearings on H.R.1,* 1971, pp. 148–149.

26. See National Manpower Policy Task Force Associates, *The Family Assistance Plan: An Analysis and Evaluation,* Washington, D.C., Apr. 17, 1970.

CHAPTER 10

1. Rambler Essays, no. 50.

2. For an extended discussion of this point, see Charles Tilly, "Race and Migration to the American City," in James Q. Wilson (ed.), *The Metropolitan Enigma.* Washington, D.C.: Chamber of Commerce of the United States, 1964, pp. 124–143.

3. Elliot Liebow, *Tally's Corner, A Study of Street-corner Men.* Boston: Little, Brown and Company, 1967.

4. All statistics in this paragraph and in the following pages are from the Bureau of the Census, *General Demographic Trends for Metropolitan Areas, 1960–1970,* PHC (2)-34, August 1971, table 4, "Population inside and outside Central Cities by Race and Age; 1970 and 1960."

CHAPTER 11

1. Educational enterprises were not alone in this expansion. Corporations, like ITT, also entered directly into the business of education through the medium of government contracts to run programs at the Job Corps centers. One of the effects of these undertakings was to drain off educators into the private business sector. See Marcia K. Freedman, "Business and Education" in Ivar Berg (ed.), *The Business of America.* New York: Harcourt, Brace and Company, Inc., 1968, pp. 364–387.

2. John K. Folger and Charles B. Nam, *Education of the American Population,* 1960 Census Monograph, 1967, pp. 169 and 176.

3. Ann Miller, "Occupations of the Labor Force According to the Dictionary of Occupational Titles," University of Pennsylvania, February 1971, p. 39.

4. Hirsch S. Ruchlin, "Education as a Labor Market Variable," *Industrial Relations,* vol. 10, no. 3 (October 1971), pp. 287–300.

5. John K. Folger, Helen S. Astin, and Alan E. Bayer, *Human Resources and Higher Education.* New York: Russell Sage Foundation, 1970, p. 39.

6. Ivar Berg, *Education and Jobs: The Great Training Robbery.* New York: Frederick A. Praeger, Inc., 1970, chaps. 2, 3, and 4.

7. John K. Folger, "The Demand for College Graduates," to appear in the *Journal of Higher Education,* 1972.

8. Eli Ginzberg, "The Outlook for Educated Manpower," *The Public Interest,* no. 26, Winter, 1972, pp. 100–111.

9. See discussion in American Council on Education, *Universal Higher Education: Costs and Benefits,* Washington, D.C., 1971.

10. See W. Lee Hansen and David Witmer, "Economic Benefits of Universal Higher Education" in American Council on Education, *Universal Higher Education: Costs and Benefits,* Washington, D.C., 1971, pp. 31–32.

11. For a more careful discussion of the complicating influence of employed women, see Theodore W. Schultz, "The Reckoning of Education as Human Capital," in W. Lee Hansen (ed.), *Education, Income, and Human Capital,* New York: National Bureau of Economic Research, 1970, pp. 297–306.

12. The neo-orthodox policies, calculated to increase the demand for manpower indirectly, included tax arrangements designed to increase business confidence. The result was to encourage investments, many of which had only a modest effect, indeed, on the creation of jobs.

13. We refer here to job requirements for education, not to its consumption benefits, and these requirements do not include those that might appear, were the nation to meet the challenge of health and other social problems. One could easily imagine a different pattern of demand—especially for professionals—were we to "reorder priorities" and opt out of neo-orthodox conceptions of economic policy. For a review of the relationship between jobs and education, and for initial data on the underutilization of well-educated manpower, see Ivar Berg, op. cit.

14. The State University has 42 percent and the City University 17 percent of all students in the state. Total enrollments have increased by 90 percent, from 403,000 to 765,000 students, in the period 1961–1970.

15. Reviewed in *The New York Times,* Jan. 29, 1972.

16. For a convenient overview, see University of the State of New York, State Education Department, Office of Planning in Higher Education, *Guidelines for the Preparation of Private College and University Master Plans,* 1972, and *Education beyond High School: The Regents Planning Bulletin,* Albany: the State Education Dept., April 1971.

17. When such a forecast was made regarding technical manpower require-

ments in New York State, it showed that the present supply of technicians is not only sufficiently educated to adequately fulfill requirements specified, but is in fact better educated than employers' *"ideal* expectations" for 10 of the 15 specified occupational groups. See Ivar Berg, op. cit., p. 82.

18. U.S. Department of Labor, *Employer Manpower Planning and Forecasting,* Manpower Research Monograph no. 19, 1970, pp. 8 and 13–16.

19. Ibid., p. 14.

20. Harry Bridges, the president of the union whose members were to share in the benefits of technological changes, was understandably upset. Many of the employers in the Pacific Maritime Association, it turned out, wanted merely to reduce the work force on the docks, and not to introduce labor-saving devices that would increase productivity.

21. See the two concluding chapters of Richard B. Freeman, *The Market for College Trained Manpower, A Study in the Economics of Career Choice.* Cambridge: Harvard University Press, 1971.

22. W. Lee Hansen, Burton Weisbrod, and William Scanlan, "Schooling and Earnings of Low Achievers," *The American Economic Review,* vol. 60, no. 3 (June 1970), pp. 409–418.

CHAPTER 12

1. The authors have presented a fuller description of the system of linkages which integrate the flow of job opportunities with manpower flows and discussed the informational implications of this system in *The Labor Market: An Informational System.* New York: Praeger Publishers, forthcoming.

2. N.Y. State Department of Labor, *Employment Review,* November 1969, p. 89.

3. In Manhattan, 119 of the 177 establishments with 1,000 or more employees in 1969 were in trade, FIRE, or other services. Moreover, it is probable that a number of establishments reporting 1,000 or more employees listed in manufacturing were in fact the central headquarters of manufacturing firms that are national in scope.

4. Thomas M. Stanback, Jr. and Richard Knight, *The Metropolitan Economy: The Process of Employment Expansion.* New York: Columbia University Press, 1970.

5. Thomas Schelling, "The Ecology of Micromotives," *The Public Interest,* Fall, 1971, p. 82.

6. It has been brought to our attention that one large firm in recent years has found it necessary to interview several hundred thousand applicants to fill the vacancies left by the turnover of its staff.

7. David Lewin has investigated the use of various types of labor market information by a number of large New York City firms. The results of this investigation are presented in Chapter 5, "Employer Utilization of Labor

Market Information," in Yavitz and Morse, *The Labor Market: An Informational System*. New York: Praeger Publishers, forthcoming. Lewin concludes that the typical large New York firm does not use government data primarily because it is not tailored to its specific needs and is, moreover, likely to be out of date by the time it becomes available in published form.

CHAPTER 13

1. Herbert Bienstock, "Manpower Directions in New York City in the 70's," *City Almanac*, vol. 5, no. 4, December 1970, p. 5.

2. Ibid., pp. 4–8.

3. Peter Willmott, *Adolescent Boys of East London*. Baltimore: Penguin Books, Inc., 1969, pp. 142–167.

4. "Industrial Society's Conference of Youth at Work," *The Times* (London), Dec. 17, 1968.

CHAPTER 14

1. Alfred Eichner, "Public Policy for Growth," in Eli Ginzberg and the Conservation of Human Resources Staff, *Manpower Strategy for the Metropolis*. New York: Columbia University Press, 1968, pp. 262–292.

2. James Coleman et al., *Equality of Educational Opportunity*. Washington: U.S. Government Printing Office, 1966.

INDEX